The Last Parade

A true American War Story
By
Carl V. Lamb

M. Anderson Publishing Company

Library of Congress Catalog Card Number: 99-95257

Printed in the United of America.

ISBN-0-9673335-0-4

Grateful Acknowledgments:
All photographs, except the authors, are from the collection
of Sergeant Marvin Childers U S M C

Published by M. Anderson Publishing company
PO Box 611
Teays, WV. 25569-0611

TO C. B. HARRIS

Carl V. Lamb 1-12-2002

CONTENTS

CONTENTS (continued)

To my father, who taught me how to stand for what I believed was right. To my mother, who taught me how to love and cry . To the Angel of God almighty for the use of his shield. And to those who were there, especially the twelve fanatics, both living and deceased.

Foreword :

This is a story by a marine known to his comrades as Psycho Sam. It is not your standard war story, which usually has a central theme, a hill or perhaps a bridge, which the good guys go out to capture; some make it, some don't. Somehow all the sacrifices are portrayed as worthwhile. This story tells the truth about war. It is shaped by the events which actually happened to make in it a tale worth telling. The author has waited fifty years to relate this tale. He has written it as accurately as possible. It is indeed a unique tale every American should read. The reader will find no other story quite like it. Here is the story of Psycho Sam.

The events comprising this story concern the men of Fox Company, Second Battalion, First Marine Regiment, First Marine Division, United States Marine Corps, and others, who fought in Korea in the fall and winter of 1950 and spring and summer of 1951. The events are all true. Names of many have been changed to protect privacy and avoid harm to any person. Many years have passed since this story took place, but the memories remain fresh and undimmed by time in the author's mind. He especially remembers his comrades who lost their lives in the flower of their youth. They are not dead to him. Waking in the night, he still hears their cries and shouts amid the sights and sounds of battle. In the author's mind, the ghosts of men long forgotten still climb the hills and haunt the valleys and even yet today, their eerie cries ring out in the paddies and mountains of that far distant land

CHAPTER 1 ... Arlington National Cemetery ...

It was a warm day in July of 1950, in Arlington National Cemetery. Although there was a hint of a breeze, the men were sweating in their stiff collar blues and white trousers. A midday sun filtered down through the leaves of the maple trees and reflected off the polished brass buttons of their uniforms and, had it not been for that slight breeze and the shade provided by the maples, it would have been a really hot day. The young sergeant in command of the firing squad stood very still as if listening for something. He gazed intently across the hill through sunlit gray-and-white tombstones standing starkly above the green grass. The men were growing restless, beginning to fidget about, when down the hill, where a blacktop road curled lazily between the stones, the object of the young sergeant's attention, a long black limousine, followed by a string of cars, rounded the bend of the road and made its way up the hill. As the limousine came to a stop the sergeant called the firing squad to attention. Off to one side of the firing squad a burial detail of eight Marines dressed in blue coats and white trousers, sunlight glinting off the brass buttons of their tunics, marched to the rear of the limousine and stood, ready to receive the casket.

Mourners, dressed in black, with an occasional bit of color showing, began climbing out of the cars. They moved slowly, deliberately, as people are wont to do at solemn occasions, gathering at the freshly dug grave, which was shaded by the limbs of a large maple tree.

The eight pallbearers took the flag-covered casket in firm grasp and moved toward the grave. The sergeant called out, "Present Arms!"

He wheeled about and saluted, holding it until they placed the casket, dropped the salute and called over his shoulder, "Order Arms."

He heard the sharp crack of their hands on the rifles, then commanded, "Parade Rest." The men assumed the position of parade rest, holding to the barrels of their rifles with their right hands, left hands behind their backs, feet spread apart, right foot in position. He put his hands behind his back and stood, feet apart.

A Rabbi quietly spoke over the casket. The sergeant did not understand what the Rabbi was saying, but kept his eyes on the Marine Corps Major who was with the funeral party. It would be he who would give the sergeant the signal to fire the volleys required at a military funeral. They were burying a First Marine Division Corporal, whose body was just now being brought home from World War Two. To the sergeant, it was a solemn occasion, and he wanted to make certain that solemnity was properly observed.

The Rabbi finished speaking and stepped back. The major signaled. The sergeant came to attention, executed a left face, called the firing squad to attention and commanded, "Ready!"

The men brought their rifles to the ready.

"Aim!" The men pointed their rifles precisely at thirty degrees skyward.

"Fire!" The shots rang out as one.

They fired three volleys. At the sound of the last volley a bugler began sounding Taps as the pallbearers folded the flag, readying it for presentation to the next of kin.

Suddenly, cutting across the mournful sound of Taps, a woman's voice cried out, "Dot's vhat my Abe vas, *a bugler*!"

As the casket was lowered slowly into the earth, the woman cried out in anguish, "Abe! Come out of dot casket."

She kept weeping and crying out for her Abe.

The tones of the bugle died, and in the silence which followed, the distraught woman was led away.

The major came over to where the firing squad was still standing at attention. "Good job, Sergeant," he said, removing his white gloves.

The sergeant saluted him, "Thank you, Sir."

He then marched the squad back down the hill toward an olive-colored Marine Corps bus which was waiting to return them back to their duty post at the home of the Commandant of the Marine Corps, at Eighth and I streets in Washington D.C.

On the way back across town, the men joked about the burial of Abe and one or two mimicked his mother. They seemed not to appreciate the solemnness of the occasion and its effect on a grieving mother, and this irritated the sergeant. As they got closer to the barracks, they turned their attention to the girls who were crossing the street, cat-calling and thumping on the sides of the bus, until he said, "Knock it off."

Someone groaned and called him a killjoy, but they indeed quieted down.

When they arrived at the barracks, the sergeant saw John Bundy standing sentry duty at the main gate. Bundy was a veteran of World War Two who had recently re-enlisted, and seeing him reminded the sergeant that Bundy, at their first meeting, had told him that a war was coming and the Marine Corps would expand rapidly and he, Bundy, who had come back in after a four-year absence, would soon be promoted to Platoon Sergeant.

The sergeant had been dubious. Why did Bundy believe a war was coming? Bundy had claimed he had met a captain whom he had known when both were enlisted men, who was in Naval Intelligence. They had been stationed together at the United States Embassy in London, England. According to Bundy, the captain had said that a country from the north would invade a country from the south and the United States would go to the aid of the southern country.

Now, it had only been ten days since North Korea had invaded South Korea and President Truman had ordered the Army into Korea to repel the invaders. Bundy's prediction had been accurate.

The bus came to a stop beside the long red brick building with its curved arches covering a long arcade. The men got off and formed one rank. He marched them in single file through the arches and down the arcade, the amplified sound of their cadenced footsteps ringing out.

"Detail Halt!" he shouted.

They halted, making a loud clacking sound of heels together.

"Order Arms!"

They bounced the butts of their rifles on the deck.

"Right Face!"

They faced right.

"Dismissed!"

He followed the firing squad in through the barracks double doors and climbed the stairs to the third floor Sergeant's Room, took off the dress blue tunic and white trousers, and put on dungarees. His duty was over for the day. He went out to the stair landing, climbed the ladder to the attic, and opened the trap door which led out on to the roof of the barracks, revealing two long lines of dozens of khaki uniforms hanging out to dry. He gathered the clothes into a tight bundle and went back down to the landing. He sprinkled the clothes with water from a quart bottle fitted with a salt shaker lid and rolled them tightly so they would dampen properly.

He spent the rest of the day pressing clothes, then drove to the small apartment that he and his wife, Charlotte, had rented five days previously.

As he drove across the city, his thoughts wandered again to the war John Bundy had predicted. The war in Korea had indeed begun on June 25th, 1950. It had come so suddenly it seemed unreal. It was not something he, in his naive trusting way, considered significant. He and Charlotte had planned to be married on July first, and they were. On that first of July, the war had not seemed important. It had been the furthest thing from his mind.

Some weeks prior, to help make ends meet he had begun the laundry business. A Chinese laundry existed two blocks from the barracks, but he had seen a way to compete. He would work on the credit. When he had started the operation he had gone downstairs to the second floor, jumped up on a locker box and chanted, "Men, why take your shirts to the Chinaman when I will do them for only five cents more?"

That got their attention, and he followed it with, "What could be more exhilarating than having a sergeant press your shirts?"

This appeal, plus providing credit, had worked. His side business was a success and he had been pressing uniforms ever since.

Once, while at his pressing station, an older sergeant had come in drunk and he had helped his comrade up the long flight of stairs. Instead of going on to bed, the drunk sergeant sat down on the landing and produced a bottle of whisky. At his insistence, the young sergeant joined him, and the two sat side by side on the top stair drinking. The drunk sergeant began reminiscing about a movie he had seen, titled 'Good Sam' starring Gary Cooper. As drunks sometimes do, he began mumbling, about the younger sergeant being kindhearted. "Just like Good Sam. That's who you remind me of," he said, "Good Sam."

It was about midnight and the men were coming back off liberty. As they passed the two, sitting there at the top of the stairs, he informed them that he was drinking with Good Sam. The nickname stuck. Eventually, it was shortened to Sam and, in jest, he became known as Sam Lewis, Laundry Man.

Life was soft and easy at the barracks. There had been many days when, had he not been pressing clothes, there would have been very little to do. Now, as he drove across the city, reminiscing, he had no premonition the burial in Arlington would be the end of civilized life as he had known it. When Charlotte greeted him at the door to their small basement apartment his reverie ended. He forgot about all else.

CHAPTER 2 ... The Departure ...

Twenty sergeants were housed in the Sergeant's Room at the top of the stairs. The usual after-breakfast banter had begun. When Sam entered, one sergeant accosted him. "Sam, where's my khakis you promised?"

"Calm yourself, Luke. I've got 'em ready. Where's your money?"

As the sergeant was about to answer, the Post Gunnery Sergeant entered.

"Alright, listen up," he said. All became quiet.

"A train will leave Washington D.C. on Monday morning bound for Camp Pendleton, California. The following named men are to be on it." He paused, making sure of their attention.

There was a hushed silence. Sam heard someone draw a deep breath.

The Gunnery Sergeant began calling out names alphabetically, ". . . Crowell, Joyner, Kriener, Lewis. . . ." Hearing his name called jolted him. Then he heard James Newton, a fellow sergeant, start to laugh.

"Sam Lewis, the Laundry Man, in Korea," he said, bending over in laughter.

Before he could straighten up the Gunny called "Newton," and Newton too was sobered. His laughter stopped.

The Gunnery Sergeant continued, "You will all become members of the Fleet Marine Force, better known as the FMF. You will be assigned to the 1st Marine Regiment, 1st Marine Division, which is now forming for duty in the Far East. You have until Monday morning to say good-bye to your families, have them relocated, and whatever else you have to do. No one will be allowed to have their families accompany them. Are there any questions?" He waited a moment, and then continued, "You all know what you have to do." And with that, he departed.

After the Gunnery Sergeant left, Newton joined Sam beside his bunk taking comfort in the fact that he wouldn't be facing the enemy alone. Sam, his friend, would be there to help him out. He grinned at Sam.

"We'll be buddies," he said.

"Sure," Sam said, reassuring him, understanding instinctively that in times of crises people always seem to search out company. He saw this in Newton, but Sam really had no time to talk. He had to get moving. As he hurried out, he observed Joyner going about proclaiming that he was going to shoot everything that crossed in front of him and he saw another of his comrades, Harvey Owen, just sitting casually, combing his hair. Harvey, a Sioux Indian, had spent four years posing for the sculptor who carved the statue of the Iwo Jima Flag Raising. He had stood in for Ira Hayes, another Indian who had participated in that famous event. Harvey had been decorated for bravery during World War Two and was reputed to be a very brave man. He was nicknamed "Chief," but Sam had always called him Harvey.

Within a few minutes he was back at his apartment, trying to explain to Charlotte their honeymoon was over. They had been married for only ten days. He moved about the apartment trying to concentrate on packing. Anything was better than the pain of parting, but that was all he was feeling. Later that day, with packing completed, he drove her to her parents home near Johnstown, Pennsylvania. They didn't talk much. Both were feeling some shock at being overwhelmed by an event over which neither had any control. Sam thought she took the news well under the circumstances. An independent observer would have seen they were just two kids caught up in an event larger than either of them. Neither had seriously thought about war. It was all happening so fast. The pain of early separation was something neither had expected.

The drive took them up through Hagerstown, Maryland, through the same hills near where the battle of Gettysburg was fought. They drove silently past the red barns and tall silos of Maryland and Pennsylvania that had changed little from the days of Civil War. Sam was uncomfortable. He wanted to get his leaving over with. When finally they arrived at her home, Charlotte's baby brother was playing in the yard. She ran to him, picked him up with a little girl cry that caused Sam to feel better. At least she would be at home with those she loved.

Her father sat him down in the living room and pressed a beer into his hand. He was a big man, a coal miner, who had been in the Navy during World War One.

"Don't you worry, boy," he reassured Sam, "those Marines are a tough outfit. They'll look after you. I saw them come back from the front in France, covered in dust and caked with dirt. Yes sir, boy, a tough bunch."

Sam sat silently and drank his beer, wanting the departure over with, glad for someone else to talk. He was really feeling the pain of having to separate from Charlotte. The reality was sinking in. He was going to war. His tension eased a little when his mother-in-law called out dinner was ready.

After dinner, he and Charlotte went for a walk in the lane between two rows of pines standing straight and orderly in the bright July sun. The pines bespoke a lie with their neat order which contrasted so with the poignant ache he felt inside. He put his arms around his wife, holding her close for perhaps one last time. He heard her whisper, "You must come back to me."

He felt hot tears roll down his cheeks. It didn't seem possible they were being forced apart. As they returned to the house, he tried to hide his tears, wondering what his father-in-law might say if he saw a Marine sergeant crying.

"Well, are you ready to go, son?" his father-in-law asked.

"As ready as I'll ever be," he replied.

The bus to Washington was due at one o'clock in the afternoon and, glancing at his watch, he saw that it was time to leave. His father-in-law drove him to the bus station. As they crested the hill at the end of the lane, he looked back. Charlotte was waving to him. He waved back. They went over the hill, leaving the memory of her, waving good-bye, indelibly imprinted on his mind.

When he arrived at the barracks, he learned a large contingent of privates and corporals were also going. John Bundy was among them and Sam supposed he was glad because his Naval Intelligence friend had indeed proved to be right. He mentioned this to Bundy, but Bundy seemed not to want to talk. Sam stood for a moment watching the activity as the men packed seabags. A bit later, Bundy came over to Sam.

"I'm not going," he said. "I went to see the Gunny and Major Ourand. I told them that they have corporals here who are younger than myself, and who have never been overseas. I suggested they let one of them go as I've already been to one war."

Sam felt some disappointment, but said nothing. Bundy's reluctance seemed unusual. He left the group and climbed the stairs. Later in the day, another corporal turned up, also asking to be passed over for the honor of fighting for his country. His name too was deleted from the list. Sam could not help but wonder how this must look to the major. As he thought about Bundy and the other corporal, he wondered. Why are they so afraid? Can war be that bad?

CHAPTER 3 ... The Train ...

The United States Marine Band, dressed in red coats and white trousers, came down to the station and played marching music while the men boarded. As the train began to puff and chug clouds of steam, the short toots of its whistle blended in and then drowned out the music and they were on their way. Within a short time they had reached the countryside and were viewing the cornfields and woods. The overcrowded train swayed and rocked its way towards California. Due to the crowded conditions the men were forced to sleep sitting up. During daylight hours, they played poker or stared out the windows at the fields and towns. The United States Marines had been reduced to a total of sixty-eight thousand men. It was, at that time, a small organization. Consequently, during the journey, many of the men discovered friends from other duty stations close to Washington, while others made new friends.

Sam wandered about the train observing his comrades on their way to war. He had seen the newsreels of the Marines taken during the battle of Tarawa in World War Two and had, ever since, wanted to be a United States Marine. The words of the Marine Hymn had always stirred his blood. The phrase, "First to fight for right and freedom, and to keep our honor clean . . . ," were words which held meaning for him and at age sixteen he had enlisted. He remembered well the entrance to the Marine Corps Recruit depot in San Diego, California. A large sign across the entrance to the main gate read, "Through these portals pass the world's bravest men."

He had often reflected on the words of that sign, but had never seen them tested. He would have liked to ask some older Marine what combat would be like but that would be disclosing the fact of his fear. He was unable to do that. After boot camp, he had spent two years aboard ship in the Atlantic Ocean, and in the Mediterranean Sea. Then, two years at Parris Island, as a Drill Instructor. With the year in Washington, he had five years of spit and polish and Marine Corps lore behind him although he was not yet twenty-one.

The troop train moved inexorably onward. Nearing the end of the second day, the train passed through Jacksonville, Arkansas. Sam and Harvey Owen stood side by side on the caboose, Sam peering wistfully at the passing little town. He stood looking intently, trying to see someone he knew. There had not been time to write to his parents and he had not seen them in more than a year and, as the train rocked and hammered along the rails past the school yard where he had played as a child, he felt a great longing to see them again.

Harvey Owen glanced over at Sam. Sam gestured with his hand at the parallel highway the train was going slowly past.

"My hometown," Sam said.

Harvey broke into a broad grin. "Good place to jump off."

Sam returned his grin. Harvey was kidding. The train speeded up. Seeing no one he knew increased his longing. Harvey left him there. The vibration of the wheels on the steel rails blended with the flow of blood in his body. Instinctively, now, he sensed he was going forward to some great adventure filled with danger and he felt vibrant and alive and yet he feared he might not survive. The little town was lost to his view and, disappointed, he went back inside the train. Someone had a battery-powered radio and Hank Snow was singing, "I'm moving on." The driving tempo of the music blended with the rumble of the train, increasing his feeling of moving towards an unknown destiny.

He followed Harvey forward and found a seat beside him. Again, he waited for the older Marine to speak, keeping his fear to himself. As if sensing that he was expected to say something, Owen looked out the window of the train, avoiding Sam's eyes. "Sam, I don't like the FMF," he said softly.

Sam waited. Perhaps he would say more. When Owen didn't, Sam prompted him. "Any particular reason?"

"I just don't like it," Harvey said.

Sam sensed a seriousness in Harvey and knew that was all he was going to get on the subject of war. He sat silently, watching the fields and meadows of America, out the window of the train. After two more days of travel, the train arrived in San Diego and they were transported to Camp

Pendleton during darkness. Long rows of tents had been set up. The reserves had been called to active duty, and these were blended in with the regulars. The base was bustling with activity. Sam was assigned as a squad leader in the Second Platoon of Fox Company.

Fox Company had three rifle platoons, each consisting of three squads. There was a mortar section, consisting of two mortar squads and a rocket section. Also, it had a platoon of machine guns, which consisted of six light 30-caliber air-cooled machine guns. Each gun had a gunner, an assistant gunner, and six ammunition carriers.

On the second day a feminine-voiced, baby-faced, blue-eyed reserve Platoon Sergeant named Tarring was assigned as Platoon Sergeant of the 2nd Platoon. Sam led the first squad. The second squad of the platoon was led by a youth from Chicago named Beller and the third squad was led by a quiet sergeant from Vermont named Ivan Jennings who had seen action on Iwo Jima. Newton was assigned to mortars. Kriener went to machine guns. Crowell and Joyner went to other rifle platoons as squad leaders. Harvey Owen led a squad in the Third Platoon.

A young lieutenant arrived to be 2nd Platoon leader. To Sam, he seemed like a baby. The young lieutenant appeared to be very young and it was obvious to Sam that his comrades had no confidence in their newly arrived leader. The very sight of him caused anxiety. When the baby-faced Platoon Sergeant announced to the young lieutenant that he, Tarring, would make Marines of the platoon, Sam began to really fear they were in trouble. Although the Company Commander was yet to arrive, Fox Company was complete. It was comprised of mostly young men, fresh from drinking beer at soft duty stations and sprinkled with reserves. An observer might conclude Fox Company did not appear to be ready to fight a war. To make good his claim to turn them into Marines, Baby-Face Tarring began giving close order drill. In a shrill little girl voice he shouted commands while the young lieutenant looked on. The platoon marched so poorly it seemed pathetic. To Sam, this was not very reassuring. It was almost surreal.

CHAPTER 4 ... Enter Captain Groff ...

The first tent in a line of a dozen served as company headquarters. Disorganization reigned. The First Sergeant, a dull, slow-witted, tobacco-chewing redneck from Mississippi, had formed the entire company to call out the names of two who he requested to fill out insurance papers. Two were called to the office, the others were dismissed and they departed, grumbling at his inefficiency. Why didn't he just send for the two? Sam chanced to be one of the two. He had just finished the papers when the tent flap parted. A small sandy-haired man entered, dressed in dungarees with captain's bars displayed on the collar. The captain stopped. His eyes wandered, as if adjusting to the light inside the tent. He seemed to have a certain cold hardness about him. His skull protruded just above his eyes somewhat like a ram. His head sloped back from this protrusion to his cap, giving the impression his sandy hair was receding. His eyebrows were light and sandy and there was a trace of freckling on his light skin. The hardness was in his pale blue, contemptuous eyes. "I'm looking for First Sergeant Homer," he declared. His voice had a distinct nasal twang which sounded more like he was whining.

First Sergeant Homer spat tobacco juice into a spittoon and lazily sat the spittoon back down. He did not rise.

"Ah recon thass me, Cap'n."

"I'm Captain Groff. I'm taking command of Fox Company." The irritation caused by his nasal voice was even more pronounced. Sam flinched inwardly at the sound of it.

"Been wait'n for you Cap'n," Homer replied, as he spat more tobacco juice into the spittoon.

"Cap'n we got the biggest bunch of shitheads ah evah seed for a company," Homer said, beginning to launch into a long series of supposed inadequacies.

Sam could scarcely believe his ears. To Sam, Homer appeared the epitome of incompetence, and here he was accusing the men of being just that.

The manner of the pale-eyed sandy-haired captain seemed to change right then, some indefinable something Sam could not exactly put his finger on. The captain turned to Sam.

"Who are you?" he whined.

"Sergeant Lewis, Sir. Squad Leader of the First Squad, Second Platoon," Sam responded, coming to attention.

"I want all the NCOs, sergeants and above, in this tent, on the double," said the captain. His tone implied a foreboding hostility.

Sam stepped out of the tent and followed his orders, "Pass the word. All sergeants and above, to the Company Office on the double."

Within a few minutes the tent filled. When it was clear all were there, the captain surveyed them with baleful eyes.

"My name is Groff—G-R-O-F-F," he spelled out slowly. "I'm the Company Commander of this lashup."

He nodded his head, indicating Homer. "The First Sergeant tells me I have the biggest bunch of shitheads ever assembled." He paused, letting his hostility sink in, watching as they turned angry eyes toward First Sergeant Homer, who continued his chewing and spitting.

Groff continued, "I've a mind to take a stripe off every one of you bastards right now. You all had better shape up." He emphasized the word bastards, drawing it out slowly, deliberately. He waited for the insult to sink in, then continued. "Another thing, woe be unto the first one of you sons of bitches who disobeys my orders."

He paused again, then continued, "That's all I have to say to you miserable sons of bitches. Now get your asses out of here."

The sergeants filed out of the tent and immediately began grumbling to each other. A tough commander they could tolerate; not so, an unfair one. Sam was seething with anger. He did not appreciate being called a bastard and a son of a bitch. He listened to some of the others mumble their hatred of First Sergeant Homer. He noticed Harvey Owen and Ivan Jennings were both quiet. He approached Ivan Jennings.

"Well, what do you think?" he asked.

Ivan simply shrugged his shoulders.

A day later, the very young lieutenant was replaced by a Second Lieutenant named Malder. No one ever knew what became of the young lieutenant, but all breathed a sigh of relief. Sam assumed the new captain must have noticed the lieutenant was even younger and less experienced than they were.

Upon his arrival, Malder ordered the Platoon to assemble on the street between tents and introduced himself as their Platoon Leader. He was a stocky, broad-shouldered, narrow-hipped type who wore paratrooper boots and had an air about him which suggested great physical strength. He had been in combat in World War Two. He approached the men in an assuring and confident manner.

As Malder began to take control, Sam began to feel more assured that everything would turn out all right. It seemed now they would be ready for war. The news from Korea was becoming more ominous every day and they were immediately put busy loading ammunition and equipment aboard the ships which would carry them to war.

CHAPTER 5 ... Anarchy ...

The U S S President Jackson, with the Second Battalion of the First Marine Regiment aboard, left San Diego, California on August 14th, 1950. The ship was alive with rumors of lost battles and heavy losses suffered by South Korea and American forces. South Korean and United States Army troops were being forced to retreat, on a daily basis, into a defense perimeter lying at the southern tip of Korea. Rumors were that there might not be any perimeter by the time reinforcements arrived. Apparently, South Korea was losing the war. To make matters even worse, although the world was only four years away from the war crime trials at Nurnberg, stories of atrocities were circulating; horrible tales of American prisoners of war being murdered by North Koreans.

The North Koreans were said to be using Russian T-34 tanks, and the rumor was that bazookas were ineffective against them. Aboard the Jackson, Marine bazooka gunners took a dim view of this. In fact, they did not believe it, and as he wandered about listening to his comrades Sam heard many conversations ensue about how his comrades would prove this wrong once they met the North Koreans.

The attitude aboard ship was that all these tales of horror, although they might be true, were merely an excuse for the U. S. Army's inability to stop the enemy. The gist of this attitude was, of course, that they were Marines and as soon as they were committed, they would eliminate the North Korean Army in short order. Naturally, after they had whipped the North Koreans they would head back to Washington D.C. and have a big victory parade down Constitution Avenue. The men were imbued with bravado, enthusiasm, and the ignorance of youth. In fairness, it must be said, these sentiments were on the surface; below the surface, each man had private fears left largely unspoken.

They arrived in Japan and were taken by train to camp at Otsu where the Army First Calvary Division had been stationed prior to leaving for Korea. Being newly organized and having had no training whatsoever as a cohesive unit, the battalion began training immediately. That first morning, they went for a hike in the hills around Otsu. It seemed obvious, that in addition to working off the fat, they were to learn the method of communication to be used in field situations. The captain produced a Confederate flag which his runner, a New Yorker named Saia, tied to the antenna of the seventy-five pound radio he carried on his back. The inference was, if you wanted to know where the captain was, look for the Confederate flag.

On the training hikes, communication between Companies and Battalion was, of course, by radio; within the company it was by word of mouth. This method of relaying commands down a long extended column of men was practiced all day.

Late that first afternoon, after marching up and down the hills and sending messages up an down the column all day, they returned to the barracks and lined up at the field kitchen, provided by the U. S. Army. As they were waiting to be fed, a Japanese civilian employee of the field kitchen arrived and went to the head of the line to get his food. Captain Groff, standing nearby, stared balefully as the Japanese went to the head of the line and picked up a tray.

"Get out of here, you gook son of a bitch!" Groff shouted. Furiously, he ran over and confronted the Japanese civilian.

"No you don't, you son of a bitch," he shouted.

This seemed to confuse the Japanese civilian. Obviously, no one had ever treated him in that manner before. He stood very still and did not respond, nor did he leave the head of the line. The Army Mess Sergeant came out of the kitchen and began to explain, "He works for us, Captain. He always eats before he starts work."

Captain Groff's face was a mask of cold fury. "I don't give a damn what he does!" he shouted. "No goddam gook eats before any of my men."

The soldier protested. "He's a civilian employee. He's been working for us for three years. He eats here everyday."

Groff gave his final word. "It's okay for him to eat, but no slope-headed, slant-eyed, son of a bitch eats before my men," and that ended it.

The Japanese went behind the food counter, served as Fox Company filed past, and then ate.

Sam was somewhat puzzled. He had been raised to respect all people and, since his enlistment at age sixteen, all his training had been that an officer was indeed a gentleman. Sam had believed that to be so. Captain Groff's conduct was proving all his concepts to be wrong. Why was the captain making such a fuss? Had he been older and wiser, Sam would have known that Groff was attempting to influence; if you are going to kill a man, it is far easier to do if you have no respect for him. To all who witnessed the event, he was beginning a deliberate process of weaning them away from civilized behavior.

The Battalion trained for a total of three days. From early morning until dark they were up and down the hills practicing commands and fanning out in skirmish lines. Sam was already knowledgeable in squad tactics, arm and hand signals and also weapons, but many of his companions were green and it seemed they were amateurish. Besides training, there was the matter of staying clean. Late in the evening, of the third day in Otsu, they went to the wash racks located in rear of the barracks, and washed all their dirty clothes. It was a long-standing Marine Corps custom to assign one NCO as Duty NCO of the barracks. As such he was to be responsible for peace and order in the barracks after Taps had sounded and all hands were supposedly in bed. By some stroke of fate Sam was assigned as Duty NCO that day and a lieutenant, unknown to him, was Duty Officer. He met with Sam briefly and gave him his orders for the night, instructing him to maintain order and that he should walk throughout the barracks at 12 o'clock and 4 o'clock to make certain all was well. Sam inquired about the clothing hanging out to dry.

"Should I post a clothesline watch, Sir?"

"No," he said adamantly. "No sentry is necessary. Let them sleep. We'll be in combat soon. They need all the sleep they can get."

At 12 o'clock Sam left on his round of the barracks. He decided to walk outside and along the area where the clothes were hanging. In the darkness, he made out the form of a Marine, with rifle at right shoulder, walking post between the lines. Sam approached to find out who he was, and to his surprise, found one of his own squad, a Mexican-American named Perea.

"What are you doing out here, Perea?" he asked.

"Oh Senor Sam. It's the First Sergeant. He don't like me. He is very drunk. He came and got me out of bed and he put me out here with orders to stay all night."

"What have you done wrong?" Sam asked.

"Nothing, Senor Sam. Nothing! It's because I am Mexican."

There is a certain instinct common to natural leaders, far too complex to describe in a sentence or even a paragraph, but it could be said that part of this instinct is the realization they have that those they lead must respect them. Perea was in his squad. Sam's instinct said he must stick up for Perea. He did not hesitate.

"Perea you go back to bed," he said, "If the First Sergeant bothers you again, tell him to come see me."

Perea hesitated. Obviously, he feared Homer. "But Senor Sam, the First Sergeant he will . . ."

Sam stopped him. "Perea, I'll handle it," he said softly. "You go on to bed."

Perea left and Sam returned to his bunk. He was soon asleep.

At 4 o'clock Perea awakened him. "Senor Sam, the First Sergeant he is very angry and he is very drunk; he wants to see you. He sent me to tell you to report to the Company Office and then I have to go back and watch the clothes."

"You go back to bed," Sam said.

"Senor Sam. I am afraid to. He is always persecuting me. I don't know how much more I can take."

"You're in my squad, Perea. I'll stick up for you. That's my job. You go back to bed. I'll handle it. If he bothers you again, come get me." Sam told him.

He reached out and picked up his pistol belt, the symbol of his authority, put it on, and went down to the Company Office. The door was wide open and Sam stepped in, seeing Sergeant Homer sitting behind his desk. One look said Homer had indeed been drinking. His eyes were a dull, baleful red and he reeked of alcohol.

"Who are you," he said slowly and deliberately, "to interfere with me?"

"Perea is one of my men," Sam stated.

"But, just what gives you the right to interfere? You have no say in who I discipline."

"I'm Duty NCO of the barracks," Sam said quietly. "It's my responsibility and I have my orders. And besides . . ."

Before he could finish the sentence, he heard the door begin to close behind him. He turned. A second sergeant stepped out from behind the door. He was wearing khakis with the six stripes and diamond of a Sergeant Major on his sleeves. He also smelled of alcohol.

"Who is this wise ass?" he snarled, glaring at Sam and addressing Homer. Sam didn't wait for Homer to answer.

"Who is this man?" he asked.

The second sergeant began to swear. Sam could see he thought himself so important that Sam should know him. He had a neat little mustache and a narcissistic manner. Sam felt his blood quicken. His anger was rising and he strove to remain cool. Calmly, he addressed Homer again.

"First Sergeant, who is this man?" he asked. The unidentified Sergeant Major grew livid with rage. He leaped in front of Sam, his face angrily contorted. He came very close, his face six inches away from Sam's. To Sam, he appeared vain and sarcastic.

"I'm your Battalion Sergeant Major," he screamed, tapping Sam on the chest with his finger, "and don't you ever forget it!"

Sam was not intimidated, feeling only an increasing anger. He spoke deliberately, wanting the Sergeant Major to understand very clearly he did not intend to back down.

"And I am the Duty NCO of this barracks," he said, "and don't you forget it."

He could see his message sink in. The Sergeant Major understood alright. He stepped back from Sam.

"I'll see you before the Battalion Commander tomorrow morning," he said loudly.

"If you don't calm down, you're going to see me before the Battalion Commander tonight," Sam said quietly.

He saw the Sergeant Major understood his threat so he pushed it a little. "I'm going back upstairs and back to bed, he said. "If I hear any more from either of you tonight I'll wake the Officer Of The Day and we'll soon discover who's in charge of this barracks tonight."

As soon as he finished speaking, he turned to leave. As he did so, the Battalion Sergeant Major called after him.

"Tomorrow morning, eight o'clock, you be at the Battalion Command Post," he said.

"Fine, I'll be there," Sam said.

He returned to bed, but lay awake for a long while, the details of the incident rolling over and over in his mind. It was bad enough to be going to war. Why did one have to put up with such? He found no answer and eventually slept again.

At the six o'clock morning roll call, they assembled behind the barracks close to the clothes racks. The entire company was assembled, strung out in platoons. A private, whom Sam had never seen before, came down through the platoons asking for Sergeant Lewis. When Sam heard this, he called, "Over here."

The Marine made his way toward Sam. "You Sergeant Lewis?" he asked.

"Yeah," Sam said.

"The Battalion Sergeant Major sends his apologies. He asks that you just forget it."

"Sure," Sam said, "tell him it's forgotten." And without any further thought, he dismissed the incident from his mind. He was inclined to respect strong men and to ignore the weak. To him, both of the sergeants were weak. He had no inkling of what lay ahead. Much later, he would reflect on that event as the beginning of anarchy.

There was a canteen on the post operated by a service organization. In what little free time was available the men would go there and always come back complaining. It was staffed by three young women who were there, ostensibly, to entertain troops, but the men had been bitching because the women were unfriendly. These women were known as the Red Cross Girls.

No liberty was granted to go into Otsu, but the night prior to boarding ship for Korea some of the men went over the wall and came back with a lot of whiskey which was disseminated around the barracks. Some of the men got drunk.

A PFC (Private First Class) by the name of Head, who Sam had trained at Parris Island, came running to him.

"Hey Sarge, you want a piece of ass?" He was very excited. "One of the Red Cross Girls is out in the bushes behind the barracks. It's twenty dollars a man!" He cried.

"I don't believe it," Sam said.

Head grinned at him. "Come on, I'll show you."

He followed Head out behind the barracks where some hedges surrounded a volley ball court. A line of Marines extended out of the hedges, each waiting in line.

"You gonna go?" Head asked.

A Marine came out of the hedges buttoning his fly. From inside the hedges, A female voice called, "Who's next?"

Sam shook his head disgustedly. "No thanks," he said.

"I'm gonna," Head said. "I'm a lover, not a fighter."

Shaking his head in disgust, Sam went back inside. When he entered the barracks the noise of the drunken men was growing louder. He heard a lot of shouting and went to investigate. One of the rocket men had barricaded himself inside the company office. A group of Marines were calling to him to come out.

He shouted back, "I'm not afraid to die!"

Nothing made sense to Sam. He failed to see how coming out of the company office had anything to do with not being afraid of death. Captain Groff was there, but instead of trying to restore order, Groff joined in.

"Who's in there?" he asked.

"Private Monegan, Sir," someone said.

"Monegan, this is Captain Groff. You open that goddamned door!" he shouted.

"I'm not afraid to die! You think I'm afraid to die?" came the response.

"I don't give a damn whether you're afraid to die or not. You open that goddamned door!" Captain Groff shouted.

This went on for some time. When they weren't shouting for Monegan to come out they were passing the bottle around. It wasn't clear to Sam why it was so important they get Monegan out. Why they didn't just leave him alone? Finally, after deciding that Monegan wasn't coming out, Captain Groff ordered, "Break the goddamned door down!"

And they did. It went in a crash of splintered wood and a rush of bodies. They grabbed Monegan and dragged him down the hallway. He was still shouting that he wasn't afraid to die.

Apparently, Captain Groff had been giving a pep talk because he resumed. "By God, we're gonna go over there and blow the hell out of that bunch of North Korean gooks!"

The men cheered.

"We'll teach those slope-headed bastards the meaning of United States Marines," he shouted.

The Navy Corpsman, Chico Carsenero, was also under the influence. "Bull shit!" he shouted ebulliently.

The men grew quiet. Who had committed sacrilege?

Captain Groff stared in Chico's direction but fastened his eyes on a Marine called Arkie.

"I'll come over there and stomp your ass."

"Don't look at me Captain," Arkie said. "It wasn't me."

"We'll show those gooks what Fox Company can do to em!" Groff shouted.

Another cheer echoed loudly.

Chico was very drunk. "Bull shit," he muttered, but this time to himself.

Sam went back outside. The Red Cross Girl was still calling out, "Next!"

He went upstairs, laid on his bunk and listened to the commotion. Someone came in from town and proclaimed in a loud voice, "Lieutenant Malder shot a Marine in the leg down in Otsu."

"What?" someone asked.

"Yeah. He went into town to catch the AWOLs. One of them tried to run from him, Malder shouted halt, the guy ignored the order and Malder shot him."

Sam felt uneasy. He had never seen such chaos in five years in the Marine Corps. For those five years the order and discipline of the Marine Corps had been unbroken. He had enlisted at sixteen, claiming that his birth certificate wasn't on file. His father had signed an affidavit stating he was seventeen, and he was on his way to San Diego. He grew up in the Marine Corps. Now, this behavior was angering him. Life was no longer normal. After some time, things quieted down a bit, and he drifted off to sleep.

Next day, they boarded a train which took them to the naval base at Kobe, where they boarded ships bound for Korea. Quite a few of the men were hung over. A few still had some saki. Among the latter was Chico, the corpsman, an Italian-American from New York city. He sat opposite Sam on the train, nursing his bottle of saki, and reading a prayer book. This made Sam angry. Chico represented part of the reason for his vague feeling of uneasiness. Sam had been raised in a Christian home and had been taught that drinking was sinful. He long since had departed from this early training but, deeper than that, what was really making him angry was that all the structured order had gone out of his life. His anger suddenly welled up. He leaned forward, snatched the prayer book out of Chico Carsenero's hand and threw it out the train window. Chico began to cry. He was twenty-seven years old and there he sat with tears rolling down his cheeks.

"What did you do that for? That was my prayer book," he blubbered.

"It won't do you any good to pray with a bottle of booze in your hand," Sam said. "The lord won't hear you."

"But that was my prayer book!" Chico cried, weeping profusely, bemoaning the loss of his book.

Sam was immediately sorry, but there was nothing he could do; the prayer book was gone and Sam began to realize that Chico indeed might need it.

"I really didn't mean to do it," Sam offered.

Chico looked at him in disgust, stopped crying and then hurled the bottle of saki out the window.

"You're a psycho. You got no judgment. You're a psycho."

A tall, dark-haired, West Virginia youth, named Beasly, came by. Chico looked up at him. "Psycho Sam Lewis just threw my prayer book out the window."

Beasly chuckled. "That fits you Sam. Psycho Sam! that's what we're gonna call you," he teased. He began to tell the others to call Sam Psycho. They seemed a little too hung over to notice. However, a sober Ivan Jennings grinned at Sam.

"Psycho Sam," he said. "That does seem to fit."

A half hour later the train ride ended and, after a short march from the train station to the dock, they boarded ship for the final leg of their journey.

CHAPTER 6 ... Hill 117 ...

Sometimes at night,
When I awaken,
Remembering, and remembering,
A single life that I have taken,
Remembering, and remembering,
I see him lying,
—On the ground,
Forgotten,—Long forgotten.

The ship that carried them to their destiny was an old Japanese troop transport which had been confiscated from the Japanese at the end of World War Two and now pressed into service again. They boarded in battle dress, with weapons, packs, canteens and helmets and found their way through the steel passageways, knocking and clanking about in the crowded compartments, expecting the worst and finding it. Sam placed his gear in a corner and went topside to observe preparations for getting underway. Watching the last lines of men board, he noticed a Japanese civilian, who appeared to be military age. He was standing on the dock and staring at Sam. Why is he looking at me so intently? Sam wondered. When the Japanese saw Sam's attention directed at him, he pointed at Sam and then took his finger and drew it across his throat. Then, still grinning, he pointed again and drew his finger across his throat again, indicating that Sam would have his throat cut. Obviously, he was an ex-soldier who had fought Americans who was attempting to instill fear in Sam.

Sam gave him the finger and grinned back at him. Standing beside him was Sergeant Walter Moss, a former prisoner of the Japanese, who remarked, "If I had ammo I'd shoot that son of a bitch."

Walter Moss hated all Orientals. He had been used like an ox to pull a plough through the rice paddies and he was planning revenge. While at Camp Pendleton, he had searched for insurance companies who did not have war clauses in their policies. When he found one, he bought a policy. He owned several. Still watching the grinning Japanese, he expounded upon his plan for revenge. "I don't plan to take any prisoners and I sure as hell won't become one," he said.

Just then, Sam went below. The ship was so tightly packed with men and equipment, it was clear it would be impossible to sleep all the men aboard at the same time. Within a short period, Sam felt the distinct roll of the ship; they were underway, so he again went topside to watch as they pulled away from shore and out into the green waters of the Sea of Japan. As the sight of land slipped away he went below again to see what sleeping arrangements had been made. The bunks were full so he found a place in a corner and curled up on the steel deck.

The bunks were always full; as a result, they had to sleep in shifts, and when you weren't in a bunk you were in a chow line. The ship's galley had not been intended to serve nearly as many men as were on board, so the line was continuous. To add to the discomfort, there were salt-water showers which made you feel just as dirty after you had used them. Sam spent as much time as possible topside.

When they were at sea, Lieutenant Malder held daily briefing sessions. The first thing he did was instruct them to not call him sir; nor were they to ever refer to him as lieutenant. He explained that, in his experience, the life of an officer in the front lines had tended to be very short, and he made it crystal clear that he was not to be identified in combat.

"What shall we call you, Sir?" someone asked.

"My friends call me Can Do," he said.

At the next training session, they practiced dismantling their weapons while blind-folded. Following that, they had a session where they discussed fire team tactics and arm and hand signals.

It wasn't long afterwards, in the Yellow Sea, they encountered a typhoon. There were huge waves which threatened to swallow the ship. All hands were ordered below deck to avoid being washed overboard. One seaman was injured topside when some barrels that had been lashed to the deck broke loose and began to roll about. One of them broke his leg. They huddled together listening to the groaning and creaking of the ship as it rode up and down in the howling wind. Serving food and eating it became a battle in itself due to the pitching and rolling of the ship. Some of the men became violently seasick. Sam wondered if the old tub was going to hold together, but after three days of heavy seas the storm began to taper off. When the storm subsided, they were off the coast of Inchon, Korea, and last-minute preparations continued

They had one final briefing, during which Malder began to talk about their mission. They were to land on the western shore of Korea at the port of Inchon. Fox Company was to seize Hill 117 which overlooked the Inchon-Seoul highway. They were to take it the first night. They would land at 5 o'clock in the afternoon, when the tides were supposed to be high enough for landing craft.

"Each of you squad leaders have three fire teams of four men each. Each one of those fire teams has a BAR [Browning Automatic Rifle]. That gives you the edge. You will keep those BARs in action at all times. This platoon has a total of nine BARs. If only nine men reach the crest of Hill 117, I want to hear nine BARs popping," he said.

And then, as if reading their minds, as they considered the possible consequences, he continued, "It takes an awful lot to kill a whole platoon of Marines. You can go a long, long, way."

Prior to the outbreak of the Korean War, President Truman had made some public remarks about the Marine Corps, inferring it was a glorified police force, and as a result he was unpopular with Marines. Malder addressed this also. "Don't let this crap of Truman's bother you. He's the Commander-in-Chief, but you'll not be fighting for him. In fact, you won't be fighting for your country. You can forget all that crap."

There was a moment of silence. Then someone asked, "Can Do, Sir, who will we be fighting for?"

Malder took his time in answering. He looked them all over.

"You'll be fighting for each other," he said. "That's what it all boils down to. And don't you ever call me Sir again."

The briefing continued. He explained that, after they had taken Hill 117, the mission of the Second Battalion of the First Regiment, of which they were a part, would be to advance down the Inchon-Seoul highway and retake the city of Seoul from the North Koreans. The 5th Regiment would land at five o' clock on the morning of September 15th, on an island off the coast of Inchon so that Marine artillery could be moved into place to support the First. The First would go in at 5 o'clock that afternoon. There was to be a regiment of South Koreans landing to back them up. The 7th Marine Regiment would be in reserve and would come in behind the First Regiment the following day. That was it. They saw no maps; no doubt someone had them, but as far as they knew, any hill could be 117.

After the briefing broke up, Sam spent the rest of the day wandering about the ship. Young Marines sat about in small groups sharpening bayonets and trench knives, acting as if they were looking forward to the coming events. Not that they really were. It was just their way of accepting the inevitable. They were trying to show each other that they were ready to do that which their country had sent them to do. One of the men, who was not in Sam's squad, approached him.

"How many of 'em are you going to kill, Sam?" he asked.

The question startled Sam. He hadn't really thought about killing anyone. True, he was a Marine. Yet, there had been no preparation in any of his training for killing anyone. He could not imagine killing anyone. His questioner's face was alight with an excitement which Sam didn't feel. It made him uncomfortable. How could one human being look forward to killing another? he wondered. He couldn't—and he didn't think the other could either.

"I'm just going to try to stay alive," Sam said.

"Not me!" his companion cried, "I'm gonna kill about fifteen of 'em."

Somehow, Sam concluded he was afraid and had chosen that way to deny his fear—not to Sam, but to himself. Sam left him and wandered on. In one of the groups he visited, a sergeant from the Third Platoon was armed with a Thompson submachine gun instead of the automatic carbine issued to him. He managed to carry it wherever he went and he exuded a bravado that Sam certainly didn't feel. Sam could not help but wonder if he was just putting on a good face.

At the rail, Sam paused beside a sergeant he knew who was a veteran of World War Two. He was staring down into the water. Sam stood beside him. The water was calm and deep, reminding Sam of the Mediterranean Sea where he had spent two years after boot camp. However, the Mediterranean was always blue and this water was yellow. For a long time, Sam stood beside him looking down at it, feeling the gentle roll of the ship beneath his feet. Sam sensed he was despondent and thought to cheer him up.

"How's it going, Mann," he asked.

Mann didn't answer and Sam stood for a while, silently.

Then Mann spoke. "I'm not going to make it this time, Sam," he said, quietly.

"Ah, come on," Sam said, "that's no way to talk."

Mann did not take his eyes off the water, but just kept looking down into it and shaking his head from side to side. "No. I'm going to die and I know it," he said, softly.

Sam patted his shoulder.

"You'll be alright, he said, "Why, some Jap tried to make me think I'll get my throat cut, but I paid him no heed."

"This is different. I've never had this feeling before," Mann said.

Sam slapped him on the shoulder and moved away. He too had fears of impending death. As much as, if not more than death, he feared being a coward. He looked all about at his comrades considering the fact that some would die soon. Will it be me? he wondered. When you got right down to it, he didn't know what combat would be like. Four or five hikes out in the hills of Japan just hadn't prepared him for what was to come. He was unsure. He didn't know himself. He wished that it was all over and he could go back to Washington D.C. and march in one of the Dress Blue Parades they had at the Commandant's home where, to impress them, he invited Congressmen, in the hope they would keep pressure on President Truman not to abolish the Marine Corps.

He tried to ask Ivan Jennings, one of the other squad leaders, what to expect in combat. Jennings was incommunicative. He would only say that he was one of two in his company on Iwo Jima who hadn't been hit. Beyond that, he had his favorite expression, "All you get from war is to be killed or wounded." And then, he would lapse into his New England quietude.

Sam could not talk to Beller. The gap between them was too great. Beller was just too straightlaced to suit Sam and he seemed somehow not to approve of Sam. The nickname Psycho Sam seemed to have taken hold and Beller, by his conduct, let Sam know that he felt that this implied a lack of respect from the men. Sam knew better.

When he had been aboard the cruiser in the Mediterranean, the First Sergeant had once sent for him to come to the ship's detachment office. Sam had gone to the office split door and the upper half swung open. The First Sergeant said, "Lewis, I'm going to promote two men to corporal. You are being considered. What is your opinion on how to lead men?"

Sam said, "If you can't lead em, drive 'em."

The First Sergeant had the answer he was looking for. "I'm promoting you to corporal effective immediately. Anyone you can't lead, you just drive 'em to me," he said

Sam had never had to do that. In his heart, he knew the only way to lead men was to earn their respect. The name Psycho Sam didn't bother Sam. It meant they felt comfortable with him. He embellished on it by referring to his squad as the Twelve Fanatics, none of whom seemed to fit the mold of being fanatical, but he hoped it would give the squad an identity and make them feel part of a special team. He stood at the rail, thinking about these things.

The Navy had been shelling the coast for several days. Now, on the day of landing, they moved in close, ready to land. Since they wouldn't go in till late in the day, they stood about watching the bombardment. One of Beller's fire team leaders, a corporal named John Paul Carpenter, joined him at the rail. "I just did it," he said. "I just re-enlisted for six more years. They paid me a bonus of six hundred dollars."

"Is that why you re-enlisted?" Sam asked.

"Partly. I was raised in an orphanage in Pugent Sound. Never had any family, been in the Marine Corps four years. The Corps is the only family I've ever had. I plan to make a career of it. I guess I'll spend the rest of my life in the Corps," he said.

Sam marveled that, on the eve of combat, Carpenter could look that far ahead. Sam wondered whether or not he felt any fear. The nearer they came to combat, the more fear Sam felt and he wondered if it was just him who was afraid. He was thinking about Carpenter's response when the loudspeaker began to blare out orders for all Marines to saddle up and prepare to go down the nets. At last, the moment of truth had come. Sam would soon know what combat was like. They began drawing ammunition and putting on packs and belts, and gathered at the ship's rail where they already had the nets in place for them. Tarring found Sam. He gave him thirteen little bottles of brandy, one for each man.

"Here," he said, "in case someone gets hit."

Then he told Sam that Malder would go in one boat with Beller. He and Jennings would go in together with part of the rocket section. Sam was to go in a separate Amphtrac (amphibious tractor) with his squad and the rest of the rockets. Sam felt somewhat reassured that neither Tarring nor the lieutenant thought it necessary to accompany him. As they climbed over the side and went down the nets to the circling Amphtracs, the ship's loudspeaker was blaring out, "This is the captain speaking. Several times in the last few years it has been my duty to land United States Marines on hostile shores. They have always acquitted themselves well. I am certain that you will all do the same. I wish you good luck and good hunting."

Sam's feet found the bottom of the Amphtrac as it pitched upwards and he moved forward to avoid those coming after him. As the Amphtrac pulled away, he saw Harvey Owen leap down into an Amphtrac. He walked to the front, waving to Sam. Sam waved back. His Amphtrac circled about as the others loaded, then the Amphtracs formed into a line and started in towards the beach. Off to the left, the flag of the Confederacy flew from Saia's radio antenna.

They were about a thousand yards away from the beach, which was no longer visible except as a cloud of smoke. It seemed as if time was standing still as they drew nearer to the beach and entered into the low hanging cloud of smoke. Naval gunfire shrilled overhead, sounding like a band of wounded tigers passing through the air, exploding in red flashes visible inside the cloud of smoke. Above this smoke, a pair of Navy Corsairs swooped down pouring out a stream of machine gun fire. Sam hunched down and began to worry if the Corsairs would know when to quit. They were about three hundred feet from the beach when the Amphtrac came to a stop. The Coxswain called out, "You'll have to unload here. I can't get in any closer."

Sam began climbing over the side. "Lets go," he said, and stepped out into the mud, almost falling down.

The bottom was muddy and inconsistent, with holes in some places. He was doing all he could to keep his carbine dry, holding it aloft as he waded in.

A stream of tracer fire came out from the beach and arced above Sam toward the ships, which now seemed in close. He looked back and saw his squad was following. Garrett, one of his fire team leaders, called attention to the fire above them by looking up at it with fear written on his face.

"Look at that," he said.

"They're not shooting at us," Sam said.

After what seemed like a long struggle they reached the beach and took shelter behind a five-foot high bank. Sam suddenly had the urge to urinate, struggled with the mud-caked button of his fly, couldn't get it open, and urinated anyway.

Someone shouted, "Move forward!"

They went over the bank and started inland. Sam called out for the men to move faster, but they didn't, so he cried out, "Follow me!" and moved out in front.

He began trotting in the direction of the single hut that he could see standing about two hundred fifty feet distant. As he moved towards it, Malder called out, "That's the way, Sam. That's the way to do it!"

No sooner had they reached the hut when Sam heard a shouted order to hold up. After a time which seemed like an eternity, someone shouted to go back to the beach.

Without the weight of the men, the Amphtracs had floated high enough to land and were now waiting on the beach. Someone shouted that they had been landed on the wrong beach; then an order was barked to head back to the Amphtracs, to be transported to the right place to make an attack on Hill 117. The men hunkered down in the Amphtracs and headed north along the beach, parallel to the water. In a matter of minutes, they were passing through a group of straw covered huts which were on fire. The Amphtrac Sam was in was knocking some of the huts aside as it careened through. Suddenly, the loud clatter of machine gun fire began. His back was against the side of the Amphtrac and he felt the bullets striking the side of the vehicle and ricocheting off.

The fifty-caliber gunner on the Amphtrac returned fire as they careened through a second group of burning huts. Sam began to fear a hand grenade might be dropped in on them. His first brush with claustrophobia began and he was terrified. To his great relief, they stopped. Orders to exit the Amphtracs were given. Again, they climbed out. By this time, it was completely dark. Lieutenant Malder knelt down to the ground looking at a map, using a small shielded flashlight. He studied the map for a short period, and then, taking John Paul Carpenter's fire team, he led out into the darkness. Following, Sam felt fear once again, as the only person who knew where they were going was Malder. If he were killed or disabled, how would they know what to do?

They were under a dark overcast sky, with the occasional break between clouds, allowing moonlight to shine through. Sam, like everyone, was miserably soaked in muddy water. Something else was bothering Sam. Something noxious besides the mud was clinging to him. He had been sensing it ever since setting foot on shore. He began to realize it was an extremely foul stench. They were moving across a rice paddy. The Korean rice farmers used human waste as fertilizer and the smell of the lowland paddies permeated the entire area. Every so often the moon would disappear and a little rain fell, threatening an added misery. They came upon a path and followed it slowly. It lead up a gentle rolling hill Sam assumed was Hill 117. Everything was very quiet. Malder was leading. He would send Carpenter forward with a fire team to scout the area ahead. When the clear signal was given the main body would move a hundred yards or so and stop while Carpenter scouted again.

The Navy fired a flare shell that exploded overhead and lit up the entire area. When the shell exploded, Sam lay over against the earth, with his hand across his helmet, preventing making noise as he went down. The flare floated slowly down and was gone. Sam was about to sit back up when he heard the Navy fire again, a single boom, from far out in the ocean behind. Instinctively, he knew a second flare was coming, so he kept his hand on his helmet and stayed down. Suddenly, someone kicked him viciously across his fingers. He sat up. Someone was sitting above him; obviously, the kicker.

"Who the hell are you?" Sam demanded, his fear giving way to anger.

"I'm Captain Groff," his kicker snarled.

"I don't care if you're Jesus Christ," Sam said, "you kick me again and you've got trouble."

"Stay awake," Groff snarled.

"I wasn't sleeping. I was waiting for the flare," Sam said.

At that instant, the flare popped overhead. When it died out, Groff got up and walked towards the rear of the column.

They were moving again. This time, Malder led forward several hundred feet before stopping. Silence fell; the Navy had stopped firing. The silence was broken by strange sounding voices out in the darkness, calling out to each other in that Oriental sing-song cadence so foreign to the American ear, "Ah chuka ba, Ah chuka ba, aliee."

The voices were very close and Sam was very tensed and afraid. As they continued slowly along the path, he wondered what they were saying.

On a high state of alert they moved forward. Eventually, they came to a place where a narrow, four foot deep trench, freshly dug, crossed their path at right angles. The column stopped. Sam halted about two feet from the trench so he might watch down the trench both ways.

With the column stopped, the night became very still and quiet. Suddenly the stillness was broken by a stumbling figure coming forward along the column, making loud footsteps, and muttering. Sam saw First Sergeant Homer coming up the path. As he stumbled past, Sam smelled whiskey, and knew he was drunk. "What's the fuckin' holdup?" Homer muttered, lurching slightly as he passed and continued towards the head of the column.

Again, he demanded, "Why ain't this column movin'?"

Suddenly, two dark figures came down the trench so near they almost bumped into Sam who was sitting on the ground. He was face to face with the nearest one. Immediately, he saw they were Orientals. He swung the muzzle of his carbine against the chest of the first Oriental and said, "Sundrah!"

The soldier stopped. The muzzle of Sam's carbine was almost against his chest. The second stopped only a foot behind the first. Both of them were totally surprised. They held rifles, but didn't dare raise them. Sam spoke to the nearest Marine.

"Raise your rifle above your head and make like you're dropping it."

He did.

The Koreans dropped their rifles.

"Go forward and tell Can Do that we've got two Oriental soldiers back here and we don't know if they are North or South Koreans," Sam said.

The Marine went forward in search of Can Do. Out in front of the column Paul Carpenter turned to his rifleman, a Marine from Rochester, New York, named Donald Petitt.

"Go back and find Can Do. Tell him it's all clear," he said.

Petitt hesitated.

"Never mind," Carpenter said, "I'll do it myself." He turned and started back down the path. At that instant, First Sergeant Homer reached the head of the column. He saw Carpenter approaching out of the darkness. He whipped up his rifle and fired.

Bang!

The sound of the single shot was loud enough to be the crack of doom. It echoed and rolled out into the darkness of the night. Carpenter pitched backwards, struck in the head by a bullet from an M1 rifle.

Malder screamed, "You son of a bitch! You've shot one of my men. Oh, you goddam dirty, drunken, son of a bitch." Malder knelt down beside Carpenter, whose brains were oozing out onto the soil of Korea, and tried to stop them with a compress. All the while, he was bitterly cursing Homer, his voice acrid with contempt, scalding Homer by the tone of it. "You goddamned miserable, drunken, Mississippi bastard! What are you doing up here anyway?"

And Homer was muttering, "I didn't know. I didn't know," over and over again as if talking to himself.

"I'll see you in Portsmouth Naval Prison if it's the last thing I ever do!" Malder shouted. "Get your ass to the rear of the column where you belong."

The Marine Sam had sent forward interrupted his tirade. "Sam has two prisoners and doesn't know who they are."

Can Do left Carpenter with Beller, Petitt, and one other member of Carpenter's fire team and came running back to where Sam was holding the two prisoners at gunpoint.

"Strip 'em! Strip 'em!" he cried.

He ran up to the first soldier and stood over him.

"Get your clothes off!" he shouted.

The soldier looked up at him fearfully, not understanding anything. Malder poked at him with his bayoneted carbine.

"Get your clothes off you son of a bitch!" he shouted.

Terrified, the soldier broke and ran down the trench.

Sam's carbine vibrated. A loud burst of fire broke the stillness of the night and echoed in all directions. The bullets slammed into the soldier knocking him forward and down, flat on his face in the trench. His feet were pumping frantically in the act of running, making a thumping sound in the dirt. Sam became aware that he had pulled the trigger. The man's legs were still pumping furiously.

"Finish him off," Malder snarled.

The Marine at the far side of the trench, a tall youth from South Carolina, stood over the kicking soldier and shot him again three times. Bang! Bang! Bang!

"Knock it off," Malder snarled, "you'll bring the whole North Korean Army down on us."

They carried Paul Carpenter over and sat him down beside Sam. Sam looked at him. He was making great gasping, sucking sounds, fighting for each breath. Sam sat numbly, unable to move. He was frozen in horror. Carpenter's words were ringing in his ears: "I guess I'll stay in the Corps the rest of my life." Now he was dying and, down in his gut, Sam had the awful feeling of having killed a man. Sam, who hadn't thought of killing anyone, became the first man in Fox Company to kill an enemy soldier. He felt an indescribable horror. Somehow, he sensed a void between what he had been and what he now was. Some kind and gentle part of him was gone and he would never be able to get it back. It was not like shooting at a person far off; he had been too close, only two feet away. Now, Sam began to wonder about the soldier's family, for surely he had one. They would know only that he did not come home from the war and Sam would always know that he had killed him and none of them would ever know each other. Not only did he feel badly about taking the soldier's life but he regretted the harm done to his family.

Carpenter made a rattling sound and gasped. Horrified, Sam stared down at him. All he could feel was an ache inside that would not leave.

Stripping the second soldier no longer seemed important. Beller, Petitt and Turner took him, and the four of them picked Carpenter up and started back toward the beach. He died on the way.

When the column moved again Sam moved mechanically. He was in a state of shock. They began to move forward without scouting. They had made enough noise to tell the whole Asian world where they were and caution no longer seemed important. At four o'clock in the morning, they found the crest of Hill 117 and began digging in. Somehow the machine gun section, the rocket men, and the mortars had stayed on the beach. Fox Company was there without any supporting weapons.

Sam's mind was fraught with four emotions; fear of what would happen next, remorse over killing a man, grief for Paul Carpenter, and anger at First Sergeant Homer. His fear was foremost. He wondered if he himself would be killed when day came.

CHAPTER 7 ... The Second Day of Fighting ...

Korea has long been known as the Land of the Morning Calm. The first gray light of dawn gradually flowed over a land more still and quiet than ever experienced by any there. There was not a sound other than the crunch of shovels biting into the earth in a lonely corn field. They had not slept. Their clothing was only half dry. The earth stank with a foul smell which seemed to permeate their clothes, their very minds. There was no escaping the stench. The universal thought was the North Koreans would be coming to try to drive them off the hill and back into the sea, and so they dug steadily with one single purpose; to dig into the earth deep enough to stand and fight. However, they were soon interrupted.

From somewhere out front came the thin, rasping, sarcastic voice of the captain, "You goddamned miserable sons of bitches!"

The men paused from their furious digging and looked up, jaws slack, mouths agape, surprised at being cursed. Groff stood twenty yards out in the stubble of the corn field. Corporal Saia, his runner, stood nearby, weighted down by the radio and his flag of the Confederacy. The captain's voice was angry, scornful.

"Are you sons of bitches gonna go with me, or you gonna stay here and dig holes in this damn stinking earth?" he cried.

"Saddle up," someone shouted.

They stopped digging and hurriedly began slipping into packs and belts. Those nearest to the captain began moving out in single-file column down the forward face of the hill following the Confederate flag. Groff, leading the way, was still cursing, "I didn't come to this goddamned country to dig holes in the earth," he snarled.

Sam fell in to the column and waved his hand for the squad to follow. They had barely gone five hundred yards when a creaking sound, mingled with the hum of diesel engines, reached them. They could see a portion of the road leading to Seoul and then a low hill obscured a portion of it from view. A thousand yards beyond, they saw the road again. Groff never slackened his pace as they tramped forward towards the hill which had been obscuring the road. The creaking sounds and the hum of engines grew louder, recognizable now as the distinct sound of tanks approaching on the road below. No tanks were visible on the portion of road near, nor on that part visible beyond the hill, so they had to be behind it. At any moment, they would come out from behind the hill and catch the company in the open field without any rockets or anything else capable of stopping them.

Captain Groff seemed unaware of danger and kept moving. Then word came down the column, "Air panels out."

Those men charged with the duty of carrying panels took them out of their packs and spread them across their shoulders. (These were panels of red cloth highly visible from above, identifying them to their aircraft.)

Within moments, a flight of six Corsairs appeared overhead. They wheeled about, the morning sun flashing off their silvery wings, and came slipping down in a long dive. As the rockets blasted off towards the tanks, their thrust appeared to make the aircraft stop in midair. They came in low, one behind the other, so low that they disappeared behind the hill then rose majestically, climbing into the sky with the sounds of their bombs and columns of smoke rising behind them. The last plane swooped in low and out of sight. A tremendous roar from beyond the hill and the plane failed to appear on the far side. Apparently, it had been shot down.

They kept moving. As they crossed the hill, six burning tanks came into view. They were walking fast and nearing the road. There were rice paddies down by the road with rice about knee high. As he walked through it, Sam began to see scraps of aluminum from the downed plane; nothing big, just little pieces, some no more than six inches across. Then he saw a large hole where the engine had gone into the earth. As he was walking along, looking at the hole, he raised his foot, but did not set it down, as beneath his foot, he saw a three foot long chunk of red meat. A black parachute trailed from this flesh. In the center remains, a perfectly undamaged human hand stuck out with a gold wedding band circling one of the fingers. The horror of the obvious added to Sam's shock. He gasped, stepped back, and circled the pilot's body.

Some half-tracks came down the road from the left carrying the missing part of the company, the machine gunners, rocket and mortar men. The half-tracks stopped and men hopped off and fell in with the rest of the column. A truck with twin anti-aircraft 40mm guns approached. The guns were going, "Pom. Pom. Pom," firing over the cab, spitting out explosive shells that were devastating the earth on either side of the road as the turret traversed first to one side and then the other. These cannon were fed by clips of ammunition, four rounds per clip. Two Marines fed ammo into the twin barrels while two others supplied them from a stack aboard the truck. One tank ran along in front of the truck, the tank commander's head and shoulders sticking out of the turret behind a fifty-caliber machine gun sweeping the road ahead with fire. Someone shouted, "Skirmishers right!"

The Marines fanned out in a line abreast of the tank. The line extended out a hundred yards or so to either side of the vehicles. A path of shellfire destruction was cut down the road and in the adjacent fields. The 40mm guns set up a constant hammering, firing into clumps of grass, at bushes, and an occasional straw covered hut. Any place or object that looked as if it could conceal the enemy was raked by fire.

The Marines marched beside the road using marching fire. As the Marines advanced, North Korean soldiers leaped to their feet and ran for it. Dozens of shots rang out, knocking them down, but they got up and ran again. Sometimes they were knocked down, got back on their feet only to be knocked down again and again.

Like everyone else, Sam was shooting from the hip. It was a horrendous experience. He came upon a North Korean lying face down, almost at his feet, quivering with fear. The soldier was babbling frantically. He seemed to be praying.

"Here's one!" Sam shouted.

"Kill him! Kill him!" came a reply.

Sam did not fire. In an instant, one of his men did. He felt relief. He could not bear to kill another man who was in such a helpless position. Why did they not take prisoners? Sam wondered. But, the answer was obvious. They were charged with destruction of the enemy. None of the enemy had thrown up their hands. Sam did not understand why there was no return fire. If the North Koreans were going to take off, why not do it when the Marines were far distant? It seemed they were committing suicide. Soon Sam realized the enemy was just as green as he was, and that awful withering fire of the 40mm guns just kept them down until it was too late. As their attack moved forward, the din and rattle of gunfire and the smoke never ceased.

Eventually, the 40mm gun trucks exhausted their ammo and turned back. As the attack continued, the terrain changed into rolling hills. As they crested one of these, about five hundred yards distant, a Korean soldier ran out of a hut. Corporal Baxter, from Santa Monica, California, dropped down on one knee, took careful aim and fired a single shot. The man sort of leaped into the air and then fell.

They pressed on, passing the body of the soldier that Baxter had just shot. He lay face down in the brown dead grass; the bullet had struck him in the side of the face, directly in front of his ear, making a wedge shaped hole. It looked just as if he had been hit by an axe. This fact imposed upon Sam's psyche.

They neared a second hut made of clay and bamboo walls, with a straw roof. Sam shouted for someone to cover him. He saw one of his fire teams drop to their bellies ready to fire and he ran across the open ground between, pulling the pin from a hand grenade as he ran. On reaching the hut, he saw it had a fly screen on the window, so he ran around to a second window, hurling the grenade in. He waited for the explosion, but it never came. Almost immediately, a group of children along with three women ran out the door. Catching sight of Sam, they were terrified, but also saw the look of surprise on his face and seemed to realize he wasn't going to harm them.

He had been in a state of semi-shock ever since he shot the first soldier, moving not by logic but essentially by reflex. Somehow, it eased his anguish to see these people alive. He did not consider them gooks; they were real live human beings, who had been spared by fate, because a hand grenade had failed to explode. He felt a little better, as he passed them by, luckily still alive.

As they continued to move through the area some of the initial shock of battle wore off. The road led into a group of steep hills not very high, yet the terrain was rugged enough to stop the skirmish line attack, and they were called back to the road to follow the tanks in columns, one on each side of the road. This continued till noon.

Easy Company passed through them and launched an attack on a large hill lying to the right of the road. They encountered the first spirited resistance and suffered enough casualties to stall the attack. A shouted cry went up for Fox Company to move up. Malder led the 2nd Platoon forward and began climbing the hill where Easy was stalled. As Sam's platoon moved forward through Easy, Easy returned carrying two men on stretchers and with several walking wounded, who were being helped along by their comrades. Their faces were grim, reflecting the shock of battle and they did not speak.

Eventually, 2nd Platoon reached the crest and lay down against it in a long skirmish line. They could not see over the crest, but at the moment just leaned against it. The side was so steep, that in the act of leaning against it, they were indeed almost standing upright.

Malder passed the word, calling for squad leaders. Sam went over to join him, Beller, and Ivan Jennings who had already arrived.

"They're right on the other side of this ridge," Malder said. "We're going to lay mortar fire on them for five minutes. When I yell 'Charge!' we all go over together. Tell your men to scream loud as they go. Tell 'em to give a rebel yell as they go."

Sam hurried back and repeated these instructions to his squad, then lay against the earth and waited. From somewhere down on the road, the mortar shells left the tubes, making hollow metallic noises, sounding like tight drums being hit, and Sam knew instinctively shells were on the way. In a barrage of explosions, the shells came raining down on the far slope where, as yet, none of them had dared look. The five minutes of waiting, lying against the crest feeling the earth shake, seemed a long time. Sam's mouth was dry and he drank the last of the water from his canteen. A minute later his mouth felt dry again.

The shelling stopped. All was quiet for what seemed like an eternity.

"Charge!" Malder screamed.

Simultaneously, a chorus of rebel yells pealed out into the hot still air. This same sound erupted from somewhere deep inside Sam and out his throat filling the air with a shrill yell.

"EeeHiii!" He scrambled over the crest, running hard. The far side was also steep; so steep, in fact, they were unable to stop. Directly in front of Sam's squad the North Koreans were bunched around a machine gun. The gun fired and tracer bullets flamed up at them as they went screaming down the steep slope. The Koreans managed only a few shots before the squad was on top of them, shooting and hacking as they went. The squad passed through and over them, keeping on down the hill, shooting as they went. Sam ran wildly forward, firing and screaming "Sundrah, Sundrah, Sundrah."

Below the machine gun, the slope of the hill decreased and they slowed. They came upon a second group and shot their way through them also and reached a low area. The hill was theirs. Sam fell to the earth and looked about. On a hill to his right, about five hundred yards distant, he saw soldiers. Expecting to be shot at, he began looking for a low place in the ground. He spied a swale, went over to it and dropped down again, looking about at the rest of the men. Luckily, none had been shot.

They had come down the slope on a secondary spine which divided like the letter Y, with the stem of the Y leading back to the crest of the hill whence they came. Sam's squad had taken the right leg. Beller and Jennings had taken the opposite and now couldn't see each other. Malder was with the other two squads. Exhausted from the charge, they lay panting, looking back at the bodies of the men they had just killed.

One was lying on his back, with his face turned away from Sam. One of his fire team leaders, Harold Garret, age eighteen, from Mullins, South Carolina, was eying this same dead soldier. The man had two canteens strapped to his waist and Garret was thirsty. The sun was roasting hot. Garret, sitting down, wanted the water, but the thought of taking it from a dead man inhibited him to the extent that he would crawl a foot or two towards the man then stop. Then, he would move again and stop. Sam was fascinated by this little drama being played out before his eyes, but he remembered the soldiers he had seen on the distant hill and looked back to see what they were doing. The soldiers were no longer visible. Sam turned back to watch Garret moving closer to the dead soldier and then stopping again. Suddenly, he noticed something different; now the soldier's face was turned in Sam's direction. Slowly, almost imperceptibly, his face turned towards the sky and as he turned his helmet slowly came loose from his head. He made no effort to stop it as he slowly searched all around to see where the Marines were. He was indeed very much alive. Sam aimed at him and fired. Immediately, there was a roar and the man was engulfed in black smoke. The smoke wafted away and as it cleared the soldier came back into view. The upper half of the man had flipped completely over, and his face was now towards the earth. Grimacing in hate and pain, his hands clawed into the earth and he slowly drew upright, into a vertical position on his rib cage, staring at Garret. His lower half was still as it was, toes pointed skyward. Slowly his arms relaxed and he sank back to the earth as his upper half died.

From the other side of the ridge Malder called out in alarm. "What's going on over there?"

"Nothing!" came the reply. "Sam Lewis just shot a gook and the bastard blew up."

Within a few moments the 2nd Platoon was on the move again. Their clothes had dried, leaving them caked in mud.

The rest of the day they assaulted hill after hill. Each time they took a hill they were promised food and water. "Chow and water on the next hill, men." Always on the next hill, yet, no chow or water ever appeared and they were nearing exhaustion.

Finally, they reached a hill on the crest of which stood one single North Korean soldier, armed with a Russian burp gun (a short barreled weapon with a drum of ammunition, fifty rounds, that makes a fast chattering sound as it fires). Malder saw him first and shouted a warning. Sam tried to raise his carbine, but was just too tired to do so.

"Shoot that son of a bitch!" someone cried. Not one of them had the strength to raise a weapon, and the soldier, obviously inexperienced, stood staring down at them, dumfounded. In what seemed like slow motion, Sam's carbine came up and with great effort he fired. The soldier toppled backwards. Malder had been unable to raise his carbine and knew that his platoon had reached the limit of endurance. He led them down to the road where Captain Groff came forward in company with a South Korean Marine Lieutenant, who he referred to as Jackson, after Stonewall Jackson of Civil War fame.

"Get back out in the hills!" Groff commanded.

Malder spoke quietly. "This platoon will have their promised chow and water," he said.

"Goddamit, I said attack," Groff snarled.

"These men are going nowhere till they eat and drink," Malder replied, determination in his voice, and that ended it. Groff introduced him to Jackson and the three conferred beside the road. The men rested in the ditch alongside the road until a truck loaded with C rations, water, and ammunition appeared. They ate, filled their canteens and took more ammunition, then climbed the high hill to the right of the road, dug shallow holes and slipped, dead-tired, into them. A fifty-percent alert was set. Half the men would be awake at all times. Those who would sleep the first watch fell immediately into it. The night sounds, the sounds of heavy mortars and artillery, began as above their heads a curtain of H and I (harassing and interdictory) fire began. These weapons fired all night long.

For those who stayed awake, the gnawing fear of tomorrow was, like the smell of Korean earth, a little weaker, but still there. They crouched down in the damp earth and peered out into the night listening to the intermittent rumble of the guns.

CHAPTER 8 ... As Things Are ...

The coming of light revealed a razor-backed ridge covered with a line of shallow holes strung out atop the ridge. Here and there a small scrub tree jutted up from between the holes, stunted, lacking nourishment, lending a bare forlorn look to the landscape. What little grass there remained between the stunted bushes and shallow holes was dead. There was a chill in the still air, dew on the earth, and that foul smell still rising off the paddies below. The guns rumbled. Shells shrilled overhead and landed out in front of the holes.

Lying on his back in his shallow hole looking up at the gray dawn, Sam again heard the creaking sound of North Korean tanks. He rolled over and looked down across the hill towards the road. This time the tanks were in full view. Little brown men, seeming like ants, were trotting alongside. They were spread as skirmishers on each side of the road coming with little short steps which made them appear to be moving faster than they actually were. Their advance was leading them directly against Fox Company's hill at a point where the road curved left and the sides of their tanks would be exposed to Fox Company rockets.

One Marine tank had crawled into a rice paddy, the barrel of its 90mm rifle jutting out, just above the level of the narrow gravel road. Only the turret might be visible to the North Koreans.

Dog Company held the hill cross the road opposite and slightly ahead of Fox. The North Koreans were advancing into a trap. Before they were fully ensnared, one of Fox's machine gunners, a big fellow named

Strange, began firing at them. He was too distant to hit them, but close enough to reveal the Marine position.

As Strange's burst of fire rang out, Malder shouted, "Kick that son of a bitch in the head!"

He leaped to his feet and ran towards the gun shouting, "Cease firing."

The machine gun stopped firing. Sam lay flat in the shallow hole wishing with every breath that he had dug even deeper. Strange had fired long enough to disclose the position and Sam expected shells to come screaming in at any moment. Instead, a sharp crack sounded from the paddy below. Flame blossomed out from the Marine tank. The lead North Korean tank exploded. Two more sharp cracks followed in close succession, and suddenly there were three burning tanks in front.

There followed a roar of rifle fire sounding up into the still air and the machine guns opened up.

The North Korean infantry never had a chance. They were slaughtered by rifle and machine gun fire from both Fox and Dog Companies. Within moments it was all over.

Word passed. Fox Company will move out in fifteen minutes.

Opening his C ration box, Sam hurriedly ate a can of navy beans. The box also contained a piece of orange gumbo candy which he traded to Kenneth Hall for a can of chicken and vegetables. He ate that also.

As Fox moved out, a new sergeant joined 2nd Platoon. Lieutenant Malder told him to follow Sam's squad. They moved out, one column on each side of the road. The tank growled up out of the paddy and preceded them down the road. All that morning, they marched steadily. Occasionally a distant shot would ring out and they would dive for the ditch. The tank would rake the likely hiding places with its machine guns. If the tank failed to eliminate a sniper, a fire team (three men and a leader) would be dispatched to hunt him down while the onward march continued. At 1 o'clock in the afternoon they reached the base of a low hill and paused at the railroad track which circled it. Orders came to hold up the advance while Corsairs bombed and strafed the hill.

Malder called the squad leaders. "When the planes stop bombing we'll attack in a skirmish line. There's supposed to be three hundred gooks up there," he said.

They lay down against the railbed waiting for the planes. Suddenly, right beside Sam, a shot rang out. He turned and saw the new sergeant clutching his foot with both hands. Apparently, he had shot himself.

"You yellow bastard!" Malder shouted. "You'll be court-martialed for that."

"It was an accident," the sergeant said.

"The hell you say. I saw you do it!" Malder said.

"No you didn't. It was an accident." The sergeant removed his shoe as he talked.

"Corpsman!" he cried.

Chico Carsenero, the corpsman whose prayer book Sam had thrown away, bandaged the sergeant's foot. A few minutes later, a jeep arrived and carried the sergeant away.

The planes appeared and began dive bombing the hill, swooping down like hawks killing young rabbits, impressive with deadliness. Simultaneously, the artillery began firing many shells. The combined air and artillery bombardment continued for some time. The shells were terrifying, literally screaming as they passed overhead.

After some time, the bombardment stopped and they were ordered to attack. Fanning out to the left and right they formed a long skirmish line stretching for five hundred feet and started up the hill. With the flag of the Confederacy flying near the center of the line they appeared little different from the soldiers of the Civil War. The nearer they got to the crest of the hill, the faster they moved, first in a fast walk and then in a trot. By the time they crossed the first trenches, they were running. These trenches were empty, with no sign of the enemy having been there. In a running charge they crested the hill and proceeded into a cornfield. Beyond, at the base of the hill, the railroad stretched out eastward. A lone figure in white pantaloons was running down the track.

"I want him alive!" Groff shouted.

The two closest men to him chased the man down and led him back. He seemed crazy. As Jackson questioned him, he kept bending over and jerking cornstalks out of the ground and eating the dirt off the roots. He was just an old Korean peasant who, apparently, had endured both the air strike and the shelling. Perhaps he was hungry but, more likely, his nerves had broken because of the bombardment. He yielded nothing of any value during interrogation and Groff ordered him turned loose. The man walked down the hill towards the west, waving his arms above his head shouting, "Tuleman and Stalin, Tuleman and Stalin."

They dug in for the night, Sam's squad in front of the mortar section. It was growing dark as Malder came over and knelt down beside him.

"Sam," he said, "if anything happens tonight I'll depend on you to hold this section of the perimeter together. Under no circumstances take any orders from Alexis." (Lieutenant Alexis was the mortar officer.)

Sam had never heard of an officer pre-countermanding a fellow officer.

"Alexis is yellow!" Malder continued.

Sam wanted to know more, but said nothing. He wondered how Can Do could know that Alexis was yellow? Malder seemed hesitant to volunteer any more, but he apparently could see Sam was puzzled.

"The first night," he said, "the mortars and machine guns weren't separated from us. Alexis kept them at the beach, instead of following us as he was supposed to."

They finished digging in. Somewhere behind them heavy 4.2 mortars had been set up, and these began firing randomly and continued throughout the night making heavy drum-like sounds followed by fiery explosions. It seemed as if some angry god were hurling hell's fire and brimstone onto the earth.

They were dug in a circle. It was similar to when the settlers made their way west and the American Indians resisted. They slept in shifts, one man awake at all times. Orders were to let no enemy penetrate the circle. It was Marine Corps practice to do so every night, no matter the circumstances.

After digging in, word came down the line. "Any man who fires a round at night had better have a body to prove why he fired."

Sam peered grimly out into the blackness of the night. He had no idea what had happened to people in the other platoons, except those in the immediate vicinity. He had been so busy trying to stay alive that he had time for little else. But now, he puzzled over what Malder had told him. He had always been proud of being a Marine and had accepted, without question, that all officers were courageous and were indeed gentlemen. He had also respected older NCOs. His concepts and long-held opinions were being destroyed. Captain Groff appeared coarse and unfair. Homer was a drunk who had killed Paul Carpenter; one sergeant had shot himself in the foot, and now Malder was telling him the mortar officer was a coward. All these things annoyed him. But on the contrary, Fox Company was advancing through North Korean held territory in such a professional way that his misgivings were counterbalanced. Before daybreak he resolved his doubts by concluding that nothing is ever completely what it seems to be.

He woke Kenneth Hall. Hall sat up in the shared hole and looked out. There was no conversation. Sam ate a can of frankfurters and beans then lay down to attempt sleep. The fear of sudden violent death gradually waned but never quite left him. The earth stank. The guns rumbled intermittently. Eventually, he fell again into an exhausted sleep.

CHAPTER 9 ... North Hollywood ...

Daybreak of the third day revealed the dead stalks of the corn field on all sides. It stretched for a hundred yards more to the east where the railroad track crossed it. Behind lay the range of hills they had spent two days shooting their way through, while to the front the hills were giving way to lowland. Some small conversations began at daybreak. The men were gaining confidence that they would soon reach the city of Seoul and have victory over the North Koreans. Lieutenant Malder spoke up. "Don't get to feeling cocky. When we reach that Han River things will roughen up. We've just been fighting their advance troops."

Even so, Sam felt more confident. He was beginning to sense that he could stay alive in combat. He wondered how far they had come and guessed they were about seven miles inland from where they had landed. To reach the city of Seoul they would have to fight their way for another eighteen miles and cross the Han River. They were making progress. They saddled up and moved back down to the road. Two tanks rumbled forward and again they moved out in columns down the narrow gravel road towards Seoul. They soon came upon a small village which the tanks passed through with their fifty-caliber machine guns randomly firing. As they entered the village the ditches on both sides of the road petered out, giving way to hard gravel sidewalks.

Lieutenant Malder was leading. He wore paratrooper's jump boots and strode confidently forward.

Sam followed with his squad behind, strung out, five yards between men. They came upon a Korean civilian lying on his back on the hard gravel sidewalk looking up at them silently. Sam saw flecks of blood on his white pantaloons, but it wasn't possible to see where he was wounded or how seriously he had been injured.

Malder strode up to the Korean, his boots making a crunching sound on the gravel. He stopped and stared coldly down at the Korean. Helplessly, the man returned the stare. Slowly and deliberately, Malder raised his carbine, aimed at the man's face and pulled the trigger. The weapon failed to fire. In what seemed like slow motion, Malder lowered his carbine, jacked the faulty round out of the chamber and a new round in. Again, he aimed at the man, whose eyes showed the horror he was feeling, knowing he was about to die. He found no mercy in Malder's cold stare and could no longer bear to look back at him. At the last moment, he turned his face away. As he did, his eyes met Sam's and the desperate expression in his eyes was so compelling Sam could not look away. Sam watched in horror as the Korean silently pleaded with him for his life. With his eyes, he seemed to ask Sam the question, "Are you going to just stand there and watch him kill me like this?"

"Don't!" Sam cried out.

At that exact moment, Malder shot him. Bang, bang bang. Once! twice! three times! Three little holes appeared just above the man's ear. You could have covered all three holes with the ace of spades from a deck of playing cards. Bubbles of air and a little yellow matter came up out of the holes. A tremor surged through the man's body, shaking him from head to toe. He grimaced. His eyes still held onto Sam's. A little trickle of blood oozed from beneath the man's head. Slowly the light went out of his eyes as they stayed riveted on Sam's.

Sam was having difficulty staying on his feet. He felt faint. He thought he was going to vomit.

Malder turned and looked back at Sam and the men behind. He saw the horror on their faces and looked at them contemptuously.

"Where the hell do you guys think you're at, North Hollywood?" he sneered.

He stepped across the body and strode off down the street, his heels again crunching the gravel sidewalk. Sam followed. All he could think of was the plea for mercy he saw in the man's eyes.

It all seemed surreal. In three days he had killed more men than he could count and yet there were certain deaths, like the one he had just witnessed, that he would never be able to forget. From that day forward, for as long as he would live, whenever Sam heard someone mention

Hollywood he would recall that pleading look in that Korean's eyes. He would never be free of it.

The tanks kept chopping away with their machine gun fire. Events seemed to flow forward like a river and wouldn't stop just because Sam was in shock. Even in this state, the urge to stay alive was strong.

The sun rose full in the east and cast its rays across the landscape. In all respects it was a beautiful day with the sun's rays warming him in a soft and gentle way that belied any hint of violence, but the sharp cracks of gunfire, the rattle of the machine guns mingled with the roar of the tanks, and the death of that single person made it all seem like a bad dream. They moved relentlessly forward.

Far ahead, a motorcycle with sidecar attached came hurtling down the road toward them. It braked rapidly as fire from the lead tank's machine gun leaped out and arched towards the cyclist. Sam saw, by the path of the tracers, the bullets reach the motorcycle as it was coming to a standstill, and indeed it moved no more. As they neared the motorcycle he saw both the driver and the passenger were in an up-right position. Going closer he saw by insignia on the uniform that the sidecar passenger was a North Korean General. His hands were firmly holding field glasses raised almost to his face, with his elbows spread wide, just below a large hole through his chest. The fifty-caliber round had removed his very heart.

His driver was sitting astride the cycle, both hands on the bars with his mouth agape and a stunned look upon his face. A bullet had passed through his forehead just above his eyes, leaving a two-inch chasm.

All morning they continued on past the dry and gray rice paddies, the stench of human dung clinging to their nostrils. Occasionally a sniper would fire at them, and they would dive for cover while the tanks raked the suspected hiding places. Then, as if instinctively, they would get up and move on.

Sam heard what sounded like the brief rustle of wind through dead oak leaves of autumn. It died away.

"Whoom!"

A loud thunderclap sent him diving for the ground. He leaped into a ditch and peered back down the road. The Third Platoon were still on their feet. Sergeant Mann was marching forward with a machine gun draped across his shoulders. The sound of the rustling came again.

"Whoom!"

Mann's machine gun rode upward upon a cloud of black smoke then fell back to earth. The smoke lifted and Mann was gone, just in that short instant. On the road nearby, another Marine had been beheaded by the blast.

His torso lay kicking, thrashing about, while his heart pumped the blood out of his body.

"Whoom, Whoom, Whoom!"

Again the mortar shells rained down like claps of thunder on the roadway, shaking the earth, terrifying, destroying his ability to think. Why am I in this ditch? Did I leap? Or, what? A few feet beyond, a bridge culvert passed beneath the road. Sam crawled into it, still feeling the earth shake and tremble.

Just as suddenly as it had begun, the mortar fire stopped and all was very quiet again. Sam could hear voices, but he stayed in his protective culvert. Then, he heard the hum of a motor and heard a vehicle come to a stop, the engine still idling and a voice asking if this was Fox Company. The driver of the jeep had brought their mail, not realizing that they had just been under fire.

"Yeah. This is Fox Company," someone said.

"I've got mail for you," the driver said.

"Okay, you had better give it to us and get your ass out of here pronto; we're taking mortar fire."

"Is that right?"

"Damn right it's right, you fool."

Sam heard him gun the engine and roar off.

Malder began a mail call right then and there, where, less than five minutes before, shells had been raining down.

Sam heard his name called.

"Here!" he shouted.

"Where?"

"Here!"

"Where the hell are you?" Malder yelled, sounding somewhat puzzled.

"In the culvert!"

A minute later, he peered in at Sam. Grinning, he said, "You can come out now, the shelling's stopped."

"Are we moving out?" Sam asked.

"Not yet."

"Hand me my mail," Sam said, as he reached. "I'll just stay in here. When we're ready to move out, you know where I am."

Sam was thinking about Sergeant Mann and his premonition about dying. He doubted Mann even heard the mortar coming.

How odd, he thought, that Mann knew and Carpenter, with his plans to remain in the Corps for the rest of his life, never suspected.

Malder passed the mail and he took it eagerly. He hoped for a letter from Charlotte. It was not to be. Instead, he received five telegrams from Lenders Loan Company. By sheer coincidence, he opened each one in sequence. Each became a little more demanding. The last one read, "Be in our office, with one hundred and twenty-five dollars, within fifteen minutes, or else."

Their office had been near the barracks in Washington D.C., and Sam had borrowed a hundred twenty-five dollars from them when Charlotte and he were married. He had not been paid ever since and so no payment had been made.

"Saddle up," someone cried.

Sam jammed the telegrams into his pocket and crawled out of the culvert.

They moved out in column formation once again. Within an hour they were again under fire. Leaving the road, they went to ground in a pea field where orders were shouted to dig in. Sam designated the position of his squad and began digging with Kenneth Hall again. They were about two hundred yards distant from the road on the reverse slope of a broad gentle hill. Below, the hill stretched out into the rice paddies. No sooner had they begun to dig than the scream of a shell passed over and landed in the paddy below in a massive ball of fire, sending smoke and earth in all directions.

They dug furiously. A second shell exploded on the hillside just above them. Whoever was firing had put one round beyond and one round on the near side; the next round would be on them. Sam clawed at the earth furiously with his shovel, but he heard it coming, screaming like the hinges on hell's door, and he rammed his head down into what little hole he had completed. The shell landed right on the line where his squad was digging. He was pushed from behind and felt something strike him sharply in the back. He raised on his knees and elbows and looked around. Roddy, one of his BAR men, lay on the ground with his clothing afire. His shattered rifle stock was smoking. His assistant, Timmons, lay nearby groaning, holding his belly with both hands. He could see that Kuhn too was hit.

"Corpsman! Corpsman!" Sam cried.

He felt something warm running down his side and felt with his hand. His hand came back bloody. Sam began to panic.

"See how bad I'm hit," he said.

Kenneth Hall fumbled with his dungaree jacket, "It's bad," he said.

"Give me my brandy," Sam said.

Hall didn't do anything, so Sam said again, "I want my brandy. Give it to me."

"I can't," Hall said.

"You can't, why not?"

"I drank it."

"You drank it! The whole thirteen bottles?"

"Yes, I drank it all. I needed it."

It was growing dark. Sam could see Chico Carsenero working on Roddy. Next he came to Sam. Timmons was still moaning.

"Help Timmons," Sam said.

Within a short time, a helicopter landed beside them and carried away Roddy and PFC Kuhn. It lifted off as rapidly as possible before more shells came in.

Timmons and Sam were left. A jeep pulled up as Carsenero was checking Sam's wound. Captain Groff knelt down beside Carsenero.

"It's not bad," Carsenero said.

Groff looked at the wound. "Better send him back. It might get infected," he said.

Carsenero tied a red tag to his dungaree jacket and Sam got on to the jeep and sat down. They placed Timmons in, on a stretcher. He was moaning softly, holding his stomach where a large chunk of steel had entered.

The jeep ride was rough and Timmons was in a lot of pain. Sam thought he would die before he reached the aid station. It seemed they rode for hours and Sam could hardly believe they had advanced so far. Timmons kept begging for water and Sam kept saying, "Hang on boy, we'll be there soon."

Sam couldn't give him water as it might kill him, but didn't want to tell him this. Then at last, they arrived at the field aid station and Timmons was rushed into an operating tent. Sam carried his carbine into the aid tent and was ordered to take it outside. A corpsman examined his wound, cleaned it, and gave him a shot of penicillin. Then he directed Sam to a nearby tent filled with folding cots. Sam went in, lay down on a cot and listened to the artillery firing, a constant rumble of rolling thunder sending death and destruction through the air to the North Koreans. A short while later, he was asleep.

Chapter 10 ... The First Aid Station ...

Sam woke with a start. At first he thought he was at the front. Light came through the open tent flap and he fell back on the cot. He heard the sounds of vehicles entering and leaving and the voices of Marines and corpsmen. He got up and walked to the entrance of the tent and looked about. The aid station consisted of a few canvas tents and a field kitchen. It was set atop hard ground, but he still smelled the foul odor of the paddies and it irritated him. Even so, he felt a great relief to get away from combat, to feel safe again. He took a deep breath. How wonderful it was to be alive; to feel human again, free of the threat of violent death. Others were dead, yet he was still alive and that gladdened him. He felt mild tinges of guilt, but now the ache was gone from his chest, and he felt lighter, more confident. Since the jeep ride the previous night, he estimated that Fox Company had fought its way a third of the way to Seoul. Somehow, he felt, when they captured Seoul the war would be at an end. No one had ever told him that, but the optimism of youth allowed him to think that way.

He ate a good breakfast at the field kitchen consisting of powdered eggs and powdered milk. It was a far cry from breakfast at the barracks in Washington D.C., where he could take a tray and go cafeteria style. He thought longingly of his old quarters at Washington. Life there was still so vivid in his mind that he compared everything as to how life had been then.

"Three eggs over easy please and home fried potatoes." That was his memory of eating breakfast back then. There had been large pitchers of cold milk at each table. And he had always loved cold milk. Now, even though the milk was powdered, it was good to have. After eating, he inquired about

Timmons and Roddy. Timmons had surgery during the night and was then flown to Japan. Roddy was on the Hospital Ship Repose. PFC Kuhn, who had been flown out with Roddy, was only slightly wounded just like Sam, and Sam found him in one of the other tents.

Stationery was available at the Medical Station and he confiscated some of it so he could write to Charlotte and to his mother. They would probably be receiving telegrams that he was injured and he didn't want them to worry unnecessarily.

As the day wore on, a steady stream of hospital jeeps unloaded more wounded and Sam began watching for people he might know. Walter Moss was brought in, his dungarees covered in blood. Alas, he was dead and Sam saw them carry him out behind a tent and place him along with the other dead.

It was very sad. Yet, he inquired no further. Sam felt Moss too had a premonition because he bought all those insurance policies.

At noon, one jeep arrived. In it were two Marines holding another Marine in a sitting position in the back. They leaped off as it stopped and beckoned to the third Marine to climb down. Instead of climbing down, he clapped both hands to his ears and started screaming. He banged his ears furiously, as if trying to free sounds from within his head, all the while screaming and holding his hands over his ears. It seemed he was trying to drown out some terrible sound that only he could hear. He looked familiar, and then Sam recognized him as Bernie Welman. He had been a ballplayer in civilian life. He was a talented pitcher. When he enlisted in the Marine Corps the colonel in charge of the Recruit Training Battalion at Parris Island was trying to build a baseball team. He learned about Welman's talent and had latched on to him and, instead of basic training, Welman played ball. When his platoon was graduated, so was Welman, without ever having learned how to march.

No amount of pleading could get him off the jeep. He just continued slapping his ears and screaming. No doubt he was still hearing the shells. Finally, he was dragged off, restrained in a straightjacket, and carried inside.

Late in the day an ambulance arrived with a Marine laid out on a stretcher. As they pulled the stretcher out of the back of the jeep, Sam recognized the stocky frame as that of Malder. They set him on the ground outside the medical station. PFC Kuhn and Sam went over to see him. His face and shoulder were bloody. Some of the flesh had been torn away from his jaw, which appeared to be broken. Sam knelt down beside him and Malder recognized him, but seemed unable to talk. Sam wanted to know how the fighting was going for the platoon, but he never asked.

Instead, he said, "Kuhn and I are going back up tomorrow, Can Do."

Malder struggled, as if trying to get off the stretcher, then fell back. He tried again, was able to get halfway into a sitting position and clenched his fist. He tried to talk and Sam could see that his jaw was indeed broken. He made a supreme effort and his eyes took on a wild appearance.

"Those damn Communists!" he cried. "Kill 'em!"

He sank back, unable to say more. Two hospital corpsmen carried him into the tent. He was making a gargling sound as if choking on blood.

All afternoon a steady stream of casualties arrived at the aid station. In answer to Sam's question as to how the fighting was going, the answer was always the same.

"Bad, very bad."

Beller was brought in late that afternoon. Some of his fingers were missing from one hand, and obviously something was wrong with the other, but before Sam could talk to him they hauled him away.

Sam went looking for Kuhn and told him he thought they should go back up. Kuhn was only sixteen, still a freckle-faced boy. He had a broad forehead, sandy hair and gray eyes. Like Sam, he had lied about his age when enlisting. He just grinned when Sam mentioned going back up. He didn't seem to be bothered by combat at all, but Sam found the whole thing deeply troubling, especially the killing of the Korean in the village. It seemed to him Malder had no need to kill him. The man did not appear to have been a soldier. More likely, he was a civilian who had not had the sense to get out of the village. He was one of the people they supposedly had come to help. Sam could not think of him without remembering that look in his eyes. What he found troubling was that, in all respects, Malder had been good for the platoon. He had counseled them so as to be able to face the reality of combat and to do their duty, not for their country, but for each other. The latter, however, would satisfy the first. Sam respected Malder. He tried to rationalize his killing of the wounded Korean, but was unable to.

That night, he dreamed the wounded Korean was staring at him and he wakened in a sweat. It was impossible to go back to sleep. He pondered what he might find when he returned to the front. He remained awake the rest of that night. After breakfast, the corpsman dressed his wound and also checked Kuhn.

"You're both ready to go," he said.

Sam looked for his carbine. He had left it outside the aid tent and now it was missing. When he asked, none of the corpsmen professed to know anything about it. He drew a new one from the supply tent. The weapon was packed in a heavy preservative Cosmoline grease. He stripped it down and cleaned it as best he could. The only thing which would break down the Cosmoline was gasoline, and he hadn't any. He had to settle for some medical gauze and wiped the parts as clean as possible. Fortunately he still had, taped back to back, two thirty-round magazines.

He drew eleven more fifteen-round magazines, and after filling all the magazines, he took two more boxes of ammo, each containing fifty rounds. The boxes he put in his pack; the fifteen-round magazines he dispersed about his waist in designated canvas pouches.

Kuhn drew a new BAR along with twenty pounds of ammo. They caught the next ambulance jeep going back to Fox Company and were soon on their way. Sam was afraid, but he had grown closer to his comrades than he realized. As the jeep wound its way past the wreckage of vehicles and bodies of dead Koreans and general debris of battle he sat quietly and wondered anxiously what he might find when they reached Fox Company.

CHAPTER 11 ... Yong Dong Po ...

At length the jeep driver slowed down and turned off the main road. He entered a pea field which was bordered by some smashed huts which were pocked with bullet holes, in a landscape which reflected the ferocity of the battle which had taken place. Here and there a little column of smoke rose from the ashes of a burned hut. Familiar figures clad in dungarees sat about cleaning weapons and drinking coffee. The jeep driver explained, "This is Fox Company. They're in reserve. Took heavy casualties yesterday."

The jeep braked to a halt. Sam got out and looked about. The first person Sam recognized was Manson, a BAR man whose face broke into a broad grin when he saw Sam and Kuhn. Sam stood, looking around for Tarring. Tarring saw him first. "Good to see you guys back," Tarring grinned. "We had a rough day yesterday. Beller got hit and we lost Can Do. I had to reorganize and I gave your squad, or what was left of it, to Baxter. If it's okay with you, take over Beller's squad. Baxter is just getting the feel of things with your squad so there's no sense disturbing him now."

Sam nodded his assent and went about finding out which men he had inherited. The first fire team was led by Atlee Shelton, from Madisonville, Kentucky, whose nickname was Arkie. He spoke with a slow, easy drawl and was a quiet thinking person. Rude was Arkie's BAR man. He was an easy going and pleasant person. Petitt was rifleman. McGarity led the second fire team. Erickson, a little Swede from Arkansas, was BAR man. Dunlap and Lewellyn were left in the third fire team with Lewellyn carrying the BAR. After Sam identified his new squad, Atlee Shelton filled him in on the rest.

"You really missed it Sam. The night you were hit they brought tanks against us again. Monegan was dug in down near the road. When the tanks came in the only thing we had was Monegan and his bazooka. I guess he figured he couldn't hit them unless he was real close, so up he got out of the hole and walked down to meet them. Perkins went along to load the bazooka. Perkins was carrying the ammo for the bazooka so he had no choice except to go along."

"Did they have any infantry with the tanks?" Sam asked.

"Yeah man, did they ever! There were a whole bunch on trucks, but Monegan just knelt down right out in the open and began firing. He nailed two tanks right off the bat. After he hit the first one he moved. It was still dark and hard to see him, but we saw the flash when he fired. He whacked the second tank and held his ground. I guess he just got overconfident. Anyhow, he bagged a third and we saw the flash from the same place as when he hit the second. By that time they were shooting at him, so just after he hit the third tank he decided to move, but I guess it was too late; they almost cut him in half with machine gun fire. All the time we were firing at their infantry and we just mowed them down."

"Was Perkins hit?" Sam asked.

"Not even a scratch," Arkie said.

"Yesterday we hit a roadblock and had a hell of a fight. Bullets were flying all over the place. We had to cross a railroad track and the enemy were defending it with a machine gun. Old Harvey Owen came out from behind a hut and was hit by three bullets in the leg. Luckily, they grazed him and it didn't even seem to bother him too much. He took a grenade and hurled it at them. They picked it up and tossed it back and the durn thing exploded in midair. Old Harvey just said, "I'll get that sucker." Then he took a second grenade and drew it back by my head with the pin already out. "One thousand one, one thousand two," he said and then he threw it. It never came back that time. Then he hollered for old Varn, his BAR man, and they went down where they could fire up the tracks. By this time the gooks were trying to pull back; Old Harvey and Varn caught 'em trying to get across the track and just stacked 'em up."

"What happened to Sergeant Moss?" Sam queried.

"I don't know how he was hit. I saw three of them with their hands up start to come in to give up. Moss just shot them down; he really hated them you know."

"Yeah, I know," Sam said, thinking he must have had a lot of hatred to be murdering Koreans to get revenge against the Japanese.

Arkie continued. "Anyway, when I looked back Moss was on the ground. He was propped up with his chest covered with blood. His face was a ghastly gray and I knew he was gone."

Arkie shook his head sadly. "What a hell of a life he had. Pulled that damn rice paddy plow for four years and now to end like this."

Sam didn't say anything. He was beginning to wish he hadn't come back.

"How did Malder get it?"

"He was hit at the roadblock along with Phippen. Phippen was lying on the ground, bawling. He had a broken leg. Malder told him to move his yellow ass up off the ground and go back to the aid station. Then mortars came in again and Malder was hit too."

"I saw Malder," Sam said. "I don't think he'll be back."

Having rested for a day at the aid station, he began to feel better. This seemed to be the case for the others as well.

Bodies of North Korean soldiers lay all about the general area. Some American soldiers drove up in a truck followed by a Negro First Sergeant in a jeep. They stopped and began looking about. The Negro First Sergeant climbed out of his jeep.

"Those Marines has been here. Look at all them bodies. You can always tell where Marines has been because they's always a lot of dead bodies lying round."

He began to shake his head sadly. "Well, les get to it."

The soldiers who were in the truck got out and began loading the dead. One of the North Korean soldiers showed some sign of life.

"This one's still alive," one of the soldiers said.

Manson had been watching. He leaped up and went running over holding his BAR.

"Where, which one? I'll put him out of his misery," he said.

The First Sergeant drew back indignantly. "Man what's wrong wid you? You ain't gonna shoot that poor old gook."

"The hell I'm not," Manson said. "Which one is it?" Then he saw the Korean move and aimed his BAR.

The First Sergeant stopped him. "If you shoot that poor old gook I'm gonna see you in prison. I'm a Master Sergeant in the United States Army and I order you not to shoot that poor old gook."

"Better get him out of here then," Manson said.

They placed the Korean soldier on the jeep and the Negro sergeant drove off. The soldiers placed the bodies on the truck and left. The mercy shown by the Negro First Sergeant made Sam glad. It was the right thing to do. It seemed to him that war lifted the restrictions of society in such a way that a keener sense of right and wrong was needed to retain some semblance of human decency.

By this time Sam understood why Captain Groff had raised so much hell when the Japanese mess employee had gone to the head of the chow line in Japan. Groff wanted the men to think of him as a gook and not a man. It would be easier to kill someone you didn't consider an equal.

The rest of the day was spent relaxing at Yong Dong Po. Sam felt fortunate because it was his second day of rest and he had a better perspective. His comrades had hardened in such a way that the show of bravado had disappeared. The change in them, while obvious, was hard to define. It could be that all were now more serious. Those who had seemed impulsive now seemed more contemplative. They did not speak of what they would do tomorrow nor what had happened in the immediate past. They just sat about making coffee and hot chocolate, heating rations, writing letters and cleaning weapons. There was no talk of taking Seoul, the city they had been commanded to recapture from the North Korean invaders. Those who had once celebrated with saki now looked at cases of same without even opening them. It seemed to Sam that everyone was waiting for what tomorrow might bring, yet no one spoke of it.

They dug shallow holes and crawled in for the night, listening to the intermittent sounds of the mortars and occasional prolonged bursts of gunfire coming from some other battalion, indicating that the North Koreans were fighting back, attempting to achieve, by night, what they had failed to do by day.

CHAPTER 12... The Patrol ...

When Sam first awakened, the smell of the earth sickened him. He closed his eyes and lay back, thinking about Walter Moss and how ironic his life and death had been. His four years of being a prisoner of war, toiling in rice paddies, had twisted him with so much hatred he had killed every Oriental possible before succumbing to death in those very same smelly paddies. Sam shuddered at the thought of death in this horrible place. The idea of being buried in the earth of Korea repelled him even more than the thought of death itself. He opened his eyes and sat up. The morning was shrouded in a light fog which hovered about the huts and dew-covered pea fields. The sickening smell of human dung seemed to intensify in the fog, making the rations taste awful. Sam ate only out of necessity. The fog hovering about them and the clinging smell combined with the anticipation the day could bring some new horror as yet unknown was depressing. The whole atmosphere seemed gray and ominous.

"Saddle up!" The cry rang out, and they readied.

Before they could move out, the shrill scream of artillery rent the air above their heads. The shells passed over and fell on Dog Company.

"Corpsman, Corpsman," someone cried.

As the shells came screaming in Sam heard them calling out again for help. The shells passed over from the rear which meant they were friendly. Not that it made any difference to the men upon whom they fell. Two were killed and three wounded. It indeed was an ominous day, enough to sober Sam with that fear of death again, crowding all else from his mind.

Under an umbrella of artillery fire, they moved out, then moved and stopped, then moved and stopped again. Each time they halted, Sam began to dig a hole. Fox Company was the second company in a long battalion column and, although they heard the frequent snap of enemy rifles, those in front of them were taking care of the enemy snipers. Marines would approach the sniper hiding places and they would fall victim to fear and stop shooting. That fear would soon be justified as a rapid burst of automatic fire ended their lives.

All day they marched and in the evening reached the western bank of the Han River and stopped.

Amphtracs were ferrying the men across. While they waited to be ferried across, Sam again dug in. His cartridge belt was rubbing his wound, removing the scab and making it raw. Just before dark, they were ferried over, the last to cross. Fox Company dug in facing the river, where there wouldn't be much chance of a night attack.

Sam was beginning to evaluate each happening, no matter how insignificant, as to its possible value in ensuring another day of life. He spent the next two hours digging a hole about two feet wide, seven feet long, and two feet deep. After making an agreement with Arkie to awaken him in two hours, he put a pad on his wound, tied it with gauze around his waist, then lay down and used his helmet as a pillow. Seven times that day they had stopped and seven times Sam had dug. He felt exhausted.

Sam had no sooner relaxed than they were ordered to move. He climbed wearily out of the hole and found Tarring.

"What's up?" he asked.

"We're going back across the river to escort some tanks back here," Tarring said.

While preparing to move again, Tarring explained that the tanks had crossed the river at a more favorable location and 2nd Platoon would escort them back to this present location.

They crossed the river in an Amphtrac. A jeep was waiting for them and they marched behind the jeep toward their destination. The driver offered Tarring a ride, but he declined and marched along with the platoon until well after midnight. Only those in the jeep were aware of the destination. Sam feared what would happen should the jeep hit a mine or somehow be blown up. When they reached their destination another Amphtrac took them back across the river. Sam swore silently, wondering why they had not just ferried them to the site and saved all the marching.

They exited the Amphtrac below a blown bridge. There was a lot of gravel underneath the bridge and several tanks were parked on it.

By this time it was about 2:00 A M.

Tarring suggested, "Just lie down beside the tanks, try to get some sleep, we'll move in the morning."

Baxter volunteered to stay awake and let the others sleep. Sam joined him. They lay down on their bellies on the gravel and agreed that Sam would watch down river to the left and Baxter to the right. Within a half hour Sam spied a column of infantry stealthily approaching from the river bank towards them. He aimed his carbine preparing to open fire as he heard Baxter click off the safety on his pistol. The two watched in silence while the infantry slowly approached in their short-strided walk. Sam took them for Orientals. As they drew near, a voice from one of the tanks challenged them.

"Halt!"

They stopped.

"Who are you!" the tanker asked.

A voice responded in English giving their South Korean unit designation.

"Pass on," the tanker replied.

The whole column, a full company of men, went gliding past and disappeared, ghost-like, into the darkness.

Baxter lowered his forty-five pistol into his shoulder holster and let out a long sigh of relief. "We never would have stopped them," he said rightly.

Sam lay silently. He shivered ever so slightly. Lying in the hard gravel was somehow better than dirt and it was comforting to know that friendly forces were somewhere about.

Soon, dawn came and they drew rations by the bank before moving on out. Sam decided just to heat some coffee using one of the little cans of canned heat. He filled the canteen cup, added some instant coffee, powdered cream and sugar, and within a minute or two he was enjoying hot coffee.

The sun rose like a great orange ball, but without much warmth. Fall chill was beginning to make its presence known. The tanks growled up out of the river bed and waited on the railroad track. A platoon of engineers, planning to sweep the tracks for mines, accompanied them. There were ten tanks, and the men mingled alongside the tanks and started east along the track. They had gone about half a mile when the Marine Lieutenant in charge of the engineers asked Tarring for a fire team to investigate the hill off to the left and ahead. Tarring relayed this to Sam and Sam sent Arkie.

He moved out at a trot, making the crest of the hill about five hundred feet away. Sam watched as he led his fire team across the paddy and up the hill beyond. Sam happened to notice one of the tanks had stopped and was swinging its cannon around, in the direction of Arkie, who was now heading back towards them. Sam ran frantically towards the tank, just as it fired a stream of thirty-caliber bullets, trying to align its cannon. Tarring took off at a run, grabbed the tank's phone and shouted to the tank commander.

"Hold your fire! Those are our men."

Arkie came back fit to be tied.

"Damn. It's bad enough gettin' shot at by the gooks. But must the damn tanks do it too?" he snapped.

They soon reached another hill and the Lieutenant of Engineers decided to dispatch another fire team. He turned to Arkie.

"Corporal," he said, "go check that hill over there."

"Fuck you! Lieutenant, if you want that damn hill checked, do it yourself. You ain't using me for target practice again," Arkie said.

The lieutenant turned red with anger.

Sam could not help but chuckle as they continued.

The episode with Arkie ended any reconnoitering of the area ahead. The lieutenant didn't protest, and Tarring remained silent.

The railroad gradually veered away from the river. It was now bordered on the left by a low rice paddy about three hundred feet wide, with some drainage ditches crossing at forty-five degree angles to the track. The paddies were dry with only a stubble of rice, yet the straw was still high in the paddies even though it was dead.

On the right, a low hill lay behind a small village of mud huts, and merged into a broad hill, with a ridge line running right-angle to the track. At its upper end, this ridge line turned away from them, and beyond that lay a valley of undetermined depth which Sam couldn't see from his position on the track, but he could see yet another hill rising beyond. Everything had that dead look of fall. Only small, scrubby trees dotted the hills. Nothing much seemed to grow on Korea's hills. If there were trees at all, they were always stunted.

As they neared the village, Sam saw men running about on the top of the hill which lay beyond the valley. Some of his squad dropped to a kneeling position and started to fire at them.

Sam shouted, "Hold your fire! only Marines are stupid enough to run along the skyline like that."

No sooner had he spoken than a series of explosions rocked the railroad track ahead. Black smoke rose beyond the tanks and it was impossible to tell whether or not any had been hit. A rifle bullet struck a rail and ricocheted away. They went down, with Lewellyn and Sam lying side by side between the rails as more explosions popped in front of them. More bullets hit the rails beside Sam and went whining off.

"Move up a few feet," Sam said. "One round might nail us both."

"If you want to move, you move," Lewellyn said. "I'm staying right here."

Tarring came running down the track, hunching low to protect himself.

"Sam, take your squad and clean out that village. I'll meet you on that ridge beyond," he said.

Sam stood up waving his hand. "Second squad, let's clean out the village," he yelled.

The men leapt up and off the railroad track and began, systematically, checking each hut in the village. They worked in two-man teams. One man kicked a door open, stood to one side, while the other was ready to fire. The village was about two hundred yards wide. They passed quickly through the place without encountering anyone.

Tarring had led the other two squads up to the first ridge where they had gone to ground in a skirmish line.

Rifle fire was coming across this ridge, making flat snapping sounds, forcing them to stay down. Sam went to ground beside Tarring. "The village is clear!" Sam told him.

On the other side of Tarring, McGarity pulled the pin from a hand grenade, rose to his knees and hurled it. As it left his hand, a bullet struck the grenade, deflected off and passed on through the palm of his hand. The grenade bounced over between Sam and Tarring. They hugged the earth, waiting for the explosion. It didn't come. The grenade was, very fortunately, a dud.

Tarring hadn't seen the bullet strike the grenade. He thought McGarity had just dropped it.

"What kind of baseball player are you?" he said.

McGarity, holding his injured hand, replied, "Dadgum bullet hit me."

Then Tarring saw that McGarity's hand was bleeding and helped to bandage it.

All the while bullets, making flat snapping sounds, were still cracking over the ridge. Something had to be done. They were unable to continue, and didn't know how many of the enemy they were up against. Also, they would not have enough ammo to last forever. The only positive aspect of their situation was the tanks. They had enough tanks with them to make it look like the vanguard of a huge army.

While Tarring was bandaging McGarity's hand, Sam decided to reconnoiter the ridge line by moving back towards the village and then circling up the hill. He slipped down away from the crest and started towards the right flank. Suddenly, he came face to face with a North Korean soldier who carried a single-shot rifle in his right hand and was apparently scouting, just like Sam. Sam raised his carbine and pulled the trigger as he brought it up. His first shot struck the ground in front of the soldier, and then his carbine jammed.

The soldier gawked at him, making no attempt to raise his own rifle. He was so surprised at seeing Sam, his mouth dropped open. Sam didn't think he realized the weapon had jammed as panic was written all over his face. Simultaneously, Sam panicked. Both took off in opposite directions, Sam excitedly screaming, "Gook! Gook!"

He returned to where Tarring was. Rifle fire was still crossing the ridge.

"Tarring, I'm going to try to flank 'em," he cried.

"Go ahead," Tarring replied. "I'll get one of those flame-throwing tanks up here."

Sam called for his squad to follow and started back. When he reached the place where he had met the soldier, he saw him watching from the doorway of the first hut in the village. Again Sam fired. This time he fired two shots before the weapon jammed. He cleared it and fired again. This time it chattered the way he expected. He shot cross marks on the hut, but could not be sure whether he had hit the soldier or not. He did not realize it till later but, when he had cleaned the weapon, he had been unable to get the Cosmoline out from the area around the firing pin. As soon as the heat of firing melted the Cosmoline the problem ceased.

Leading the squad, he circled the ridge until he reached a point where he could look down into the swale where the rifle fire had come from. The squad followed him and dropped down. Manson, on his own initiative, had accompanied them. He fired a burst from his BAR down through the swale. To Sam's amazement, dozens of Oriental heads popped up in front. They were dug in very close to one another, a strategy used not to repel infantry attack but to avoid being killed by air attack or artillery.

The whole squad fired at them, literally raking them with a hail of bullets. They kept popping their heads up, but weren't even looking in the right direction. The squad fired rapidly as they kept popping up. They were slaughtered by the fire. As Sam poured fire at them he shouted, "Sundrah! Sundrah!"

They now knew where Sam's squad was, and began coming out of their holes towards them. Some were obviously surrendering, but some not, forcing the squad to be selective as to whom they shot. Farther down, where Sam had parted from Tarring, a plume of flame billowed out across the ridge, devastating everything it touched. Many had been in a cave, in front of the flame-throwing tank, but far enough away that the flame was unable to reach them. They came out with upraised hands and headed towards Tarring. Those closer to Sam were coming with hands extended skyward in surrender. Manson was sitting cross-legged, not even bothering to take cover, still pouring automatic fire at them. Sam kept yelling "Sundrah!" as loud as he could. It seemed as if the earth was full of them. One trotted towards the squad still holding his weapon.

"Here comes one who looks like he wants to surrender," Manson said, "but he's got the wrong thing in his hand."

He fired, knocking the man backwards.

Even as Sam fired he felt a revulsion at all the killing. It was horrible. He was aware, from the expression on Manson's face, that when Manson shot the one who still had his rifle Manson was enjoying killing them. He felt even more revulsion and was sorry for the man Manson had just killed. It all seemed so utterly cruel. But such emotions had no place in their situation, and he kept firing as rapidly as he could. It was kill, or be killed. Later on, when he had time to think about it and remember seeing his bullets tearing off pieces of their skulls, he would define war not as kill or be killed, but as kill—and be killed.

Much later, Sam realized that, as surely as you take a human life, some part of you slips across an imaginary boundary and goes with him, never to return.

The heads still kept popping up and Sam kept shouting, "Sundrah, Sundrah," and pouring fire at them.

They had so many prisoners they couldn't guard them and still keep shooting, and it began to look as if they would be overrun by the sheer numbers of prisoners. The men stopped firing and covered the prisoners. Sam knew that if he did not keep those in the swale pinned down with fire, they would even yet destroy him.

"Arkie," he shouted, "guard prisoners; the rest of you keep firing."

Down where Tarring had brought up the tank, over a hundred had surrendered to him, and he was stripping them.

While all this was taking place the Engineer Lieutenant, who had suffered a rifle bullet in one hand, was talking to the Battalion Commander on the tank radio. The Battalion Commander sent orders to stop the fight and bring back the tanks, saying they were needed to attack the enemy in the streets of Seoul. This hill had no strategic value. The lieutenant relayed this news to Tarring. Tarring sent a runner up to Sam.

"Break it off!" The runner shouted.

"What about all those still out there?" Sam asked.

"Leave em," he said. "We're supposed to strip the prisoners and use them as hostages!"

Sam backed away from the ridge and took his prisoners down the hill to where Tarring and the rest of the platoon were guarding the others. Some of these were wounded and were placed on the tanks. The rest were stripped, but three proved to be women, so were allowed to put clothes back on.

They returned to the railroad track and moved towards Seoul. The column now consisted of engineers, tanks, naked North Koreans, and Marines. As they went along, Sam opened a can of cold beans, took two or three bites and happened to glance to the rice paddies on the left. The paddy was alive with North Korean soldiers, crouched down in the paddies, scarcely fifty feet away, sneaking towards the column. They hadn't dared to fire when 2nd Platoon attacked the hill because the tanks had been between the platoon and them and they feared the tanks. Now they were trying surprise, still not daring to fire because their comrades were shields.

Sam hurled the beans aside. "Gooks!" he screamed.

Everyone began shooting at the same time. The North Koreans broke and ran for it. One group of five leaped into a ditch, clawing to get up the other side. Sam dropped to one knee and fired into them. One fell face forward. The others tried to claw across him to get away.

One of the tanks shot straight down the ditch into the scrambling group, hitting them with a 90mm shell at point blank range, blowing them up in a jumble of parts, arms, legs, heads, and smoke. Sam emptied his last magazine with the burst of fire. He got down below the railbed, took out the two boxes of ammo and began loading magazines. Around him the gunfire roared and rattled and popped. The machine gun fire from the tanks, intermingled with the sharp high cracks of the cannon and the fire from the platoon, was deafening. Before he could load new magazines the firing died down and then stopped. A large part of a North Korean battalion lay dead in the paddy. They lay in the ditch they had tried to cross or sprawled on the banks on both sides of the ditch, blood soaking their uniforms. Some were parts of bodies, here an arm, there a leg, sometimes half a head and sometimes unrecognizable chunks of humanity. The Marines stood looking at them, awed by the results of their fire. No one spoke. Except for the hum of the engines of the tanks it was quiet and still. After a minute or so the tank engines roared and they moved out again, continuing to follow the track.

Eventually, the railroad intersected a gravel road and they left the track and followed the road, entering into a village where the people came out to meet them. A young Korean, who appeared to be about seventeen, got very excited when he saw all the prisoners and a whole line of tanks. He ran up to Sam and pointed at some distant hills. "Fiivve thooousand communeests! that a way, go get em!" he screamed. He couldn't contain his excitement and kept yelling to "go get em."

Arkie was laughing at the Korean. The thought of being sicced on to the enemy amused him. Finally, Sam said, "Okay don't worry, we go get em."

This seemed to satisfy the young Korean, because he stopped shouting go get em, but began to yell, "Banzai!"

They moved on, hearing his cries ringing out behind them.

The next village they reached, the Mayor had gotten all the inhabitants out to greet them. The entire village population, about three hundred people, lined the dirt street. At his signal, they raised their arms skyward and bowed down touching the earth, letting out a thunderous, "Banzai!"

Three times they bowed and each time they cried, "Banzai!"

The word can mean many things, but as they used it then it meant, "Hurray!" Sam never forgot the word. Many times after, when visiting his comrades, he greeted them with, "Banzai."

Within an hour, they reached the main body of the 1st Regiment, the force which would attack down the main street of Seoul. They turned one hundred fifty-six prisoners over and Tarring reported to the regimental commander, the famous Chesty Puller. When he began to tell the commander about the action, Chesty told him that he had no time for tall tales, but said that he had done a good job, and dismissed him.

Tarring came back and related Chesty's comments to the platoon.

Sam sensed they had been lucky. If it had not been for the presence of the tanks, they would not have been able to prevail against a whole battalion of North Koreans. They had killed twice as many as they had captured, but the fact they had captured so many was a welcome sign. Now, all they had to do was take Seoul and they could go home. The day had been one truly horror-filled day, one which Sam would never forget.

After turning over the prisoners they located the rest of Fox Company. All were glad to see them and some of the men began telling the rest of the company about the firefight. Fox Company had had an uneventful day and had been held in reserve because of being short 2nd Platoon.

It was growing late. The advance of the main body stopped for the night. They prepared to sleep on top of the ground. Since there were so many others between them and the enemy, it was not necessary to dig in.

It was almost dark when a young lieutenant arrived who was to replace Can Do Malder. Sam saw him report to Captain Groff. They immediately clashed. Although Sam didn't hear it begin, he overheard portions of the argument. He first heard the captain's nasal whine and then he heard the lieutenant say, "I don't give a damn who you are. I don't have to put up with your shit."

He was very adamant about it, and it sounded as if the captain had really made him angry.

Then Captain Groff responded, his voice filled with arrogance, "I'm top dog in this outfit!"

"You may be top dog, and I may have to follow your orders, but I don't have to take your crap," the lieutenant said.

"I can have you sent back to battalion," Groff snarled.

"Then do it!" said the young lieutenant.

As they argued, Sam got a good look at the new lieutenant. He was blond and fair-skinned and was about the same stature as Captain Groff. They were walking past as they argued and now they were walking away. He did not hear the rest of their conversation. He wondered why Captain Groff was always so hostile. Was he concerned that he would lose control of the company? This made no sense, because the people he seemed to feel threatened by were obviously not destined to take command.

After going without sleep the night before and fighting all day, Sam was exhausted and he soon fell asleep. During the night, he dreamed about the fighting, and was holding his carbine and spraying a literal sea of heads that kept popping up out of the ground, and then he dreamed he was on a warm beach with Charlotte and he reached out to touch her, but she turned into a chunk of raw meat with a hand sticking up out of the meat.

At about 2 o'clock, he woke with a terrible headache, and began to vomit. He needed aspirin desperately. He began searching for a corpsman. Looking about at the sleeping forms, he could not recognize any as Doyer or Chico Carsenero. His head was splitting apart and he began to wake people and ask where he could find a corpsman. Cursing him, some didn't know, but one directed him to the general area where the lead corpsman for Fox Company was sleeping. He was a Chief in the U. S. Navy. Sam knew him simply as "Chief."

Sam shook him. Disgruntled and half asleep, he snarled, "What do you want?"

"My head is bursting," Sam said.

He rolled over, coming awake, and sat up. He pulled out a pack of cigarettes, put one in his mouth, lit it and extended it to Sam.

"I don't smoke," Sam said.

"Yeah, but smoke one anyway."

Sam was growing desperate. It felt as if the top of his head was coming off. "I need some aspirin," he pleaded.

"I'm getting you some. Here, swallow these." He dropped three aspirin into Sam's outstretched hand. His hand was shaking violently. He reached for his canteen and with shaking hands gulped the water and aspirin down.

"Now, lie down and smoke the cigarette," Chief said.

"I don't need it," Sam said.

"Yes you do. You're all upset. You're waking everybody up and we need our sleep. We're going to lead the attack on Seoul tomorrow," he said.

Sam followed his suggestion and smoked the cigarette. After a time, the headache began to subside. All the while, the guns and mortars were pounding the city. You could hear the hollow drum-like sounds of the huge 4.2 mortars as they left the tubes and arced high into the air and fell like thunder. These blended with the distant sounds of the artillery as if the whole world was a constant rumble of sound. The wounded tigers passed overhead, followed by more explosions. The North Koreans were making a counterattack with T-34 Russian tanks. Offshore, the battleship Missouri was throwing 2700-pound shells at tanks from 25 miles distant, huge projectiles from its 16-inch guns forced through the air by 490 pounds of black powder. Sam lay and listened to it for a while. The sound of artillery chills the bravest man's blood. To a soldier, it is the most terrible of sounds. But, this was outgoing and it was reassuring. Within a few minutes, he was again asleep.

CHAPTER 13 ... Seoul, Korea ...

Just before dawn he awakened to the sound of a tremendous heavy battle. The North Koreans had attacked another battalion with T-34 tanks. Sam got up and moved to a point where he could find cover. All about everyone was stirring awake, alarmed by the volume of sound coming from the battle. From the position he had taken Sam could see a thousand yards towards the city where the fighting was going on. Yet, he was unable to determine any details. He decided to eat breakfast and opened a can of beans. His squad followed suit. He looked about for the new lieutenant without finding him. The new lieutenant was no longer with them.

They had a breakfast of C rations, drew supplies of ammunition and grenades, replenished their drinking water, and fell in on the tail of the other battalion that was forcing its way. The outskirts of the city stretched a considerable distance and they followed along behind the constant rumble of the battle which was taking place ahead. The day was just a march. At nightfall they took up defensive positions in the outskirts of the city where buildings on both sides of the street showed evidence of the fighting which had taken place.

Once the squad was placed for the night, Sam found time to think. The fact of being in Seoul was reassuring. He was an idealist and an optimist. Naively, he believed they were close to the end of the war. His attitude was such because he had not yet analyzed the situation. Although he was idealistic he was also extremely curious. Nothing escaped his observing eye.

Sam noticed one building on the street was experiencing a lot of traffic. He saw the Battalion Operations Officer, Joe Perrigo, enter the building. Major Perrigo was a short man, very dark, with a heavy beard that required daily shaving, and extra long arms that seemed to swing to his knees. He looked like an ape. You could not fail to recognize him anywhere. Sam wandered down the street to see what was going on. The door of the building was open so Sam stopped and looked in. Inside he saw a dim flickering light from a candle.

A North Korean soldier sat in the center of the room in a straight-backed chair. His shoulder epaulets said he was an officer. His eyes had a glazed look about them. Major Perrigo was questioning him. There was an interpreter present, but Sam couldn't determine what he was asking. The North Korean soldier had a bullet hole in each of his upper arms on the outer portion of his arms. His blood was soaking his sleeves, causing them to adhere to his wounds. Perrigo stood directly in front of the soldier, the interpreter to one side. The interpreter barked a question. The soldier just looked at him with a dazed look and did not reply. Perrigo grabbed the man by each arm, letting his thumbs anchor in the bullet holes, and shook the man vigorously, shouting, "Talk, damn you, talk," while rocking the man's head back and forth. A tall lanky Marine Corps officer stood to one side watching. He chanced to see Sam watching through the open door and came out.

"What are you doing here?" he demanded. Without waiting for Sam to answer, he continued, "You have no business here. Move on."

He stepped back inside and closed the door. Sam went back down the street and got settled in for the night. He could not help but wonder why he had been ordered to move on. Were they torturing the soldier? Had they shot him in both upper arms or had they just happened on to him? He could not say they had shot him, but he knew Major Perrigo's thumbs in the holes in the man's arms did not represent medical attention. It seemed cruel. He could not fit this in with his concept of American character. Then, Sam thought they might get some information which could save a lot of lives, perhaps even his own. Thus he rationalized, but he still couldn't reconcile to the cruelty of the interrogation. He was left with a vague feeling of dismay. He wandered back to where the 2nd Platoon was digging in.

There was a huge shell crater in the middle of the street. The machine gunners had set up a light thirty there and this tied in with his squad, so he decided to spend the night in the shell crater. He saw to it that the disposition of his squad was adequate and settled in for the night.

Except for the intermittent H and I firing of the mortars, the night proved uneventful. When morning came rations were issued and they set about heating their breakfast before the inevitable command, "Fox Company, saddle up," sounded. It came before Sam could finish eating and they packed up and moved out in a single column. If there was a battle plan for the day, it wasn't known to them. Obviously, the attack which had begun the prior day was to continue. Word was relayed that Easy Company would lead out, Fox Company would follow, and Dog Company would bring up the rear of the battalion. In this marching order, they passed through the battalion which had led the day before and became the lead battalion.

The morning began with tanks going forward, taking the lead. They soon came under small arms fire and Easy Company began to kill whomever they could find. Fox came along behind, with the constant rattle of fire ahead reminding them that their turn would soon come. The smoke of battle thickened. Hospital jeeps made their way back and forth picking up Easy Company's casualties and hauling them back, filling Sam with dread.

"Fox Company, forward!" The cry came back down the street relayed from man to man and passed on as they obeyed and moved ahead. The North Koreans had built barricades across the street out of whatever they could lay hands on—furniture, pots and pans, straw mats—and intermingled them with sand bags, bedding and stones. They fired from behind these and from buildings on both sides. The first tanks shot holes in these and ground through; behind these a bulldozer tank came forward and plowed paths through the barricades. 1st Platoon was leading. They ran forward, passed through Easy Company, and went into no-man's-land firing and flipping grenades into doorways, but soon began to slow down.

The roar of gunfire permeated the air with the constant sound of battle. The advance stalled again. A layer of smoke hovered all about them. Sam saw two Marines from the 1st Platoon carry Sergeant Crowell back down the street on a stretcher. Then shortly after the platoon leader, Lieutenant Snyder, and some others whom Sam didn't know were carried past.

Easy Company was called forward. Sam rested on the sidewalk, leaning back against a building, watching them go past into the firing. A young boy, known only as Chicken, whom Sam had trained at Parris Island, came running past. His hair was so blond that it was almost white. He had never shaved in his life. Sam called out to him. "Hey Chicken, you be careful!"

He recognized Sam, giving him a broad grin. "Those bastards can't hit me," he cried, as he ran forward into the fire ahead.

The sun was up high, warming them, somehow making the battle routine. Occasionally progress was made ahead and they moved up to maintain communication. A short time later another stretcher was carried past. Sam barely recognized Chicken. His face was covered in blood, his mouth open, he was unconscious, might have been dead as far as Sam could tell, but the urgency with which they carried him said he was alive. A steady stream of wounded came past on stretchers and Sam moved up a few yards.

"Fox Company! Move up!" the cry rang out.

Sam repeated it and went forward. He reached a Russian T-34 tank that appeared deserted. The barrel of its cannon had been pierced by a rifle bullet which had gone through both sides of the barrel. They were running forward, a column on both sides of the street. Mortar shells were falling ahead and on both sides. One struck some ammo stored in a building on the right and the whole building went up with a roar.

Opposite from Sam, Bontempo, who back aboard ship had said to Sam he was going to kill about fifteen of 'em, was running forward, bullets striking all about. He leaped into a hole in the street which had been dug by North Koreans. A Korean soldier crouched down in the hole holding a Russian burp gun. The soldier pulled the trigger.

Brrripp!

Bontempo reacted as if his legs were steel springs. He came out backwards, dropping his rifle and clutching his left arm. At least one bullet had struck him.

"Gook!" he shouted.

Sam started across. Before he could get there, Tarring emptied his carbine into the North Korean.

Smoke hung low over the street, making it difficult to see. Buildings blew up, throwing bricks and debris everywhere as others collapsed adding more dust to the smoke. The roar and rattle of fire never stopped. It was just a din of noise, smoke, explosions, and flame. From somewhere in front, an enemy machine gun was chopping and sawing away, bullets tearing down the street. Now, suddenly, Sam couldn't see anyone ahead, but knew they had to be there, and he kept going. As he went past an open door he heard someone call out to him. A Marine from the 3rd Platoon motioned for him to come in. Sam looked through the door into what appeared to be a courtyard. It was surrounded by eight foot high concrete walls. A half dozen Marines were inside, just standing, doing nothing. The sergeant with the

Tommy gun seemed to be in charge. Sam hesitated. The Tommy gun carrying sergeant motioned to him.

"In here!" he cried.

Sam looked about, trying to fathom what was happening. In an instant, it became clear; they had ducked into the courtyard to escape the fighting. Not only were they failing to attack, but what they had done was stupid. It might appear safer, for the moment, than out on the street, but they were blind; they couldn't see what was happening outside their shelter. At any moment, a grenade could come sailing over the high wall and they would be dead. Remaining there, with no way to see through the walls, made fools of them. They were blind when they needed to be able to see. More important, those ahead of them now had no way to relay the word; communications had been broken. Sam could see by the expressions on their faces they were acting cowardly and knew it. Instinctively, he blamed the sergeant and concluded if the sergeant could get another sergeant to join him it lessened his chances of facing a court-martial if his actions were discovered. In the instant, Sam saw it all and wanted no part of it. He looked at each one as he spoke, seeing their eyes drop, their gazes not meeting his.

"I'm going out that door," he said. "I advise the rest of you to follow."

"Stay here! Stay here!" Tommy Gun cried. Sam went out and looked back once. Two of them were following. He kept running through the smoke until he saw Marines in front and recognized Arkie. Sam ran towards him as a building blew on the right side of the street, showering bricks across the way. Sam caught up with Arkie and followed him as Arkie moved forward. A little farther down the street the smoke cleared a little. A red tracer fired by some North Korean lifted up from the street to a height of about seven feet and came arcing down, coming directly at Sam. In reality, it was coming fast but it seemed to be slow motion. In the second which took place, he dived headlong into the street behind the body of a dead North Korean soldier. His face had been run over by a tank. His head was crushed into a thin pancake, round like a Halloween pumpkin, his teeth flattened out perfectly into a broad grin. Where his eyes had been, there was now just outlines, shadows which said eyes had been there. The eye lashes and eyebrows were intact, but the rest of his eyes were almond shaped dark matter. Sam lay behind him, his face six inches away from what was left of the Korean's face, using him as a shield.

The round passed over and exploded beyond Sam. He leaped up and ran forward. Rounds of high explosive were going off in a building to the right. One explosion, then he ran, hearing a second behind him, then another in front, showering him with fragments of brick and dust. The 2nd Platoon was now in front of the fight, shooting it out with the North Korean defenders. They fired, cursed and fired again, running from one place to the next, bullets striking all around, making snapping sounds.

All the while, those long, slow, arcing tracers kept streaming down the street. They charged from one barricade to another, blazing away at the enemy as they sometimes tried to run. There were no shouted commands. No word was being passed. The 2nd Platoon was exploding on them, but they fought back. Baxter went down, lying out in the street, in a spreading pool of blood. One of the high explosive rounds struck Chico Carsenero, knocking him flat in the street. Erickson dragged him off the street back against a wall and sheltered him in his arms. Jackson, the Korean interpreter, joined them, his face expressionless, impervious to Carsenero's screams, the shots, explosions, and sounds of a city on fire. They might as well have been in hell.

Sam knelt down beside Carsenero.

"Shoot me. Shoot me!" Carsenero cried.

"Oh shit, Chico," Sam said. "We're not going to shoot you. We're going to get you out of here."

"No! Oh God—I can't stand it! Shoot me," he cried.

"You'll be going home, Chico. Think about it. Home boy, home!" Sam said.

Arkie and two others joined him. Someone had a stretcher. They pulled Carsenero on to it and started back down the street, keeping low as they trotted along with him, bullets whining off the buildings. A combat photographer knelt down and took pictures of them as they passed.

Sam found the forward aid station less than two hundred yards to the rear. Carsenero was still begging to be shot when the corpsman gave him a shot of morphine.

Sam turned and ran back up the street to get Baxter. He had to go about two hundred yards. When he got there, the pool of blood Baxter lay in was now several feet in diameter and he appeared to be going into shock. He had raised his chest off the street and was looking at Sam silently. His face was stone gray. His buttocks had been torn by a bullet, and this was where all the blood was coming from. Sam had no stretcher so he tore a door from a building and they placed Baxter face down on it and carried him back to the aid station, running low, trying to avoid the fire that was still coming. Two corpsmen were at work at the aid station when Sam reached it a second time.

A jeep had already taken Carsenero out. They placed Baxter on the ground and started back. Sam came upon an aged Korean man who sat upright on the sidewalk on a handmade quilt. An aged Korean woman, apparently his wife, had dragged him out to the street. She was on her knees, with her arms outstretched, pleading for help. Tears streamed down her face as she cried out in Korean. Sam knelt down beside them. The old man's leg had been broken above the knee and flesh ripped apart. About two inches of white bone jutted out pointed towards what was left of his knee.

"Get a door!" Sam said.

Arkie looked about, found one, ripped it from its hinges and brought it over.

The old woman was still weeping, but now, in a different voice. She was thanking them.

"Careful, now," Sam said, "we don't dare disturb his leg."

They dragged him in his sitting position onto the door, trying not to move his leg. The old man was in terrible pain. You could see it written on his face. His wife was overcome with relief, but her tears were still streaming. They hurried back to the aid station again. First Sergeant Homer was there, sitting back against a building. They sat the old man down. "Can you give him morphine!" Sam asked the corpsman.

"I don't have any more. I've used it all up," he said.

Two other Marines were there, smoking cigarettes. Sam concluded they were walking wounded.

"Anyone got any morphine?" he asked.

"I got some, but I ain't usin' it on him," Homer said.

Sam was seared with contempt. It was inconceivable to him that Homer should refuse to give a poor old wounded Korean man morphine. He acted instantly, by reflex, without any thought at all. He swung his carbine around and pointed it at Homer, finger on the trigger.

"Give it to him," he said.

Without hesitating, Homer moved over to the old man, took out a morphine syringe, and stuck the needle in the old man's arm.

The old woman was still crying and thanking them as they left. They caught up with the fighting, coming to an intersection where a second street entered the main street at an angle. The flag of the Confederacy was flying beyond the intersection. Sam started across the intersection, moving perhaps a little too slow considering the situation. Captain Groff appeared on the street ahead waving his arms above his head and shouting at Sam. The din of battle was so loud Sam couldn't hear what he was saying and he stopped right in the middle of the intersection.

"What did you say?" Sam cried.

"Get down! You crazy bastard!" Groff shouted.

"Why?" Sam asked, seeing Groff was standing.

"There's a goddamned machine gun firing right down that street!" Groff cried.

Sam looked about. "They're not shooting at me," he said.

Apparently, only moments before, the North Koreans had been firing from the side street, but had abandoned their position.

Sam was growing too careless. The day had been so long filled with danger he was beginning to ignore it. That incident did it. Groff ordered a halt for the day.

"Dig in right here," he said.

Sam led his squad into a small building on the left side of the street. They knocked a big hole in the floor and punched holes in the outside wall. Sam found a machine gun crew and they set a gun up with a field of fire able to cover the street in front. They tore out more floor and dug holes at various places and knocked firing slots at the bottom of the outside walls. Sam went outside and looked about. Across from him and slightly to his rear a tall building which appeared to be a hotel stood intact. The sounds of battle were fading, but all around the city was burning. He thought he saw some movement down the street in front. Peering through the smoke, he wondered what it was. Then he saw it again and this time he could tell what it was. A white rag, tied to a rifle, came out of a building ahead on his right and waved back and forth. There was no mistaking it.

"Sundrah!" Sam shouted.

A young North Korean soldier stepped out of the building into full view, holding the white flag aloft.

"Sundrah, Sundrah," Sam shouted again and again.

They came out by the dozen, holding their hands aloft. Sam was surprised at how young they looked. All appeared to be in their late teens or early twenties. As they came in, he and his squad kept them covered. When it became clear that no more were coming, they marched them towards the rear. Easy Company was right behind, so they turned them over to Easy Company and went back to their house. His men settled in for the night. Sam stood outside the fortress looking up and down the street. The city was on fire. He was bone-tired, but glad to be alive. So much had happened so rapidly it was impossible to assimilate the events of the day. The taking of this second large group of prisoners was especially an encouraging sign.

They were halfway through the city and this surrender brought the promise of an easier day tomorrow. With a half smile he remembered Bontempo leaping into the hole with the North Korean, and his boast, aboard ship, he was going to kill fifteen. His chance had come to kill one, not fifteen, and he had come out of that hole like a jack in the box. It seemed funny and yet Sam remembered that he himself had run from one only two days before.

There came a long swelling burst of gunfire that reached a crescendo, died away, then reached a crescendo a second time and died down to random shots, then ceased. At first, Sam thought a counterattack had begun, but he didn't see anyone coming at him. No need to be concerned. Whatever it was, it had been dealt with. He went back inside the fortress. Some of the squad were already asleep. In spite of his tiredness, Sam had a rare good feeling of having survived a day of furious fighting. It was good to be alive in the very heart of Seoul. If he could survive for just a few more days he would soon be going home to march in the victory parade. How nice it would be to return to Washington and pick up life where he had left off. With the thought in mind, he settled in for the night. He slept soundly.

CHAPTER 14 ... The Swimming Pool ...

Sam woke to the sounds of many Korean voices all speaking at the same time. The voices of women and children were mingled in with fewer male voices. It sounded as a flock of birds sometimes does and he was immediately curious. He got up and stepped outside to investigate and saw a crowd of civilians across the street, not quite bold enough to mingle with the Marines, but not seeming to be afraid either. They had left their homes to escape the fighting and now had returned. This was a very good sign. The main danger had passed. Sam wondered where they had gone to escape the destruction, and how they had known it was safe to come back. He stood still, watching them. A young Korean, perhaps twenty-five years of age, saw Sam come out of the house and left the crowd and came across towards him.

"Excuse me sir, do you mind if I enter my house?" His English was perfect.

"No. Go ahead. I'm sorry you're going to find it torn up inside."

Sam followed him in, announcing to the squad that, "The owner of the house is here."

The young Korean looked about in dismay. Half his living-room floor was gone. The machine gun still jutted out from beneath where the floor had been. To Sam's amazement, he did not show any anger. He struck up a friendly conversation with the squad and Sam went back outside. Little cooking fires were springing up at various places up and down the street as Marines gathered about heating coffee and hot chocolate.

The sun was already well up and, aside from the devastation, shell holes in the buildings, burned out or blown up buildings and shattered barricades, it might have been an ordinary morning.

"Sam!"

Tarring was coming towards him from the direction of the hotel. As he drew near, Sam saw he was visibly excited. He was a small man with clear blue eyes and turned-up nose that made him look much younger than his twenty-seven years, especially when he smiled. But, now he wasn't smiling; quite the contrary. His eyes had the look of desperation.

"Sam!" he cried, "come with me."

He waited until Sam caught up to him and then turned and hurried down the street. Sam began walking beside him, having difficulty keeping up. "What is it?" he inquired.

"I'll show you," Tarring said.

Sam had never seen him so agitated and could not imagine what was wrong. He kept walking fast and Sam hurried even more to keep pace with him.

"Can't you tell me what it is?" he asked again.

Tarring seemed about to choke. "No, you'll see. I can't tell you what it is. You've got to see it for yourself," he said.

He led the way to the tall building that looked as if it were a hotel. They came to a broad series of concrete steps which led up to the double-doored entrance. Crowds of South Korean civilians swarmed on both sides and watched as they climbed the steps and went through the entrance. The lobby of the building was over on the right. On the left, a set of broad steps went down from the lobby, reached a landing and turned, to the right. Tarring pointed down the stairs.

"It's down there. Go down and see," he said.

Sam went down. When he reached the landing it was somewhat darker because it was a basement and the electricity had been knocked out. He had a great curiosity to see what was so mysterious that Tarring felt he had to see for himself. Why didn't he just tell me? Sam wondered. He stopped at the bottom and let his eyes adjust to the changed light. Two tall windows on the east wall allowed rays of sunlight in, shafts of light which reflected off the minute particles of dust and debris that seemed to be swimming in the air. He looked away from the windows to where the sunlight fell and saw what appeared to be handrails bordering a rectangular hole. A ladder extended up out of a swimming pool. A stench like he had never smelled before emanated from the pool. Sam walked closer. The sight struck him. He felt a shock, like a blow from a club, more powerful than anything he had ever felt before. He was staring into a dry swimming pool full of dead naked human beings. They were covered with rivulets of blood, their bodies laced with bullet holes. Some had moved their bowels and the stench of death and human excrement rose from the ghastly pile, threatening to suffocate him. He began to faint, his legs buckled, and he sat down, beginning to weep. It occurred to him one or more of them might still be alive, lying there helpless, unable to do anything, and he searched the pile, looking for any sign of life. Some had held up their hands, in the last terror of their lives, attempting to ward off the bullets. Their faces were young, nothing more than youths like himself. Then, he recognized the one who had waved the white flag. Now, he knew the source of unexplained gunfire he had heard! It repelled him. He could not bear the truth of it. Why? Why? Why? Why would Americans do such a thing? The question could not be answered. It was incredulous. He didn't want to believe it. My God! he thought, what was the difference between the piles of dead Jews killed by Nazis, and these North Koreans? He could see, from the patterns of holes, that after they had gone down, their killers had stood over them and sprayed the pile with bullets. Blood was everywhere, running from one man onto the next, and running over the layers of bodies underneath, dried and caked. It was horrible beyond description. He could only see death in that horrible pile and struggled with the horror, tried to stand. Fighting to keep from fainting, he fought to get to his feet. He had to get out of there! He started back up the stairs, holding to the hand rail, but fainted and fell down. Tarring came down and helped him climb the stairs.

"Those are the prisoners we took yesterday," he said.

As Tarring helped Sam along, the Korean civilians, lots of women and children among them, stood watching them. Sam was still weeping. If Tarring had not supported him, he would have been unable to stand. The people stared at them curiously. Apparently they didn't yet know what was down there. My God, Sam thought, what will they think of us? We are liberators to them now, but what will we be when they see that horrible pool? They will remember us as murderers.

"Does the Captain know?" Sam asked.

"That's why I came and got you. I complained about it, but he wouldn't listen to me. He just cursed me. We can't have this kind of thing. We're Americans. The more of us who complain, the better it will be," Tarring said.

"Where is the Captain?" Sam asked.

"Come on, I'll show you," Tarring said.

He released Sam and again walked rapidly. Sam followed him a short distance to a side street where Captain Groff squatted in the street, before a small fire, drinking coffee. Sam was crying unashamedly.

"Captain!" he cried.

Groff looked up at him and at Tarring who stood back a distance behind.

"Captain, have you seen that awful sight in the swimming pool?" Sam cried.

Groff stared at him without answering.

Sam demanded of him again, "Have you seen it, Captain?"

He couldn't believe anyone who had seen it would not be horrified. If the captain had reacted as Tarring had said, Sam wanted to hear it for himself.

Groff gave his answer.

"Hell yes, you son of a bitch. I've seen it!—And I'll not hear another word about it!"

"Captain ... Captain," Sam choked. Tears streamed down his cheeks. He didn't want to believe he had heard.

"Not another goddamned word—you hear!" Groff shouted. He looked about, saw others watching, and began to ridicule Sam. "Would you look at that?" he said. "Crying over a bunch of dead gooks." He grinned, looking about at all who were within earshot, jeeringly making fun because Sam was crying.

"If that don't beat all I've ever seen," he said, "and over a bunch of dead gooks."

Sam was weeping unashamedly, deeply shocked. He knew he must insist the thing was wrong, or be forever a party to it. He couldn't believe he was being taunted for weeping. He tried to stop but couldn't, becoming very angry. Someone had to take a stand against this thing. If the captain wouldn't, then he must.

"Alright Captain," he said, "have it your way. But there's something you better know. From this day forward, if any man in my squad ever kills a prisoner of war I'll execute that man right on the spot."

"Get the hell out of here," Groff cried. "By God, I can't believe you're cryin' like that—over a bunch of dead gooks. ..."

He laughed again, mirthlessly, looking about for approval from those watching. Sam was unable to accept this. He thought perhaps the captain had not understood how serious he was.

"Don't you forget, Captain. I'll kill anyone who kills a prisoner of war," Sam said. "I'll not be a party to murder, Captain."

As he walked away, Sam was well aware many had watched the confrontation. He resolved to oppose Groff, or anyone else, should such a situation ever again arise. He could not do otherwise.

He returned to the house where he had spent the night. His squad was in the street heating their rations over a small fire. Arkie stood up, watching him approach. He reached the squad fire and knelt down. Arkie pressed a canteen cup of coffee towards him.

"Here Sam," he said gently, "drink this."

Sam sat on the ground, crying softly.

"It was a whole swimming pool full of naked dead men who surrendered to us. Come on, I'll show it to you. You've got to see it."

But, Arkie pressed the coffee at him.

"If it has done this to you, Sam, I don't want to see it," he said gently.

Sam sat clutching the coffee in both hands. He was unaware of what was happening around him. The order to saddle up was given. Later, he would vaguely remember reaching for his carbine and being on the move again.

They continued down the same street past the North Koreans who had fired at them with the tracer bullets. These had died behind their long barreled rifles. (The weapons used a 20mm anti-tank shell and had wooden stocks and bipeds to hold up their eight foot long barrels). The North Koreans had dug foxholes right down through the concrete streets and now lay sprawled in death, victims of the fire Marines had poured back at them. Fox and Easy continued the leapfrogging tactic of the prior day and still took some fire but nothing like before.

Sam passed through Easy Company. Now, he felt a deep contempt of them. As he passed one of their BAR men, a big, broad-faced, red-haired, freckled Marine, Sam taunted him.

"There's big brave Easy Company, looking for prisoners to shoot," he said.

The red-haired Marine responded.

"Damn right we shot that bunch of gooks. I'll shoot every one of the sons of bitches I can get my hands on."

"Prisoner killers," Sam shouted back.

Even though there was fighting, his mind was on other things. He was out of touch. He kept remembering parade grounds at Parris Island and Washington D.C. at the Commandant's home and being thrilled with pride at the sound of the Marine Corps Hymn, "First to fight for right and freedom, and to keep our honor clean."

The reality of the pool overlaid these memories, making lies of them. They were now illusions, made so by those who had murdered the prisoners. They had robbed him of the pride of being a Marine and, instead, he felt shame. He ached inside with a hurt which wouldn't go away.

Two days later, when they were dug in on a hill north of Seoul, Tarring again came to Sam. He said he had news that he felt Sam should hear. He had not talked with Sam since the pool, apparently realizing that showing the pool to Sam was a mistake. It seemed to Sam that Tarring had doubts as to whether or not Sam was going to be able to cope. There was nothing Tarring could do, but he tried.

"Sam, the Gunnery Sergeant in Easy Company was setting a trip flare when it exploded and killed him," he said. Sam stared at him dully. To Sam, Tarring seemed glad. Why would he be glad at the death of another Marine?

"Blew his damn head off," Tarring said. "Serves him right too. He was in charge of the detail who killed the prisoners."

"How do you know?" Sam asked.

"I don't. But, that's what they told me," he said.

Sam took no comfort from this. Some things happen which can never be rectified. They are stains on the human soul which remain forever. The swimming pool had destroyed Sam's faith in the United States Marines of which he had been and still was a part of. The event seared Sam Lewis's mind and he was unable to sort it out. He saw life through different eyes.

The entire regiment rested north of Seoul. They had taken the city in three weeks of fighting. Of the forty-five who had been the 2nd Platoon of Fox Company, twenty-eight remained. Of those, eight had been wounded including Sam, but Sam was also wounded inside.

As a nineteen-year-old corporal, he had been a Senior Drill Instructor at Parris Island, responsible for training platoons of men, when some Platoon Sergeants in the same battalion were Junior Drill Instructors. Sam was different. Some people feel more, see more, and experience more than the average person. They have a heightened awareness. Artists and musicians and idealists, of which Sam was one, live life closer to the edge than their comrades.

The combat objective of Sam and his comrades had been achieved. Seoul, Korea, was freed from the hands of the North Koreans. The long hard days of fighting ceased and the men began speculating on how soon the war would end. The break in the fighting was a most welcome respite.

Sam sensed Tarring felt sorry for him and regretted showing Sam the pool. He was not ashamed of his grief and didn't want anyone feeling sorry for him. He was deeply aware of Captain Groff's ridicule of him for being so distraught over the swimming pool. In adapting, he grew tougher inside, but he had lost respect for authority and found ways to show his contempt.

Sam observed that, when the company dug in against light or no opposition, its first position was never final. Apparently the executive officer, a First Lieutenant named Sorenson, was being allowed to determine the position, then Groff would inspect and make changes. The next time Fox Company moved, Tarring assigned an area to Sam which his squad was to defend. Sam sized it up and made mental notes of where his BARs should be placed and gave the order to dig in. As the men began to dig, he strolled over beside a scraggly pine and began to heat his meal.

Erickson was the first to notice Sam wasn't digging in. Erickson was a little pimply faced youth who had a way of laughing that wasn't laughter at all, but just a little chortle. He was digging and had dug down about a foot when he stopped.

"Sam, are you gonna dig in?" he asked.

"Nah, I'm not gonna dig today. I'm tired of diggin' in," Sam said. And then, he borrowed one of Groff's lines, "I didn't come to this damn country to dig holes in the earth."

Erickson went back to digging and thought about what Sam had said. Then he stopped again and called over to Lewellyn, "Lew, Psycho Sam's gone off. The crazy bastard's not gonna dig in."

Lewellyn straightened up and looked over. Sam had his cocoa hot and took a big sip.

"Sam, have you gone apeshit?" he asked.

"Nah, just tired of diggin'," Sam said smugly.

Erickson chortled to himself, shook his head, and dug again. Finally, he decided to try again. "Sam, those gook mortars could start coming down any minute. Ain't you gonna dig a hole?"

He was genuinely concerned.

"I've got one," Sam said. "As a matter of fact, my hole's being dug for me."

By this time, he had the attention of the whole squad. He began to draw some real concerned looks.

Erickson glanced about, exchanging looks with the rest of the men. They had all stopped now.

"Just who is diggin' it?" he demanded.

Sam gave him a big grin.

"You are," Sam said. "I'm gonna take your hole."

Erickson chortled, "You'll take this hole over my dead body," he said.

They had almost finished when Groff came around, looking things over. Shortly thereafter, Tarring came back. "Sam, you're going to have to extend your line down to that little pine tree down there," he said, pointing to the tree. As he was leaving, Sam instructed the squad, "Okay men. we'll have to change a little bit," he said. "Erickson, you'll have to move your BAR over to cover the ravine; you can take the hole that Lew dug."

"I'm not movin'," Erickson said.

"Oh yes, you are," Sam said. "Look at that gully. We have to have your BAR cover that gully. Besides, there's a hole already dug for you."

Sam's logic was sound; Erickson could see it was. "Where are you gonna go?" he asked.

"I'm taking your old hole," Sam said, with a grin.

Erickson grabbed a dead pine limb off the ground and came at Sam. Sam ran just fast enough to keep out of reach as Erickson chased him downhill. When he gave up, Sam came back up, got his gear, and got down in the hole.

They were in a two-company perimeter and had the front side of the hill. Dog Company had the rear. Someone didn't have a hole. At nine o'clock that night some Marine just over the ridge to their rear was digging his second hole of the day and cursing.

Arkie watched the cruel joke. "Sam, you better hope that guy don't come over here asking questions," he chuckled.

"Survival of the fittest," Sam said. "From now on, no matter what happens, I intend to survive."

CHAPTER 15 ... Margurite Higgins ...

The hills were low, rolling, and brown. Early October was a dry time of the year. The hills stretched north from Seoul for some distance and beyond the rugged bare mountains showed themselves. Each morning revealed a dense cloud of white fog that lay in the valleys leaving only the tops of the brown hills exposed. The men rested.

In their foxholes, during daylight hours, they kept little cooking fires and played hearts and poker. No one had any money. It was just a way of killing time. Some of the debts got as high as one thousand dollars but none ever expected they would be paid. Garret owed Martin one thousand four hundred until Sam got into the game on Garrett's behalf and won it all back.

Sam was restless. The underpinnings of his concepts had been destroyed. He roamed from one fire to the other, seeking the companionship of his comrades, trying to find reassurance in them of his American heritage and values. He habitually greeted each group with "Banzai! Five thousaaand communeeists, that a way, go get em." This always brought smiles of friendship. On the surface, he hadn't a care; below the surface, the trauma of the swimming pool was raw. His shrapnel wound healed, but his psyche did not. He had lost respect for authority.

The machine gunners were playing hearts with Sam's squad. One of these, a Mexican-American named Murgia, took a trick with a key card. "The cat came back!" he cried out with glee. "The cat has struck again."

Peterson, seventeen years old and freckled-faced and serious, stood beside the hole watching. He grinned broadly. Boduch, one of the machine gun sergeants, came over and stood beside Peterson.

Sam, about to deal a new game, looked up.

"Could I talk to you Sam?" Boduch said quietly.

"Sure," Sam said.

Boduch nodded his head, indicating he wanted Sam to follow him. They walked over and sat down on the side of the hill, looking down the brown grassy hillside in front of them towards the stinking paddies. Boduch spoke quietly.

"Sam, I know how you feel about the swimming pool. I saw some of the same thing in the Pacific. It was true that the Japs fought to the death, rather than surrender, but it wasn't all principle. Some of it was fear. Some who did surrender got shot anyway. On Saipan they soaked some in gasoline and burned them alive."

"But we can't have that," Sam said. "If we're going to do such things we might as well not be here."

"I just thought it might help if you knew you had done the right thing," Boduch said.

He patted Sam on the shoulder and walked away. After he left, Sam sat for a long time thinking. He was glad his complaint about the murders had attracted so much attention. If Sergeant Boduch knew about it, he surmised that everyone did. He still ached inside with contempt for Easy Company even though he knew most in Easy Company had no part in the murders.

A little later, word was passed to clean rifles. Sam took out the back-to-back magazines from his carbine and inspected them. They were clean. He placed the weapon on single fire, jacked a round in the chamber and pointed the weapon at the sky and fired.

"It's clean," he said.

He expected to draw some response from Captain Groff.

Word came down the line, "What was the shot?"

The answer went back. "Psycho Sam is cleaning his carbine."

Again, he waited for reaction from Captain Groff.

None came.

Sam sat for a time looking down the hillside in front. The slope leading up to the position was gradual and covered with brown dead grass and little scraggly pine bushes thinly dispersed, where a soldier might hide at night. It was his instinct to study how the terrain lay at each position where they dug in. The ground they occupied was not an ideal position.

He looked over to his right, where Easy Company was dug in. Unlike Fox's hill, they occupied a hill which had a fifty-foot high vertical rock cliff in front. Anyone who attacked them from the front would have to scale the cliff. He rejoined the card players and the day passed uneventfully. About two o'clock that night, a tremendous volume of gunfire began in Easy Company's area. The firing increased to a crescendo. Mingled with the rifle shots and machine gun chatter, Sam could hear the fast-firing "brrrppp" of the burp guns. From the number of audible bursts from the burp guns he knew the North Koreans were all over Easy Company. As the battle increased in intensity everyone was awake, expecting to be attacked, but no attack came. Sam listened anxiously to the battle sounds. With each passing minute it became clear that Easy Company was in trouble.

About four in the morning, Tarring passed word for squad leaders. Sam responded. In the darkness he worked his way downline to Tarring's foxhole.

"We've got to go help Easy Company," Tarring said.

"In the dark? How do we get through the lines?" Sam asked.

"They're sending a runner who will lead us through."

The runner arrived. They left their position, each man holding to the belt of the man ahead. Tarring held to the belt of Easy Company's runner. In this manner, they made their way through the darkness, all the while hearing the fast staccato sounds of the burp guns intermingled with the steady rifle and BAR fire.

They reached Easy Company's perimeter and went through the lines. It was near daybreak. The enemy had begun to withdraw, so they were held in reserve at the company command post. As the fighting waned, some of Easy people came to the CP to give casualty and situation reports. One Marine came back and reported his section of the perimeter had been overrun. He had placed a large timber across the top of his hole and at the height of the battle a gook had stood erect on the timber firing his burp gun until the Marine had shot him off with his pistol. He was very excited about it and had to tell someone.

As dawn broke in the eastern horizon, Easy began to carry their dead and wounded back to the CP. Two Marines on stretchers were set on the ground beside Sam. He sat there listening to the noise of their breathing. It was the same sound Paul Carpenter had made the night he died and Sam had to force himself to look at them. Each had been shot in the head. Somehow, one looked familiar. Then, he recognized him. He was the BAR man Sam had taunted in Seoul. He had been shot just above his right eye and slightly to the right of it. His brains trickled down his forehead and turned off towards his ear. He was unconscious. Each breath he drew came in a rattle and a jerk. Sam sat spellbound, remembering his saying he would kill every one of 'em he could get his hands on. Seeing him in this condition made the futility of the situation almost overwhelming. Sam felt a great sadness well up inside. He wondered if the enemy had known that Easy Company had been responsible for the swimming pool. He got up and walked forward a few yards. Out in the valley, in front of the position, a heavy fog lay low over the paddies. Only the tops of the brown hills showed above the clouds of fog, and he looked down on the fog knowing the North Koreans were withdrawing beneath its cover. Just white clouds of morning mist, Sam thought, but they had known it would be there, we hadn't. Occasionally, black smoke broke up through the mist as Marine mortars tried to interfere with the North Korean withdrawal.

Tarring was informed they were no longer needed and they returned to their own perimeter without having fired a shot. Later in the day, they heard the Army 1st Calvary Division would relieve them and push farther north. The Marines were to reboard ships to make another landing. They also heard their pilots had reported seeing huge convoys, hundreds of miles long, extending from China across Manchuria and into North Korea.

Petitt came back from the Hospital Ship Repose, still limping from his wound. He reported to Captain Groff. Groff was sitting beside his hole, his feet dangling over the edge. He looked up at Petitt.

"What the hell good are you?" Groff said, his voice taking on his sarcastic twang. "What the hell you think I'm running here, a home for cripples?"

Petitt began to stammer, "I . . . I—I thought you needed help. They said the company had a lot of casualties."

"Help!" Groff exclaimed. "Look at you. You can hardly walk. You don't even have a goddamned rifle."

"I thought I'd get one here, Sir."

"Oh. You must think I have boxes of rifles just laying around. What good are you, anyway? You can't even kill anybody. Get the hell over to your platoon." With that, he let Petitt off the hook.

Tarring brought Petitt to Sam.

"You're going into Sam Lewis's squad. Here Sam; he's all yours," he said.

Petitt grinned at Sam, "Jesus, I don't know if I wanta."

"Wanta what?" Sam said.

"Become one of the Twelve Fanatics," Petitt replied.

Sam stamped his foot on the ground and pointed at the distant hills. "Banzai!" he screamed. "Five thouusaand commuunisst, that a way, go get em!"

Everyone laughed.

Then, Petitt said, "Listen you guys. I heard Easy Company murdered a whole bunch of gooks in some hotel building in Seoul. Margurite Higgins, the war correspondent, she found out about it. They said she was pissed. They had to call her in and talk to her to shut her up."

Everyone got quiet. They all looked at Sam.

"How do you know Margurite Higgins knew about it?" he asked.

"That's just what I heard. Everybody at Battalion was talking about it," Petitt said.

Sam absorbed this silently. Time after time he wrestled with it. No matter how he tried, he was unable to accept the truth. Those who filled the swimming pool had killed for revenge. Or had they just killed because they could? It was senseless, so it made no sense to search for logic to excuse the act. For Sam, the problem had no solution, only a consequence, which was, as yet, unknown.

CHAPTER 16 ... A Lull in the Fighting ...

While they rested on the hill replacements arrived. Five were assigned to Sam's squad. Tarring brought the five to Sam simultaneously. With a gesture of his hand he indicated Sam to them,

"This is Psycho Sam Lewis, your squad leader." Then, addressing him, "Sam. They're all yours."

"Don't stand so close to each other," Sam said. "One mortar might get us all."

They spread apart a little. Sam set about determining who he had. Sergeant Fitwell was from Lexington, Kentucky, of German-American descent, tall, blue-eyed, and his face was pockmarked, probably from adolescence. In civilian life he was on the Lexington police force. He seemed calm and mature. Two others, also ex-policemen, were Reserve Corporals. One, a chubby round-faced sort named Irving Rose was from Cleveland, Ohio. The other, James Causey, from Shreveport, Louisiana, was tall and erect with a military bearing. He carried two long-barreled 45-caliber Colt revolvers, and appeared as if he knew how to use them. The fourth was a reserve corporal from Toledo, Ohio, named Hank Prior. He wore thick prescription glasses which made his eyes appear really large. Sam didn't think he would be able to see anything in a firefight, but kept this observation to himself. The last was a young Italian-American, from Cleveland, Ohio, named Benny Vesuvius. Sam looked them over.

"Anybody ever been in combat before?" he asked.

"I have," Causey said. He sounded sure of himself.

"Where did you see action?" Sam asked.

"I was on Saipan and Okinawa. You can call me Jim."

"Okay Jim, you'll be fire team leader of the second fire team," Sam said.

Fitwell spoke up. "I'm a sergeant, but I was an Airedale [member of a Marine air group]. I don't know anything about this infantry stuff."

"Don't worry about it," Sam said. "You'll lead the third fire team. Since you guys all know each other, I'll put you together. You'll have Prior and Rose in your fire team. Jim you take Vesuvius in your fire team. He pointed out the position held by the squad.

"My squad is dug in along this line from the pine tree down to the big rock. Get dug in. We can all get acquainted after you dig."

A moment later, Rose and Causey were back. Rose said, "Sam, there's something you should know. We would've been here sooner, but Benny Vesuvius wrote home and told his father we weren't getting enough training. His old man wrote to President Truman and they held us up for two more weeks."

"Is that right?" Sam said.

"Yeah. There's something else," Rose said. "Our last night of liberty, Vesuvius was uptown in Cleveland in dress blues, sergeant's chevrons, and a chest full of ribbons."

Sam had to laugh. "No kidding!" he said.

Causey said, "I'll take care of him."

"You won't hurt him?" Sam said.

"Nah. I'll make him BAR man. That'll straighten him out."

"Alright," Sam said.

A few moments later, Vesuvius came to see Sam. "Sarge," he said, "Causey made me de BAR man. Sarge I don't know nuttin' about dat BAR."

"That's alright, Benny," Sam said.

"But Sarge! I don't even know how to pull da trigger!"

"That's okay Benny. All you have to do is carry it. When it comes time to use it, one of us will use it."

Poor Benny was trapped. Sam felt sorry for him, but he couldn't show it. He would just have to toughen up. Benny saw it was no use, hung his head dejectedly and walked away. Next day, trucks arrived at the bottom of the hill to transport them back to Inchon. The company went down in a long column behind the Confederate flag, still had youthful confidence, expecting to go home soon to the big victory parade. They had survived and had grown tougher. Sam had also, but the pool still troubled him. They boarded the trucks, headed back towards Seoul, and were soon passing through the Army 1st Calvary Division, whose trucks pulled aside to allow them to pass.

The Marines were ragged, filthy dirty, and smelled of the human dung of a dozen rice paddies, but 1st Calvary was clean and wore bright yellow scarves around their necks. Some 1st Calvary began calling the Marines jarheads, and some Marines began calling back, suggesting the yellow should run down their backs instead of around their necks. All the news they had heard about the war had suggested the U. S. Army had been unable to hold off the North Koreans, while Marines had not only held them off, they had soundly beaten them. They did not respect the U. S. Army. The mood began to turn ugly.

In the truck behind Sam some Marine stood up, pulled the pin out of a hand grenade and tossed it to a truck full of soldiers. "Purple Hearts for everybody!" he shouted.

In a wild scramble, the soldiers emptied the truck. Arkie grinned at Sam. "He dumped the powder out, then screwed the detonator back in," he said.

The dust curled up from the road. Sam wrapped the mechanism of his carbine in tin foil from the C rations to keep the dust out, and didn't say anything. He didn't feel the same exuberance the others felt. He could have been proud of what he had done and the way he had conducted himself under fire, but for the swimming pool. Sam was ashamed; the others were proud.

They reached Inchon. The trucks pulled in next to a large warehouse which was surrounded by streets of mud huts. A shower was provided where you stripped, got sprayed with DDT to kill the lice, and then entered the shower. Coming out of the shower, you were given clean dungarees. Sam and Arkie both saw the shower and made for it right away. As they left the shower, a galley had been set up to serve hot food, and they went over to the galley to eat and discovered instead of hot food they were serving cold Spam.

"Oh shit," Sam said, "I can't eat that crap."

"What else can we do?" Arkie asked.

Sam spotted a large stack of rations which were guarded by a Marine private who was armed with a rifle.

"We'll raid that chow dump," Sam said.

"Shit man, they've got a guard on it."

"Don't worry about it," Sam said, "We're clean. We look like officers. Just act like you own the damn chow. Come on." He started towards the dump. Arkie caught up and walked alongside. He grinned at Sam.

"Man, I sure hope you're right," he said.

Sam reached the dump and began reading the labels on the boxes, studiously taking his time. The guard stared at him, somewhat with suspicion, somewhat with curiosity. Sam ignored him. He picked up a large box which looked as if it contained enough food to feed a platoon, hoisted it to his shoulder and proceeded back to the warehouse, never bothering to look back at the guard. Arkie accompanied him, chuckling with delight. Sam slammed the box down on the floor of the warehouse and shouted "Banzai!" Then opened it with his bayonet. It contained, among other things, some canned fried bacon. Everyone was hungry, and he shared freely, and the food was soon gone. Sam ate the last strip of bacon, which was the most delicious feast he had had in weeks, but he was still hungry. "Let's go get some more," he said.

Arkie hesitated. "Ah . . . I don't know," he said.

"Come on. Remember, be arrogant. Act like an officer."

Arkie went along, but this time he wasn't grinning. They approached a second time. This time, the guard really stared at them. Sam saw more suspicion in his stare than curiosity and decided to get just any kind of carton. He picked a smaller one and again walked away without being challenged. Back at the warehouse he discovered he had confiscated 24 cans of canned cream.

"Look at this shit," he said, feeling disgust. "Next time, I'll get some more bacon. Let's go."

Arkie shook his head. "Not me. I didn't like the way that damned guard looked at us the last time."

"Ah, come on," Sam said, "we can do it."

Arkie was positive. "You go ahead. I ain't gettin' shot over any bacon."

Sam returned to the dump alone. A red-haired Warrant Officer was lying in the grass a few yards away from the stack of food. He appeared to be somewhat curious. Sam pretended to ignore him and took his time, scrutinizing each box till he was certain he had one which contained bacon. All the while, both the Warrant Officer and the guard were scrutinizing him. He calmly shouldered the box and started to walk away, seeing a long line of men had formed at the galley, some fifty yards distant, for Spam. Over on the right, there were four streets of mud huts, slightly beyond the chow line. Sam started towards the chow line, but within a few steps a voice challenged him.

"Hey! where you goin' with that chow?" It was the Warrant Officer.

Sam half turned and looked back, but kept walking. The Warrant Officer was getting to his feet.

"I'm taking it to the galley," Sam said, continuing to walk towards the chow line. The Warrant officer, who appeared about 45 years old, was following him. Sam could outrun him. If he ran towards the chow line the guard wouldn't dare fire at him.

The Warrant Officer quickened his pace. "I thought the galley was feeding Spam," he said.

"How in hell would I know?" Sam answered, and broke into a run. He ran alongside the chow line. It was mostly Fox Company. They all knew him and a cheer went up.

"Hey look, it's Psycho Sam!" "Hot damn! Run, Sam, run!"

And he was running fast, hearing the cries of "Run, Sam, Run!" blend in with the Warrant Officer's shouts of, "Stop that man. Stop him!" and the guard shouting, "Halt!"

He ignored the shouts and really put on a burst of speed, feeling dismay as he ran. Even if they didn't catch him, they could identify him, but he kept running. On the second row of huts, he turned into the street between, ran past two huts, made a hard right and went through the door of the second hut, expecting it to be empty. To his dismay, he found himself in Dog Company's CP. A captain, a lieutenant, and three Senior Sergeants sat cross-legged around a GI blanket, playing poker.

Without hesitating, Sam dropped the box on the floor by the wall, jerked a straw mat over it and plopped down cross-legged between them to the left of the dealer.

"Deal me in!" he panted.

Their mouths dropped open in astonishment.

"This is a money game," the dealer said.

Sam reached to his pocket pretending to have money. "Come on, I've got money, deal me in!"

The dealer flipped him a card, "Five card stud," he said.

Suddenly, the guard appeared in the open doorway. "Oh, excuse me, Sir. Did you'all see a guy run by with a box of rations on his shoulder?"

They roared with laughter. All except Sam. He was breathing too hard to laugh. The guard recognized him. "You're the guy!" he exclaimed. "Where's that chow?"

One of the poker players stopped laughing.

"You may as well give up," he said.

The Warrant Officer appeared in the door way and recognized Sam instantly.

"You're under arrest," he said. "Get that box of rations and come with me."

Reluctantly, Sam uncovered the box, shouldered it, and went out the door. They were still laughing. As they walked back towards the dump, Fox Company started laughing and calling out very subdued, like they hadn't wanted to see him caught, but couldn't resist laughing. Sam looked in their direction.

"Banzai!" he cried.

The Warrant Officer was startled. He stared at Sam incredulously.

"Just who the hell are you, anyway?" he asked.

"I'm Sergeant Lewis from Fox Company," Sam said.

"What . . . why are you stealing chow when there's plenty to eat at the galley?" He seemed genuinely puzzled.

"I'm a vegetarian. I can't eat Spam. Put yourself in my shoes. If you were hungry and couldn't eat Spam, what would you do?" Sam said.

He could tell his logic had swayed the Warrant Officer. He seemed to be considering. "You put that chow back where you got it. If I catch you here again I'll have you shot," he said.

"Am I free to go?" Sam asked.

"You can go," he replied.

Sam returned to the warehouse. A lieutenant, whom no one but Tarring had met, had arrived to take command of the platoon and the men were speculating on how this might affect them. They wondered why he hadn't introduced himself. In addition to the arrival of a new lieutenant, Joe Goggins, a black Sergeant from Chicago, had been assigned as platoon guide. He wasn't a really big man but was thick-chested and broad-shouldered. He looked as if he could take care of himself. There were only three blacks in Fox Company and rarity made them conspicuous.

The position of platoon guide was a spare-tire position for Tarring. Goggins had been a cook on Saipan and had been decorated with the bronze star for taking some Japanese prisoners after the battle was over. He was becoming acquainted with the men when Sam got there. If there was prejudice Sam couldn't see it. A few minutes after Sam arrived, Goggins asked for their attention. "Fellows, there's something I want to say."

The men grew quiet. Goggins looked slowly about at the faces he saw around him. His voice was low and calm. "You all see I am black. What I want to say is, I just doesn't think I am as good as you is, I takes it fo granted."

Causey asked him if he could sing. Joe looked at him with a puzzled look. He had the age-old problem of black people in a white society. He was trying to ascertain whether he was being addressed as friend or foe. "Sure I can," he said.

Sam wondered if there was going to be a problem but, within a few minutes, Causey had persuaded him to sing and Goggins was singing a Negro spiritual at the end of which the platoon clapped and applauded.

Next day, Tarring approached Sam.

"You're to report to the Company CP," he said.

"What for?" Sam asked.

"A ceremony. They're going to award Purple Hearts."

It just leaped up inside him. He had no idea it would happen, this sudden thought that awarding medals would be hypocritical, but it did. The good would be glorified: the bad would be covered up. The evil men do is hidden while the fine courageous acts are glorified. That is how the game is played and Sam didn't want to play the game.

"No thanks," Sam said. "I don't want to go to any ceremony."

"Why not?" he asked. "They have a photographer. He's going to take your picture and send it to your hometown newspaper."

"I don't want my picture in my hometown paper," Sam said.

"It's the same photographer who followed us through Seoul," Tarring said.

"Where was he when they filled the swimming pool with those prisoners we took?" Sam asked. "Maybe he would like to send a picture of that to my hometown newspaper."

Tarring breathed a long sigh. It was obvious he could see Sam had been traumatized by the pool and he regretted having shown it to him. Tarring was not an idealist. But he seemed to understood Sam's dilemma.

"I don't know, Sam," he said softly.

"I just don't want any part of it," Sam said.

"You have to go," Tarring said.

Sam felt trapped. He grew desperate.

"Tell them you couldn't find me," he said. "I'll stay out of sight."

Tarring left. Sam went outside and circled around to where he could watch the ceremony. All the others who had been wounded but not hospitalized stood lined at attention. Captain Groff proceeded from man to man, pinning the Purple Heart Medal on each one. Each time he did so, the photographer's camera flashed.

Watching from his hiding place, Sam was unaware of how badly he had been damaged. The change in him, like the change in the goals of his government, was insidious. He had looked eagerly forward to capturing Seoul and going home victorious. Seoul had been taken and going home had not been mentioned. Rumors persisted that since the North Korean Army had collapsed the main goal had been changed. The new goal was to unify Korea under one government. The news was that the U. S. Army was advancing rapidly through North Korea. When they reached the Yalu river which separated Korea from Manchuria the war would be over. So Sam watched from his hiding place, watched the camera's flash, without being fully aware of the incongruity of his conduct. He wanted as far away from anything military as possible.

Next day, orders came to board ship.

CHAPTER 17 ... An Exercise in Futility ...

An old Japanese transport plowed slowly south away from the coast at Inchon. The water was fairly calm and the ship rode heavily, groaning and creaking a little, rolling just a bit. It was heavily laden with the men of the Second Battalion and crowded beyond belief. Below deck it was dark, dank, and smelly. Sam had found a spot above deck to sit and write a letter to Charlotte. He had just finished one to his mother in which he did not mention the fighting, saying only that his wound had healed, he was back aboard ship, and he was alright. They were in the Yellow Sea and true to its name the waters had a yellow muddy color. An American destroyer approached and began pulling alongside to transfer mail. Sam hurriedly finished his letter and sealed it hoping to have it transferred across to the destroyer.

The destroyer shot a line across the transport which was hurriedly secured and sacks of mail were transferred across. They received a letter from Sergeant Crowell which was addressed to Fox Company, and this was passed from man to man. Reading it, one could feel his depression. They had amputated his right leg above the knee and he would be maimed for life. His letter read, "I don't think a single one of you would trade places with me." He went on to say where he was being sent for treatment and ended with good-bye to all of them.

Chico Carsenero wrote to the 2nd Platoon, telling them his leg also had been amputated, but just below the knee. He said that he had experienced great pain and would have shot himself to escape it, had he not been given morphine. He ended his letter by saying, "Tell Sergeant Lewis I shall never forget him."

Sam wondered whether this was because he had thrown Chico's prayer book away or because he had carried him to the aid station. It was saddening to know each would spend the rest of his life with an artificial limb and Sam wouldn't have traded places with either, but he still envied them because their war was over.

The transport turned and rounded the southern tip of Korea and the water began to change color from yellow to blue to green as they turned north and entered the choppy waters of the Sea of Japan. The battalion stayed aboard ship for several days while minesweepers cleared the waters of mines adjacent to the beaches, where they were to land. What lay ahead of them, no one knew. Once again, fear of the unknown gnawed at Sam, as he was sure it did for all the others, but no one voiced it as none wanted to admit being afraid. They knew a new landing was intended, but didn't know where or what awaited them. This was like the journey across the Pacific, except this time all the bravado was gone. None sat about sharpening bayonets and boasting about how many men they would kill. They had been bloodied. There was no need, or desire, to pretend they were not afraid.

The new lieutenant, Alexander Von Ludwig, didn't bother to introduce himself. One day he came below, saw someone smoking, and chewed the guy out.

"Put that damn cigarette out. You know there's no smoking below decks."

Physically he was a large man, about thirty years old and over six feet tall. He had been a beer salesman after World War Two and he obviously had enjoyed demonstrating his product, as he was indeed overweight. He soon became known, behind his back, as Lard Ass. Tarring came to know him before the men did and when Sam asked him about the new lieutenant he concluded Tarring didn't like the lieutenant.

They steamed back and forth in the Sea of Japan, hearing the Army was mopping up the North Korean Army in record fashion, and Bob Hope had landed at the beach where they were to go in. It looked as if the war might end very soon.

"Sam, it looks like we'll just do occupation duty," said Harvey Owen.

"Do you really think so?" Sam asked wistfully.

"Yeah" he said, grinning at Sam. "Just drink beer, and kick shit out of the Army."

Then, a day or so later, the word was passed for Fox Company to assemble on the fantail. They went back and ganged around some ammo crates that were lashed to the deck. Captain Groff stalked out, climbed up on the ammo boxes and glared at them.

"You miserable bastards," he began. "You think you've seen some fighting. You sons of bitches ain't seen nothing. You bastards don't know how to fight. I wouldn't even be talking to you bastards if Battalion hadn't ordered me to make a speech. Well, since I've been ordered to, here's my speech. If anyone wants to know who's top dog in this lashup, I'll tell you right now. By God, it's me!"

He climbed down off the crates and stalked away.

Sam thought the speech was disgusting and unfair. Captain Groff still seemed preoccupied with being the most powerful person in the company. After all, he was the Company Commander. Who was he afraid of? Certainly, no one of the enlisted men could be construed as challenging his authority.

To the newer men, he was impressive. To the rest of them, he was just the captain. By giving no praise for the job they had done on the Seoul-Inchon highway, and by his profane abuse, he managed, once again, to leave them angry.

Shortly after his speech, they went ashore at a place called Wonsan. They landed on the afternoon of a gray overcast day in October on a sandy beach that was almost devoid of vegetation. It was a little bit cold. They moved about two hundred yards in from the water's edge and set about gathering wood to make fires to heat their food. The fall wind was blowing bits of dry beach sand. The squad fires began to leap up, fanned by the breeze.

Joe Goggins joined Sam's squad fire. He subscribed to the Kiplinger Letter, and it contained some news that he was just bubbling to share. "Listen to this!" he cried, looking excited. "We foresee an early end to de Korean war."

"What's a nigger like you doing with a Kiplinger Letter?" Causey asked.

"Watch yourself, Causey. I don't have to take your shit," Goggins said.

"Watch what? You?" Causey said.

"Yes, Me!" Goggins said quietly. Something in his voice said that he meant it. Causey didn't reply.

Subdued, Goggins continued reading the letter until he finished with the portions pertaining to the war. It seemed that Kiplinger knew far more than they did.

While they were drinking their coffee and cocoa, Tarring came towards them at a fast pace.

"Sam!" he cried, "Saddle Up. The 1st Battalion landed fifty miles south of us. They just got the shit shot out of them. We're going down there to help out!"

The men fell silent. Some had pitched pup tents. They began to tear down the tents and pack up. By dark, the 1st Platoon was moving out. Captain Groff was leading, using a walking stick. Saia was a few yards behind. The Confederate flag was fairly snapping in the breeze. 2nd Platoon fell in behind the 1st Platoon and began marching silently into the night.

As they marched inland, the moon came out from behind rapidly moving clouds. Lieutenant Von Ludwig was carrying a large valise and a seabag in addition to his carbine and a 45 automatic pistol. He struggled vainly with his gear and soon stopped. The men ignored him as they went silently past. He saw Tarring and called to him.

"Tarring, get me some volunteers to carry this damn gear," he said.

Tarring caught up with Sam. "Sam, give me two volunteers. The lieutenant needs help."

Sam turned back and saw Petitt coming past.

"Come on Petitt."

Petitt grinned, "I ain't helping that bastard, let him carry his own gear."

"You will if I will," Sam said.

Petitt followed him back. Von Ludwig saw them coming.

"I asked for two men. I didn't want a squad leader," he said.

Sam ignored him, picked up the seabag and put it across his shoulder. Petitt got the valise and they hurried to catch up. Von Ludwig was right behind them.

"Careful with that valise," he cried.

Sam had hoped to distance himself from him but, without anything to carry, Von Ludwig was able to keep up. He followed along behind Petitt, berating him constantly not to drop the valise.

The column was moving quietly. The men had all been sobered by the prospect of more combat and each was lost in his own thought. They never knew what the plans were. For them, it was to follow the man ahead and hope that someone knew where they were going. The wind was rising, and above them were intermittent dark clouds that occasionally parted to let moonlight come through. Now, in the moonlight, Sam saw the glistening rails of railroad tracks extending in both directions and the flag turning to the right beginning to follow the rails. They had marched about a mile and were now in the heavy gravel of the track trying not to stumble on the cross ties and listening to the curses of those who did. The rails they were following split off and formed another pair of rails, and in a few hundred feet they were in a rail yard with many sets of parallel tracks.

They went past an antiquated steam engine and alongside a long train composed of a series of flat open cars. Von Ludwig had known where they were going because he got ahead of them and climbed up on one of the flat cars.

"Put the seabag down here," he said.

Sam went back and found Petitt.

"Where does his excellency want his valise?" Petitt asked angrily.

Sam took it from him, found that it was heavy, and swung it aboard the flat car beside the seabag. Von Ludwig pulled the bag to the center of the car, arranged the seabag to one side, then sat down on the car with his legs stretched out, his back against the valise. All up and down the train, men were climbing aboard. Some 3rd Platoon began to board the car.

"2nd Platoon only on this car," Von Ludwig shouted.

Sam found a place near the end of the car. Petitt followed.

"If you're not 2nd Platoon stay off this car," Von Ludwig cried.

Sam looked about, making certain all his squad had gotten aboard. The train creaked a little, seemed to roll both ways, and then went forward as it picked up speed. The wind began to whip across them and it was getting cold. Everyone was bitching at the same time, trying to wrap in shelter halves to get protection from the wind. Sam was afraid again, wondering what awaited them at the end of the ride. They were traveling through mountainous country. You could see the hills rise up on each side of the train. The train began to slow a little and the wind died down. Suddenly, darkness enveloped them before they knew what was happening. They were inside a long dark tunnel and still slowing down. The whole train was inside now and came to a stop. Sam's claustrophobia was very strong. This was North Korea! What in hell were they doing, stopping inside a tunnel! At any moment the enemy could dynamite the tunnel shut and they would suffocate. The train whistle blew, filling the tunnel with deafening sound. A chorus of shouts and cries rose up from the train. "Move this son of a bitch!"

In response, the train whistle sounded again. Sam wondered whose idea it was to stop an entire battalion of Marines inside a tunnel in known hostile country. Didn't anybody have any sense?

Finally, the train began to move again and a cheer of relief went up. Although the men didn't know it, Joe Perrigo was inside the cab of the train. He was holding a 45 automatic pistol to the Engineers head and giving him a choice, either move the train or die.

When they cleared the tunnel, Sam felt great relief. Then, to his dismay, they entered another and inside the second tunnel the train was beginning to slow again. A moan of despair rose up from the entire train, but this time the train only slowed, and then gradually increased speed. They passed through several tunnels in this manner, feeling an almost unbearable fear; then at last the train broke out of the last tunnel into more level country and ground to a halt. It was about four o'clock in the morning.

"Everybody off!"

Orders were shouted to dig in on both sides of the railbed facing outboard. The train went into reverse and backed up into the entrance of the last tunnel and stopped again. The roadbed was about ten feet higher than the rice paddies that stretched to both sides and it was a relief to dig in the side of the bed rather than the stinking paddy. Off to their left, planes were making a night air strike, the only one Sam had ever seen. They would come screaming down firing, with machine guns, cannon and rockets going down in fiery trails. The planes seemed to stop in midair and hang there when the rockets were loosed.

Sam dug in with Petitt. By daybreak, they had a hole two feet deep and seven feet long. Petitt took the first watch. He wrapped his shelter half about his shoulders and sat on the bank just far enough down as not to show on the skyline. Sam got down in the damp earth and slept for an hour. As soon as it was light enough, he went out in front of the position and strung a trip flare.

Word was passed that Fox Company would patrol into a village that lay off to the right front, and they hurried to eat rations and prepared to move out. Groff walked out in the paddy and stopped. He no longer cursed them because they now knew when to move. As they followed Groff out, Lieutenant Von Ludwig struck the fine copper wire of Sam's trip flare, with his foot pulling the pin out of the flare. He didn't know he had touched anything. The flare popped like a rifle shot and Von Ludwig dived headlong into the paddy and lay face down with his buttocks quivering.

Someone laughed. Then everyone laughed. He got up and looked about.

"I wasn't ready for this," he said.

They continued marching. As they neared the village, several villagers came out and watched them approach. They did not greet the Marines with three Banzais as the South Korean villagers had done.

Captain Groff moved to the head of the column with Jackson, Saia, and the ever-present flag. Jackson spoke in Korean to the nearest villager, a young Korean boy. The boy turned and ran into the village. A moment later, he returned with an elder Korean. The old papa-san approached Jackson and bowed from his waist down, a low sweeping bow. Jackson turned to Captain Groff.

"He's the village elder," Jackson said.

The old man bowed again, this time to Captain Groff.

"Ask him how many soldiers are here," Groff said.

Jackson spoke again to the elder, listened to his response, then turned again to Groff.

"None, he says."

"Tell him to get all the people out in to the street, pronto," Groff said.

Jackson turned again to the elder and relayed Groff's command. The old man babbled to those around near him and they ran back into the village shouting in Korean. The villagers came out into the street. One of them was a young girl who appeared to be twelve or thirteen. Erickson grinned at her.

"Baby doll," he said.

"Knock it off," Sam said.

"She looks just about the right size," Erickson said.

Captain Groff turned. "Check the huts," he said.

Jennings's squad began taking the left row of huts. Sam's squad took the right. At the third hut, Sam found a cache of wooden rifles buried under a straw mat.

"This one has a lot of wooden rifles!" he said.

Captain Groff came over and looked in. He turned back to Jackson who had followed with the elder.

"Interrogate this bastard!" Groff said.

Jackson began barking at the elder, firing questions in rapid order. The old man answered quietly, speaking quickly, but not showing any excitement. Jackson turned back to Groff.

"He says there were soldiers here, but they are all gone. The soldiers had them make the wooden rifles. The soldiers were training them to defend their village because the Americans would come and rape their women and burn the village."

"Burn the hut the rifles are in," Groff said.

Two men from the third squad came forward, went into the hut and then backed out with flaming torches. They touched these to the roof of the hut. The inside was already on fire.

Groff spoke again. "Tell him if the soldiers come back he must let us know. If he doesn't, we'll come back and burn the whole goddam village."

They left then. Sam kept looking back to see how the villagers were doing with the fire. It looked as if they were not going to be able to save the hut, though they were scurrying about with pails of water. Sam thought to himself that war had not changed much since Sherman marched through Georgia. Only this time, the burners followed a Confederate flag.

The rest of the day was spent improving their position at the track. They strung trip flares out in the paddies and went about the task of heating rations. They heard the 1st Battalion, whom they had come down to assist, had beaten off the enemy, but portions of the 1st Battalion had been overrun and many men were killed. Some of these had been caught in their sleeping bags and had been hacked and stabbed beyond recognition. Their own comrades had been unable to recognize them.

That night, a trip flare went off in front of the position. Immediately, a hundred rifle shots rang out, then an old greyhound loped contemptuously along, parallel to the line, unscathed. A relieved laughter went up from the entire line and died into little snickers.

Later in the night, Lieutenant Von Ludwig came walking from hole to hole, asking, "Anybody awake in that hole." Then repeating it at the next hole.

Petitt did not like him at all. "I was asleep," he said, "till that bastard came by."

Sam had tied a trip flare to a stake in front of his hole and ran the trip wire back to the hole and tied it to a little stick that hung down inside the hole. At two o'clock, Von Ludwig came back again. As he drew near, Sam pulled the wire. The flare popped and Von Ludwig leaped into the top of Joe Goggins's hole, while Goggins was asleep, scaring both of them out of their wits. Von Ludwig got up out of the hole, apologizing as he did so, not knowing what had made the flare go off. He broke off his inspection trip without completing it and the rest of the night passed uneventfully.

The town of Majong Ni lay south of them. The powers that be sent them on another patrol at daylight. As yet, they had seen no enemy, and now were to venture into Majong Ni to attempt to contact the force which had attacked the 1st Battalion. They followed the track towards town, came to a place where a road crossed the track, went past a hole where a man and a woman lay dead, curled up beside each other as if they were sleeping. It was not apparent how they had died, but it appeared they had been dead for three or four days.

As they drew nearer the town, a Korean came walking slowly towards them. His entire lower jaw was missing. In its place only raw flesh showed. The man seemed dazed. Some cruel Marine called out, "Hey, Gook, why don't you talk to us?" The man stumbled on without taking any notice of them at all. Sam wondered whether he knew where he was headed or was just in shock. Petitt looked at the man as he passed.

"He's going to die someplace," he said.

They passed through some stinking rice paddies and got into the town on a street that was lined with palm trees. A destroyer was out in the harbor throwing shells over their heads to screen their approach. A combat photographer was accompanying them and looking about for something to take pictures of. Sam noticed the photographer hadn't bothered to take the jawless man's picture. Apparently, Sam thought bitterly, no hometown newspaper would be interested in it. The column held up and they stood about, waiting impatiently. Big Jim Causey sat down beside the road and leaned back against one of the palm trees. He had grown a goatee and looked the part of a picture-poster Marine. The photographer aimed his camera. At that instant, one of the destroyer's shells fell short. A tremendous explosion hit the middle of the road about twenty feet away. The photographer hurled the camera aside and left the road on the opposite side.

Most of the platoon had wisely left the road before the explosion. But Sam had stayed. When the shell landed he went up in the air about two feet, his feet pumping, but he was going nowhere. He came down and in two great bounds he cleared the road, to be greeted with laughter. Everyone was looking not at the photographer, but at Sam.

"What's so funny?" he asked.

Arkie grinned at him. "You, Sam; you were up in the air, your legs were pumping and you were going nowhere."

"I guess I'm gettin' kinda fast," Sam said.

The patrol ended shortly thereafter and they returned back past the dead man and woman without seeing any sign of the jawless man. Sam got down in the hole and went to sleep. It was always best to sleep whenever you could. One never knew what might happen at night or when you might be required to be awake for two or three days.

When he woke it was almost dark. Petitt was sitting above the hole looking out across the paddy. He had a blanket wrapped about his shoulders. He saw Sam was awake and came down beside the hole.

"Sam. Do you think Joe's Kiplinger Letter is right about the war ending soon?"

"Hell, Petitt, I wouldn't know. It came within a few feet of ending for me today."

"I hate this damn war. And I hate some of these people we're with," he said.

Sam could see that something was bothering him. "What's wrong?" he asked.

"While you were asleep, me and Causey went out to that first village where we burned the hut. We just wanted to look around, thought we might find some eggs. Off to one side of the huts they had a winch that pulled cars or something out of that mountain beside the village. We could hear Marines talking so we went over and went into the hut where the winch was. They had her in there."

Sam's heart seemed to skip a beat.

"Had who!"

"That little girl. They had her top off. They started to cut her pants off with a bayonet and she shit all over herself."

"Did you guys stop it?" Sam asked.

"No, we were going to. We started to say something, but it was, well, it was like somebody was gonna get killed. They were acting real crazy. Causey, he started to stop them and they made it clear that it was none of our business. Causey said we better get out of there. So we left."

"You mean the two of you just walked away and left that little girl with them?" Sam asked.

Petitt didn't answer. Sam could see that he felt awful.

"What happened next?"

"One of 'em said, 'Wipe the shit off her and we'll fuck her.'"

"Who was it?"

"That corpsman in the Third Platoon was one of them. They're over there talkin' about it now."

Sam got up, picked up his carbine and went down the track. He saw the corpsman and two others together. They were cooking a chicken they had killed. The corpsman was clean-cut looking. You could not imagine him doing what he had done. One of them was a big PFC who had been fourteen years in the Marine Corps. Back at the barracks in Washington D.C. he had once helped Sam recover from over-indulgence in alcohol by bringing mashed potatoes for him to eat when nothing else would stay down.

"Hi Sam," he said.

Sam nodded, but didn't say anything. Under any normal circumstance he would have gone to the Company Commander, but that was out of the question. If Groff wouldn't do anything about the murders at the swimming pool he wouldn't do anything about rape. He realized that all he had expected of the captain that day in Seoul was that he speak out against killing prisoners of war. He knew that the captain had not ordered the massacre at the pool. He had not considered that in order to speak out the captain would be admitting to higher authority that he knew about it. Then there was the matter of Petitt's coming back through battalion and learning of it. Someone higher in authority than Captain Groff would have to know about it. Who at battalion had persuaded Margurite Higgins not to reveal the atrocity?

Sam sat down on the track and placed his weapon across his legs. How could he kill them? Could he make it look like an accident? He felt such contempt it showed on his face. If he could get them with one burst it might work. But, if he did, his deed would be as bad as theirs. While he was wrestling with the thought, they moved apart. He knew then it wouldn't work. He didn't dare let them know what he knew. To do so might open him up to a bullet in the back. He sat for a moment and then got up and walked away. He was trapped. We're doing the very things we came to stop, he thought. He got up and walked slowly back down the track in despair. He looked back once. The corpsman's mouth was open and he was gaping at Sam.

The words of the Marine Corps Hymn echoed in Sam's mind, "First to fight for right and freedom, and to keep our honor clean; We are proud to claim the title of United States Marine." Where did this lead to? He couldn't go to a superior officer. He had no authority over the offenders. He was angry enough to kill and couldn't, because he knew it was wrong. He went to see Causey who confirmed what Petitt had said. Sam looked at him. Causey was five years older than Sam, a combat veteran who had fought Japanese. He had a baby daughter at home. Why had he not drawn his Colt 45 and ordered them to stop?

"Why in God's name didn't you stop them?" Sam asked.

"Sam, it just wasn't worth getting shot over," he said.

CHAPTER 18 ... The Horseshoe Bend ...

From the position on the railroad track Sam could see the village where the young girl lived. On the following day several Marine trucks appeared at the village. Sam sat on the embankment of the track and watched them load the villagers in the trucks. Petitt came and sat down beside him.

"What's goin' on over there?" Sam asked.

"They're going to blow the village up." Petitt replied.

"Why?"

"To keep the enemy from using it," Petitt said.

The trucks departed. Shortly after, the village was destroyed by naval gunfire.

Sam never learned whether the three had killed the girl or not, but the question gnawed at him. He approached Causey again.

"Jim why in hell didn't you stop them from raping that girl?"

"Look Sam. I know how you feel. But forget it man. Forget it."

"I would have stopped them," Sam said.

"Don't ask me about it again," Causey said angrily. "I've said all I'm going to say about it."

Sam thought Causey felt guilty for having walked away. He knew that he would not have done so. He was confronted with the inescapable conclusion that such things have always happened in all armies at all times, that in society the criminal element is always a small fractional part. He could accept that. What he could not accept was the fact that his superiors would not act to halt these things from happening. He wondered just how far up in Battalion did the knowledge of the pool go.

They stayed at the railroad track for several days. Each day they made daily patrols past the dead man and woman who lay curled together in death. No one ever buried them. They just lay in the hole and rotted, symbolic of what was happening all over Korea.

Then an Army Captain arrived who was an expert on cold weather survival. The men were assembled and the captain began lecturing on cold weather survival. Soon they would be going where it would be very cold. He showed them the winter boots they would be wearing, the thick socks to be worn with the boots, and the mittens that had a trigger finger pocket. He demonstrated the lined parkas with big hoods. It would be necessary to keep canteens of water and food inside their clothing, next to their bodies, to prevent them from freezing. Then he did an odd thing. He was supposed to be giving a technical lecture but he departed from his usual speech. "One of our great presidents once said, 'All we have to fear is fear itself.'"

His lecture over, the officer left them with that thought.

After they drew the clothing, word was passed that they would go out into the mountains to set up a roadblock to prevent the North Korean Army from escaping further north. Because Easy Company was closer to the road, they boarded first; then Fox Company followed.

When they moved out, Lieutenant Von Ludwig latched onto two luckless Marines from Ivan Jennings's squad to help him carry his gear from the track to the trucks, a distance of about a half mile. As they moved along, he assisted them with commands, "Careful with that valise! Don't drop it now."

When they reached the road, both Dog and Easy Company had already moved out, leaving an insufficient number of trucks. They boarded. Sam found a fender and climbed up on it. He liked the idea of riding on the fender. You got a lot of wind and dust, but you also got the heat from the engine and in an emergency you could get off quickly. The rest of the company were packed into the trucks with no room at all to move about.

They headed northwest into the mountains in country so poor the land seemed only capable of growing scrub trees. The road was dry and dusty and the trucks kicked up a column of dust that could be seen from the high peaks for miles. Sam wrapped the mechanism of his carbine in tinfoil he had saved from a chocolate bar to keep out the dust. As they began to climb higher into the wild country, the road became little more than a pair of ruts on the sides of the mountains.

Ahead of them the column wound around the mountain on a ledge that led into a horseshoe shape before weaving left again to clear the horseshoe. Sam was riding the lead truck. Suddenly, as they began to enter the horseshoe, the driver rammed on his brakes, nearly throwing Sam off the fender. The entire column stopped. Sam could hear a lot of firing around the bend where the horseshoe was and saw the tail of the Easy Company trucks enter the bend. They waited for some order to come. None did. To the left, the mountain rose almost vertically. Climbing it would be nearly impossible. To the right, a huge abyss led across to the other end of the horseshoe. Unwilling to enter into the trap and unable to do anything to stop it, they waited, listening to the hammering of heavy machine guns and volumes of rifle fire. The firing continued for about ten minutes, then died to a trickle and stopped. The trucks began to move again. They went round the bend into the horseshoe.

Dead and wounded Marines lay everywhere. The corpsmen were moving among them giving plasma and bandaging wounds. Once again, Easy Company had suffered heavily. They were placing them aboard trucks and moving out again, leaving those trucks no longer operable to be shoved against the mountain to get them out of the way. On one of the trucks a young Marine clung to the handles of a fifty-caliber machine gun that was mounted above the cab. The back of his head was gone. A half-used belt of ammo hung from the gun. They went past and reached a second truck. A Marine hung halfway out of the truck on his back, facing the sky, his face was turned towards them. Sam had known him at Parris Island and remembered him well. His face, in death, was as gray as the tombstones at Arlington, that now seemed so far distant, not only in space but in time. One of his eyes had been shot out. It was like seeing an old friend and rushing to greet him only to see him freeze in death before your eyes.

After a while, sobered by what they had seen, they reached their destination. Saia and the flag were following Captain Groff up the slope of the hill. Tarring found Sam beside the fender of the truck.

"Sam, will you send some men to help Lard Ass with his valise? I haven't the heart to order anyone."

"He'll find someone," Sam said.

They left the trucks and made their way past the place where Captain Groff was setting up his command post. Captain Groff never dug his own hole. This task was reserved for whomever had broken fire discipline. You broke fire discipline by firing a round at night and not being able to produce a body to show what you had shot at. If there were an abundance of violators these were used to dig latrines. He now had the habit of surrounding himself with the company clerk, another runner besides Saia, and a Technical Sergeant. The Technical Sergeant was a spare tire for old Homer. Someone had said that the Technical Sergeant was from Battalion Intelligence. Homer had been ineffective as anything other than just a body. He certainly would not have been capable of writing letters to the next of kin of those killed in action.

As they climbed past the Captain's CP, one offender was busy digging the captain's hole. Sam's squad dug in in front of the captain, slightly uphill and facing west. Sam placed the BARs by showing the fire team leaders the area each was to cover, and after they got dug in they carried some barbed wire up the hill and strung some of it back downhill in front of their position. Working parties were a part of combat. No one ever delivered anything. Everything they got they carried themselves.

Each day a working party was formed—usually two, sometimes three, men from each squad. Sam rotated the men in this task, being careful to make certain that he included himself. Sam had observed the men hated Von Ludwig because he didn't lead. Neglecting to carry your own weight is a fatal flaw in anyone who would be a leader. Von Ludwig was supposed to be a leader. In actuality, he was just something else to carry.

The first night proved uneventful. Next day, Captain Groff led 2nd Platoon on a patrol to look for the enemy who had ambushed Easy Company. They made their way across the ridgetops until they found the area where the enemy had lain in wait above the horseshoe. It was a vantage point unexcelled. They had had a turkey shoot. Empty rifle cartridges were scattered all about. Finding no further sign of the enemy, Groff proceeded back west and descended to the road and began following it.

At length, they rounded a bend in the road which revealed two huts built back against the mountain in a curve in the road. On the opposite side of the road a sheer cliff dropped into an abyss. Two Korean civilians were in front of the huts walking towards the patrol.

"Take them prisoners!" Captain Groff commanded.

Two Marines ran forward and apprehended the two Koreans at gunpoint and brought them back. Jackson began questioning them.

"Check those huts!" Groff commanded.

Erickson and Sam ran over to the first hut. Sam stood by the door and kicked it open while Erickson covered with his BAR. The hut was empty. They went to the second hut and repeated the procedure. It was also empty. Sam ran around the hut to the rear and stepped into a pile of excrement. The odor nauseated him. Looking about, he saw several piles, and went back to where the captain was waiting.

"They've been here," Sam said.

"How do you know?" Groff asked.

"They've been shitting all over the back yard. It's still fresh."

Groff turned to Jackson and, indicating the younger of the two prisoners, said, "Ask him where the soldiers are who've been using his house."

Jackson barked the question.

The Korean gave a short reply.

Jackson turned again to Captain Groff.

"He says that it isn't his house. The house belongs to his friend here. He only came over to visit his friend."

Captain Groff gave a hard look at the older man. "Ask him!" he said.

Jackson barked the question.

The old man answered.

Jackson turned again to the captain.

"He says, what soldiers?" he said.

"Goddam that son of a bitch," Captain Groff said. "Take him to the cliff. Make him think you're going to kick him over." Then he added, as if an afterthought, "Or kick him over, if you're a mind to."

The Technical Sergeant grabbed the old man and jerked him to the edge of the precipice. Drawing his pistol, he cracked the old man on the side of his head and knocked him to his knees.

Sam's nerves went taut like banjo strings. He knew he could not stand by and watch a helpless old man be murdered. He leaned back, braced himself against the mountain, and raised his carbine waist high. Perhaps the captain had forgotten that Sam had told him that he would shoot anyone who killed a prisoner, but Sam certainly had not. He decided to warn them first. If any made as if to shoot him, or the prisoner, Sam would kill him. Captain Groff cast one quick furtive glance at Sam as Sam raised his carbine. Although he made no other sign, Sam knew he was watching and that he had not forgotten Sam's warning at the swimming pool. Sam stood easily, not wanting to convey his intention. His life depended on not doing so. With his finger on the trigger, he prepared to defend an old Korean civilian. His heart was racing.

Jackson began to question the man again. This time the old man babbled for his life. Jackson turned back to the Captain.

"There are about a hundred soldiers. He had no choice but to let them use his house. They left here yesterday before we got here. He doesn't know where they went, but he has done nothing."

"Let them go," Captain Groff said.

Sam breathed a sigh of relief and slowly lowered his carbine. Jackson spoke in Korean to the two and, with much bowing and scraping, they gave thanks for their lives.

They continued along the road and returned to their defense perimeter. As they came back to the position, Easy Company had been out in a different direction. They had taken about a dozen sullen prisoners who were now lined up for Jackson to interrogate. Groff and Jackson stopped in front of the prisoners. Groff picked the first man. He said, "Ask him how many men are in his company."

Jackson spoke to the prisoner in Korean and turned back to Captain Groff. "He says twenty-seven."

Captain Groff turned to one of the Easy Company Marines and snatched his M1 rifle. He struck the soldier in the forehead with the butt of the rifle, knocking him down to his knees.

"Now, ask him again," he said.

Sam stepped forward. "Captain, how would you like to be in their shoes?" he asked.

Groff laughed. "That's just it. I'm not in their shoes." Then he turned his full attention on Sam, "Do you think if I was in their shoes, they'd treat me any better?" he demanded.

"No Captain, I don't," Sam replied, "but you're supposed to be civilized."

Groff didn't answer, but he stopped clubbing the prisoners, and Sam felt his criticism had been effective. He went slowly up the hill to his hole. He had been on the verge of mutiny and did not like the feeling. Sooner or later, he thought, there'll come a time when I have to confront the captain.

In thoughtful moments, in the dark of night, Sam began to see the truth about war. What it really meant was the lifting of all the restrictions of civilization. With these lifted, a man was free to be what he really was. If a man were a murderer in his heart, he became one in reality. If he were compassionate, he remained so, provided he had strength of character. If a person had been taught to respect his fellow man, he deluded himself if he thought he could kill his fellow man, in the belief he was defending his country, and therefore justify doing so, without suffering the pangs of guilt. War was not kill or be killed, war was kill and be killed. Sam knew he couldn't survive simply by killing. If he was going to survive, he would have to do so by every instinct and by using every fibre of his being in the effort; and finally, by luck. No amount of will could keep him alive if he were unlucky. While luck could be influenced by attention to the details of survival, there were no guarantees. Much could not be reasoned out. Twice he had seen Easy Company take heavy casualties. Was there some great unseen power who exacted revenge for acts committed during war? Then, Sam dismissed the thought. He was just being superstitious. Besides, why should a whole company suffer for the crime of a few?

CHAPTER 19 ... A Razor Blade ...

The mountains were formidable. From atop the hill Sam could see for miles and all that lay about was hill after hill, in all directions. The leaves had fallen from the scrub bushes and the mountains were almost bare, which added to their formidability. Sam did not want to die but, more than death itself, he feared to die and be left in this cold desolate unfriendly land, far from the fires of home and the love of life and family. Gradually, the hardship of their lives intensified. Each day became harder than the day before.

While they were encamped upon the huge hill, winter found them. It came so gradually they didn't notice at first but the wind picked up, grew stronger little by little, and never left. Within a day or so firewood in the immediate vicinity became scarce and they sometimes ate the C rations cold. It proved impossible to open food cans with the heavy mittens on, and in the few minutes each day in which they removed them, the cold cracked their fingers. They didn't bleed; they first dried out and then developed raw cracks and became very sore. The place became known as Icicle Hill.

Every carton of C rations contained two small cans of fruit, usually pears or peaches, occasionally plums, and either two round pieces of gumbo candy or a round piece of chocolate bar and a single gumbo candy, powdered cocoa, instant coffee with little packages of sugar, and a small jelly. In addition, each contained three cans of something. The best would be scrambled eggs and bacon, sausage patties and gravy, and hamburger patties. The worst ration you could get was called the deadly three. This would be a can of meat and beans, except that the meat would be inedible gristle, a second can of so-called beef stew, where again the meat was gristle, and a third can of spaghetti and tomato sauce. Between best and worst, at random intervals, you would find chicken and vegetables, of which there was very little chicken and mostly carrots, green peas and filler. Then there was beans and franks, which weren't too bad, and just plain beans. On this food most everyone lost weight. Sam had weighed one hundred ninety pounds at the barracks. Now, a bare three months later, he had lost twenty-five pounds.

Sam traded rations constantly. The trick was to horse trade, and fruit was the key. He became expert at trading. If he drew the deadly three, he traded one of them for one can of fruit. He traded the can of fruit for a can of chicken and vegetables and a can of the deadly three, like he had begun with, then trade the deadly three can again for fruit or candy. The profit lay in making each trade improve his daily ration ever so slightly. He hawked his trades the same way that he had advertised the laundry business back in Washington. He would join a group at a fire, give them a friendly cry of "Banzai!" and after getting their attention begin to chant, "I have one can of sausage patties. What am I offered for one can of sausage patties?"

Unless they were under fire or on patrol, his trading was incessant. He roamed restlessly from fire to fire, getting to know all his comrades. Arkie had gone to college (after being in the Seabees on Okinawa) and had taken literature as a major. He had failed to fit in college and had enlisted in the Marines without graduating. He had a fondness for his English professor, Mrs. Finwilly, and her name always came up. Apparently, she had been a gentle sensitive person, and he seemed always wondering how she would react had she been unfortunate enough to witness the conditions of his life. He would get off on the subject, and mimic her bitterly.

"Oh, if a little bird goes tweet tweet. Arkie, oh Arkie! recite for the class your composition on the robin." He would pause and laugh bitterly to himself.

"And now class, Arkie has a new poem to read. Yesterday a round passed overhead. Tomorrow, no doubt, I'll surely be dead."

This drew bitter grins from everyone and put a little humor into their lives. In between the daily scratching for food and trying to cope with the increasing cold they patrolled, looking for the enemy. They never found the soldiers who had ambushed Easy Company; instead, the enemy found them. One dark night the North Koreans encircled them, some on all sides. They began firing different colored tracer bullets, and as they fired, the Marines could see the tracers flaming across the sky. One of them positioned himself upline of the line of holes occupied by Sam's squad. Sam heard a short rush of running footsteps from in front. Simultaneously, a burp gun chattered and a spray of bullets struck around him. Sam ducked down in the hole. Each time he came up, a spray of bullets struck around him. The burp gun sounded quite like an automatic carbine, and Sam began to suspect the company rocket squad leader, a Marine named Cheek, was attempting to fire over his head.

"Cheek! Cheek! Is that you?" he cried.

He got a burst of fire in reply. Each time he shouted, bullets answered him. Finally, he concluded it wasn't Cheek.

The sound of many running feet, somewhat like quail taking flight, said they were coming. Out of the blackness of the night they rushed. The Marines met them with a barrage of hand grenades and rifle fire. All the while, the tracers streamed overhead. All about came the heavy thud of Marine mortars, the fast chatter of the Russian burp guns. Almost as suddenly as it had started, the firing died down. All was quiet. Then, from somewhere out in front, the wailing sound of a wounded Korean cut through the darkness. It was a voice of despair and desperation, the wail of a human voice in a language they did not speak. It continued unceasingly for the rest of the night. At daybreak it stopped. In front of Sam's hole, the bodies of five North Korean soldiers draped across the barbed wire. Then the wailing sound came again, a haunting pitiful sound of a man crying out. Sam thought he might be praying.

Captain Groff walked out and stood looking down at the Koreans. He drew his pistol and shot the first man in the head. The wailing sound came again. Groff walked from man to man shooting each one in the head. Each time he fired, the pistol bucked in his hand and he laughed a strange laugh. When he shot the third one the wailing stopped, interrupted by his bullet, but he shot the others anyway.

Groff laughed a hard bitter laugh. "Ha ha, I never liked bloodshed," he said.

He holstered his pistol, strode back to his foxhole and began eating breakfast. Sam's squad went out to look them over and stood gawking at them. One, obviously an officer, had a set of red epaulets on the shoulders of his uniform. Petitt took his bayonet and began to cut one of the epaulets off. The man made a sudden noise, a whirring sound, like a rattle snake. Air was escaping from his body. Caught by surprise, Petitt leaped backwards away from the man.

"Petitt, you son of a bitch," Groff called out, laughing, "I'd sure like to check your shorts because I know you just shit your drawers."

Then, Tarring came over and stood looking down at the dead men. His little girl face was set with a grim look.

"Maybe he had to shoot them. But he didn't have to make such a show of it," he said.

Sam had hardened without being aware. He had not recoiled in horror when the captain shot them. He stood looking down at them. One clutched a stick with a double-edged razor blade set inside a split. The stick was tightly bound together at each end of the blade so that the blade would not come out. The weapons of the others were gone, no doubt carried away by their comrades, but the stick was obviously the only weapon the soldier had. Sam wondered what he might do if he were ordered to attack North Koreans armed only with a stick and a double-edged razor blade. Instinctively, he sensed harder times coming. Men who attack at night with sticks and razor blades would not be easily defeated. Sam looked away from him, out in the direction from which they had come. The cruel mountains of North Korea stretched as far as he could see, one behind the other, rugged, bare, and forbidding. They jutted skyward, jagged, ominous and impassable. He shuddered. Silently, he turned and walked back to his hole. He sat down, tore his carbine down and cleaned it.

CHAPTER 20 ... Manchurian Wind ...

One morning, Sergeant Oliver made his way along the line of their holes. He was clean shaven and had a broad smile on his face as he stopped and talked to the men. He reached the area where Sam was dug in. Out in front, the bodies still hung on the wire. Oliver gave Sam a broad grin.

"You have no idea why I've shaved, do you?" he asked.

"No," Sam replied.

"Guess what day this is?" Oliver said.

Sam looked out at the wire. "I have no idea," he said.

"It's November 10th, the birthday of the Marine Corps," Oliver said with a big grin. Then he continued along the line urging his comrades to clean up and shave. A few did. Water was scarce and it took water to shave.

Soon thereafter, they left Icicle hill and returned to Majong Ni. Sam rode the fender again. This time the truck ride was uneventful. After a journey back through the horseshoe bend they reached the plain below and became warm again. It was warm enough you could take your hands out of the mittens, and Sam's fingers began to heal. A field kitchen set up in an open field and served a Turkey dinner. It was the first good meal Sam had had in months. Although it was not yet Thanksgiving Day, word was passed that it was Thanksgiving dinner.

The day after, word was passed they were headed north. After the horseshoe bend, Sam would never ride in the back of a truck. Some might have thought it perfectly alright to be riding around in territory occupied by the enemy in the back of a truck, but it was not Sam's idea of common sense. He found a fender and climbed on. He had a good feeling about it. If the first shot didn't hit him he would be off the truck and moving when the second shot came.

Perched on the right front fender, his head lowered to avoid the wind, he leaned close to the engine as the truck moved out. They were moving for about an hour when the trucks slowed and shifted to lower gears and began winding about. The hills kept getting steeper. They entered a section of roadway on a ledge of the mountain which was barely wide enough for a single vehicle. Sam looked down for a thousand feet before he saw bottom and up a thousand feet, on the opposite side, at a seventy-degree angle. It was like being perched on the edge of the world. The day was waning. Late in the afternoon they reached a plateau. It was bitterly cold. The Manchurian wind came howling down upon them. In the center of a valley, which was shaped like the letter Y, they dismounted and formed a circle around the trucks, just as settlers had, when wagons went west and they circled to fight off Indians.

"Don't try to dig in," Tarring said, "we're moving in the morning."

They lay down on the hard cold earth. It was like lying on a block of ice. The earth was frozen solid. The wind kept howling past. During the night, it began to snow. It came down in a fine white powder and keened along the earth, cutting it bare in some places and filling in the lower areas. It put a frozen coat of ice and snow on their clothing and forced them to keep moving to avoid freezing to death. It had been cold in the central mountains, but nothing compared to what they were experiencing now. A thirty mile an hour wind was coming down out of Manchuria, the huge land mass that touched Siberia on one side and Korea on the other.

Morning arrived. The men shook the snow off their sleeping bags. A line formed for breakfast. They stood in line and shivered, filing slowly past a field kitchen for corn meal mush, powdered milk, and two stewed prunes. As soon as the food hit the tray it was cold. Sam ate quickly before it could freeze. Each man received a small can of tomato juice and drank it gratefully. Cold corn meal mush does not sit well in your stomach at thirty degrees below zero.

"Fox Company, Saddle up!" someone cried.

They dumped their trays, struggled into packs, and moved out behind the Confederate flag, heads bowed against the wind, trying to keep it from coming inside the hooded parkas and freezing their ears. They marched west into the left leg of the Y, parallel to a small stream which was frozen solid. A half mile ahead lay the village of Koto Ri. Instead of going into Koto Ri, the flag turned left and began ascending a high hill. The captain went a hundred yards up the hill, then dropped out of the column, leaving the rest of them to continue on to the crest. There, they attempted to dig in. Four picks were shared by two hundred fifty men. Each got the pick long enough to break through the frozen crust of earth and then passed it to the next hole.

"Keep digging so it doesn't freeze." someone said. Sam dug in with Lewellyn and Vesuvius. Lewellyn had been a BAR man but was too lazy to carry it. He always found a way to pass it to someone else. Vesuvius, the BAR man, had never pulled the trigger. He was untested. While they were digging in, Tarring came from hole to hole. "The Eighth Army over on the west coast is under attack by the Chinese Army," he said.

Sam felt his heart skip a beat. "How do you know?" Sam asked grimly.

"It came in over the battalion radio. I don't know anything else. Just that they were under heavy attack."

Sam remembered the reports they had heard about the long Chinese convoys. This news was ominous. It put real urgency into the digging. By nightfall they had a hole wide enough for three of them to sit side by side in and about two feet deep. They couldn't lie down, but could stretch their legs and lean back against the side. They sat down. Lewellyn began a long tale about a Marine who had gotten his throat cut at night in a foxhole. Sam got interested right away, thinking it had been something he hadn't known about. Then, Lewellyn said, "You remember that guy, don't you Sam? The one we found with his throat slit from ear to ear."

"No kiddin'!" Vesuvius said. "Wit a knife?"

"Yeah, a big knife. But, it could have been done with a razor blade in a stick just as easy."

"You remember, Sam, when you put him on watch and went to check him next morning and found blood all over his sleeping bag?"

Lewellyn was just trying to scare Vesuvius. Sam reluctantly went along with it.

"Yeah, I remember that," he said.

"Has dat happened very often?" Benny asked.

"Oh yeah," Lewellyn said. "Not to us, but to Easy Company. It usually happens late at night. If those Chinese have come into the war and they find us it could happen again."

Sam took two hand grenades out of his pack and put them on the parapet. It was still snowing, but the wind had died down. Lewellyn suggested to Benny that Benny take the first watch. "Just wake me up when you get sleepy," he told Benny.

Sam lay back against the bank. Benny got on his knees and leaned against the front bank, peering out over the parapet.

The ridge fell away so rapidly in front of the hole that, if a man stood six yards in front of the hole, Benny would be looking down at him. When Sam fell asleep Benny was peering out over the parapet.

Sam woke suddenly. It was daylight. He was covered with snow. After a moment of panic, he saw Vesuvius, still awake, peering out over the parapet. Lewellyn was asleep.

"Why didn't you wake Lewellyn?" Sam asked.

"I just didn't get sleepy," Vesuvius said, "but I could sleep now."

All up and down the line men were beginning to stir about. Sam waited before making any move.

"Keep still," he told Vesuvius, "one way to get killed is to be the first to move about in the morning."

When he felt that it was safe, he stood up. On the hillside, not five yards from his hole, the enemy had beaten a foot path. The snow in the narrow path was packed hard and Sam could tell immediately that a large number of soldiers had passed one behind the other in front of the hole.

"Benny," he said, "look at that path. They almost walked on top of us. Didn't you see them?"

"I didn't see nuttin," Benny said.

"You stayed awake all night? You didn't fall asleep did you?" Sam asked.

He followed the trail with his eyes. They had come up the hill, no doubt to reach the crest, then stumbled onto his hole and turned away. Probably had instructions not to fight; otherwise they would have killed him. The footsteps followed the crest of the hill then turned to the right and went out along the crest of the hill to an intersection. About seven hundred yards out, Sam saw a lone soldier get up out of the ground and walk towards him with a big German Shepherd dog. The Chinese soldier stopped.

Tarring came over and stood beside Sam, watching the soldier with field glasses. He passed them to Sam. The soldier was urinating in their direction.

A single shot rang out. If it came close to the soldier he didn't show it. Fox Company's sniper, a tall black man named Brown, armed with a Springfield rifle with telescope, had shot and missed. He took careful aim and fired again.

The soldier ignored him.

Word came up the line that Easy Company had been on patrol and had taken some prisoners that were definitely Chinese. Then word came that the Fifth and Seventh Regiments were under heavy attack from Chinese forces. This news was very grim and Fox Company's efforts to construct a defensive position increased. Barbed wire was strung downhill in a single strand, by driving the steel posts down through the frozen earth with a sledgehammer. Lieutenant Von Ludwig borrowed four prisoners from Easy Company and set them to digging a hole the size of a squad tent. He erected the tent over the hole. From somewhere, he came up with a small wood-burning stove and had it erected inside the tent. Word was passed that it was to be a warming tent, but most of the men had come to detest Von Ludwig so much they refused to go in, even in below-zero conditions. A second tent was erected on top of ground beside the dug-in tent. Further back, inside the perimeter, Captain Groff erected the command post tent, also dug in, but not as deeply as Von Ludwig's.

A wooden bridge spanned the frozen stream in the leg of the Y. Von Ludwig ordered Tarring to send a detail of men to the stream to cut up the bridge using an old fashioned crosscut saw.

Again, in one of those moves unanticipated, Groff had 2nd Platoon exchange positions with the 3rd Platoon and as a result 2nd was moved downhill almost to the bottom. By coincidence, the warming tent Von Ludwig had erected proved to be in the right place and did not have to be moved.

The 3rd Platoon had failed to dig properly and the hole Sam inherited wasn't large enough for three men. A small pup tent had been erected behind the hole. Although he was dissatisfied, Sam decided to sleep there. If anything happened he would move to the hole with Vesuvius and Petitt. He didn't trust Lewellyn to remain awake. He had made a mistake in helping him scare Vesuvius. He wasn't going to take a second chance with Lewellyn.

Lieutenant Von Ludwig never left the warming tent. A fire was built in the stove. He had the jerry cans of water taken inside where they wouldn't freeze and seemed intent on telling anyone who would listen, "I wasn't ready for this" or, "Boy I'd give anything to be back in Baltimore tonight."

He appeared about thirty years of age, was a veteran of World War Two, but showed no leadership ability.

Tarring came around to Sam and complained.

"Someone is going to have to straighten Lard Ass out," he said.

"Why don't you do it?" Sam asked.

"I can't," Tarring said. "If I attempt to, they'll just say I resent him because he took over as platoon leader. I've talked to Jennings and Baker about it. They agree the way to handle it is for one of you squad leaders to do it, then I'll step in and support the squad leader. What do you say?"

"It sounds like mutiny," Sam said. "We shouldn't have to be worrying about some big mama's boy lieutenant."

He didn't want to commit himself to insubordination. Without doing so, he crawled into the pup tent. Once inside it, he cleaned all his magazines, taking out the shells and wiping them with a clean cloth which had just a trace of gun oil in it. He placed all except the two in the weapon in a plastic bag. Then he took off his boots, stuck his feet down in the sleeping bag, and zipped it up.

The wind made an eerie sound through the cracks in the pup tent. No matter which side of his body was against the earth, within a few minutes that side would be cold. He kept turning and turning, first on one side then the other. At length he fell asleep.

He woke to a bright orange glow and it took half a minute to realize the glow was from a trip flare. He sat up in alarm. Down in the hole, Petitt was aiming the BAR. "What is it Petitt?" Sam asked softly.

"There's a gook out there, squatting down with a bunch of brush on his back. I'm gonna blow him away," he said.

"Don't start a firefight till I get in the hole," Sam called out to him softly. He didn't want to be caught above ground with bullets blazing back and forth.

He looked around for his boots. The flare died out and he groped about for them in the darkness. A light snow was falling, carried horizontally by the wind. By chance, Sam happened to look downline from his position. He could see soldiers walking slowly forward towards the hole occupied by Lewellyn and Erickson. The soldiers were almost on them! Why were they not being fired at? Were Lewellyn and Erickson both asleep? For some unknown reason, he began to count the soldiers. When he reached seven, the danger hit him hard. Forgetting the boots, Sam made one big running leap, carbine in one hand, ammo bag in the other, into the hole, on top of Vesuvius. Half asleep, Vesuvius tried to get up. Sam rammed him back down. Vesuvius tried again. Sam pushed on the top of his head again, pushing him down.

"Stay down," he hissed. "Get some magazines ready for the BAR."

He found a grenade on the parapet and threw it, watching the sparks trail out. Before it landed, he threw a second grenade. The first grenade fell short by a few feet. It exploded. The soldiers stopped, stood very still, and looked in Sam's direction, from which the second grenade was sailing through the air, trailing sparks. It knocked some off their feet as they were turning to run. Three came back and helped their fallen comrades. Petitt had Sam's carbine, but wasn't firing. Sam grabbed it from him and began to spray. Quickly, helping each other, the Chinese retreated rapidly and disappeared in the driving snow.

Barefooted, he stayed in the hole till dawn, then climbed out to find his boots covered with snow that had blown in the open flap of the tent. While he was putting the cold boots on, some of the squad went out and recovered a Thompson sub machine gun one of the Chinese soldiers had dropped. They squabbled over it until they discovered it had a damaged rear sight, then lost interest.

Sam asked Erickson and Lewellyn why they didn't fire. They claimed they had. Even so, he had a suspicion they might have been asleep. The Chinese had been almost on top of their hole when he shot at them.

Later in the morning, Brown went back to the crest of the hill. He had taken his rifle down to the valley and duplicated the conditions, and zeroed the rifle in. The Chinese soldier came out for his morning urination. Brown killed him. When Brown saw the soldier fall he said, "And that goes for your damn dog too!"

This raised the spirits of everyone. They knew the Chinese were behind them, but the soldier had seemed so arrogant, in his daily urination, rather contemptuous of them you might say, that Brown was cheered and congratulated as he came back down from the crest. He had been so far distant it was doubtful the Chinese had even heard the shot that killed their comrade. Although the Chinese remained on that particular hill, they were careful to keep out of sight.

CHAPTER 21 ... The Woman ...

Sam, Petitt, and Vesuvius worked all day on the hole, digging it deeper and wider. They finally got it large enough that two could lie down and the third had enough room to stand. The dirt displaced from the hole onto the parapet froze into a hard block of ice. Petitt urinated in a can, poured the urine on the parapet, and it froze before it stopped running. All up and down the line the men worked to dig deeper into the frozen earth. Down in the other leg of the Y, Easy Company used dynamite to blow holes. Cries of "fire in the hole," followed by explosions, rang out all day.

During the night, it got colder. The wind came howling down the valley and carried the snow in on them, coating the sides of the hole, their clothing, weapons, hand grenades, freezing everything even harder, penetrating right to the marrow of their bones. There was only one consolation; it was just as hard on the enemy. Sam gave Vesuvius the first watch because that was the least likely time for the enemy to attack. Petitt took second.

Petitt shook him awake at 2 o'clock.

"Sam, those guys next to us are asleep on watch. They're ain't nobody awake in that hole. I been trying to raise them for five minutes now."

Sam got angry. He couldn't understand why anyone, in a life or death situation, would lay down and go to sleep. He got on his feet and leaned forward, turning towards the hole on the right. The wind cut his face like a knife.

"Rose?" he called out.

No answer.

"Prior?"

No answer.

"Fitwell?"

No answer.

He pulled the pin from a grenade and tossed it in front of their hole. Wham!

It exploded in a red flash, blowing snow and shrapnel.

"Rose?" he called again.

"Yeah, Yeah! What do you want!"

"Stay awake!"

"Prior was on watch."

"I don't care who it is," Sam said. "Just make sure someone is awake at all times!"

Morning came. The wind continued incessantly against them, piling snow deep at the base of the hill, laying in ocean waves out in the Y and, to the left, between them and the village, turning everything into a great white wasteland. You could not describe conditions by saying it was thirty degrees below zero. The cold reached through their clothing and went right to the center of their bodies. They kept moving to keep from freezing to death. Sam went to see Tarring about a working party to carry food, and learned they had run out of C rations. The road behind had been cut and the trucks could no longer get through. If the weather cleared there would be air drops, but it didn't look as if it was going to clear.

Then, the morning air was rent by half a dozen wounded tigers that screamed overhead and fell on the road by the village, throwing great clouds of smoke and snow into the wind. Tarring knelt on one knee holding the field glasses to his eyes. "Would you look at that," he said, handing Sam the glasses.

The shells were passing over steadily in twos and threes as the whole battery seemed to be firing at will. Two columns of Chinese infantry, keeping ten yards between men, were marching down the road at a fast hard pace. As the shells fell among them they spread out a little and kept coming. A shell knocked one off his feet, and another dropped out of the column, knelt down beside the one who was hit, then got up and kept marching. Sam gave the glasses back to Tarring. He watched for a few minutes.

"Those boys have been shot at before," he said.

They turned to the right and began to climb the high hill where Brown had killed the urinating soldier. As they climbed, the artillery kept laying the shells in among them. Surprisingly, few of them were hit. They were so well dispersed that one shell would never hit two men. Obviously, they were well disciplined to march through artillery fire, as they were doing. Sam felt a grudging respect for them. All morning long they kept marching through the fire and climbing the hill.

There was lots of activity at the center of the Y as a contingent of British Royal Marines, some Army units, and Dog Company of the First Battalion prepared to move up nine miles to Hagaru where heavy fighting was underway. Sam went into the tent beside Von Ludwig's warming tent. Some of the men from the 1st Platoon were in there discussing the fact that the Chinese had entered the war. Harvey Owen sat, combing his dark, almost black, hair. He grinned at Sam, as if to say whatever was to happen would, but in the meantime, he would sit and comb his hair. He showed not a trace of apprehension.

Petitt found a discarded steel drum, cut an opening in the front of it, and from somewhere came up with two short lengths of stovepipe and a piece of tin to lay against the opening. Now they had a fire in the hole, but still couldn't get warm. To make matters worse, sparks exited the stovepipe, marking the foxhole for the Chinese.

During the night, word came along the line that the Chinese were working their way along the wire. Sam, Petitt and Vesuvius, each in turn, urinated on the fire and left a smelly smoking mess. When morning came, they threw the stove away.

They spent another day without rations. The relief force for Hagaru had been turned back by encountering Chinese roadblocks they were unable to overcome. They started out again with tanks. By the end of the day they had not returned. Sam decided to look for something to eat. He told the squad, "I'm going down to battalion to get some chow. With all those trucks down there, there's bound to be some food someplace."

He could tell the squad thought it was futile, but went anyway. It was almost dark when he got there. He began looking in the trucks, going to the rear and then searching the cabs, not finding anything. He got close to a tent and was challenged.

"Who goes there?"

"Sergeant Lewis, from Fox Company!"

"Sam Lewis!" The voice was familiar and he approached to see who had recognized him. It was Frank Lyjina, who he had known in Washington.

"God, Sam, what are you doing down here?" He shivered from the cold as he spoke.

"I'm looking for something to eat. I've not eaten since yesterday morning," Sam said.

"Come on," Lyjina said, "I've got an extra C ration you can have."

He took Sam into a warm tent and they talked for a short time. Sam had not seen him since they had left Washington. He took the box of rations, thanked Lyjina and left.

"Take care of yourself, Sam," Lyjina called after him.

As Sam went back, firing was beginning over where Easy Company was dug in and it kept increasing in intensity, so he hurried, head bowed against the wind. He reached the line and dropped down in the hole and grinned at Petitt and Vesuvius.

"Let's eat," he said.

"How'd you do it?" Petitt wanted to know.

"Some can and some can't," Sam said. "Just met an old friend, who felt sorry for me."

The firing from Easy Company's area died down and everything was quiet. The night passed uneventfully.

When morning came the overcast cleared sufficiently for planes to make an air drop of food and ammunition. They dropped it right on target, down near the center of the Y. Then, as if preordained, the sky closed in again and filled with snow in an unceasing blizzard, becoming an icy wasteland, cold beyond belief, wind that never ceased, cruel to both friend and foe.

Out of the driving snow, about a hundred yards out, two Chinese soldiers appeared. They raised their hands above their heads and made their way towards Sam. Word was passed to Captain Groff that prisoners were coming in. He and Jackson came down to interrogate the two. One of the men wore a beautiful fur cap which was made from the hide of a red fox. The other wore the standard Chinese cap with ear flaps turned down. They walked stiffly, having lain in the snow during the night to be able to approach in daylight. Captain Groff met them at the line. He allowed Jackson to question them uninterrupted. Apparently, they were able to communicate. Jackson turned to Captain Groff.

"They are from the Two Hundred Forty-fifth Company of the Chinese People's Volunteers. They wish to be honorable prisoners of war."

Groff was staring at the prisoner who wore the red fox cap. It was a beautiful cap with the red tail still intact and the symbolism of it was obvious.

"By God, I've got to have that cap," he said.

He snatched the fox cap from the prisoner's head and tried it on. It fit him perfectly. He smiled with pleasure.

"Tell them we don't take prisoners of war," he said.

Jackson turned to the two men and repeated the message.

The men pleaded with him.

Jackson repeated their plea.

"They beg to be honorable prisoners of war."

"Tell them I am sparing their lives," Groff said coldly.

Jackson spoke to the prisoners and turned again to Captain Groff.

"They say that if we don't take them they'll be shot. Their comrades have seen them surrender."

Captain Groff drew his forty-five.

"Tell them to dance," he said, laughing cruelly.

Jackson did so, but they did not dance.

Captain Groff began firing at the feet of the former owner of the red fox cap. "Dance, you son of a bitch, dance," he said.

They backed away, holding out their hands as if to ward off his bullets.

He shot twice more and they began to run. Within a few minutes they were out of sight in the swirling blizzard.

When night came, Sam again gave Vesuvius the first watch. Vesuvius woke him at ten o'clock. Sam's two-hour watch seemed to last forever. He thought about the implications of the Chinese entering the war and could find nothing to be optimistic about. A portion of the Marine Corps Hymn came to him, ". . . In the snow of far off northern lands . . . ." There was truth to it, after all, he thought. He wondered if the war would escalate further and Russia would come in, and knew that if she did he would never see his homeland again. It was not a pleasant thought and he felt the cold fear of the reality of the situation.

At twelve o'clock, he woke Petitt, who got up out of the bottom of the hole to begin his watch. Sam lay down in the same spot and found that it was almost warm. He soon fell asleep and dreamed a dream of being beside a warm lake that had a sandy beach and he was lying on the beach beside Charlotte. He reached out to touch her but she turned into a chunk of raw meat with a black parachute trailing out.

Petitt was calling out. There was urgency in his voice.

"Sam! Sam! Wake up! They're on the wire."

He was wide-awake almost immediately. He got up and stood beside Petitt, peering out into the eerie howling snow. He couldn't see anything. Petitt aimed Vesuvius's BAR.

"Hold your fire," Sam said.

"They're out there," said Petitt.

"Yeah but wait," Sam said. "They know about where we are. Just wait."

There came a metallic knocking noise from out in front.

"What's that?" Petitt cried.

"He's hitting the steel post of the wire with a gun barrel," Sam said. "He wants us to fire. If we do, they'll be all over us."

He called out to the adjacent holes. "Pass the word. The Chinese are on the wire."

He listened as it was relayed in both directions, then got a hand grenade ready. Although the wire was only thirty yards distant, the wind was carrying the snow as a fine white powder that stung his face and made it difficult to even look in that direction. They would have it at their backs. They were coming in. Sam threw the grenade. At the same time, rifle fire sputtered, then swelled to a tremendous volume as they came out of the swirling snow. Screams rent the air, intermingled with the firing. They were crying out and screaming, but something was wrong. The screams were from women and children. They were forcing women and children in.

"Stop shooting," Sam cried.

The firing continued.

"For God's sake, stop shooting!" Sam shouted.

The firing died away. Out in front, everything was still. A baby was crying, its thin cries carried on the howling wind, crying out for its mother, but there was no answer. It filled Sam with dread. They had forced the villagers of Koto Ri from their homes and driven them in, hoping the machine guns would fire and disclose their locations. It was such cruelty Sam didn't want to believe it, but it was true.

It seemed to take a long time for daylight. Just when he thought the baby was dead, it would cry again. As morning neared it cried less. The Marines peered anxiously out into the blizzard.

It began to grow light. Sam saw two bullocks, lying in the snow, feet stretched out in death. Farther out, a woman knelt in the snow, her head bowed, but otherwise, she was upright. He made out forms lying on the ground partly covered with snow. Beyond these, he couldn't see. Visibility was less than a hundred yards.

Jackson made his way downhill.

Sam called out to him.

"I'm going out, Jackson, you come with me!"

"I'm not going!" Jackson cried.

"But you speak their language," Sam said. "Some might be alive."

"I'm not going out there!" Jackson insisted.

He felt only contempt for Jackson. There was really not much more danger a few yards away, but Jackson wouldn't risk those few yards, not even for his own people. Sam went without him, approaching warily, his carbine at ready. He reached the woman first. He knelt down beside her. Her face had turned blue. She wore an expression of intense pain. Her hair was knotted at the back of her neck. Strands had come loose, and the keening wind carried them around and wafted them across her face. The baby was bundled up in a pouch on her back. Sam reached to get the baby. It gave a little whimper as he gently pulled it up out of its pouch. Accidentally, he leaned against the mother. She was frozen to the earth. The wind kept her hair moving about her face. Her face mirrored pain and anguish. Sam had never seen such an expression on a human face. What an effort it must have taken for her to remain erect! Sam felt a great pity and at the same time an admiration for her. He turned and looked back. Erickson and Causey had followed him out. He handed the baby to Erickson. "Take it to the warming tent," he said.

He began checking the people to see if any were still alive. There were three dead Chinese soldiers, three dead Korean old men, and three children, one a little boy who was still clutching a dead puppy. He found a young girl, about twelve, who was still alive. She had been shot in such a way that the bullet had passed behind her breasts and apparently exited without touching her heart. Causey found another young girl, also still alive. Sam looked all around, making sure that there were no other survivors. He saw three dead pigs and a couple of dogs.

They carried the children back to Von Ludwig's warming tent. Sam opened the tent flap and carried the girl in. Von Ludwig was leaning back against his valise. He seemed irritated at seeing Sam enter with the girl. Rose and Fitwell were warming their hands by the stove.

"Rose," Sam said, "get battalion on the phone. Tell them we have two wounded girls and a small baby up here. Tell them the baby's not wounded, but they'll need a nipple and some milk for it."

Causey came in with the other girl. Rose was already on the phone.

"What did you bring them in here for?" Von Ludwig demanded. Sam was surprised. "They need help; they're wounded," he said.

"Yeah, but why bring them in here?"

"Because it's warm in here," Sam said.

"I don't give a damn if they're wounded. Get 'em out of here! They stink!" Von Ludwig said.

Sam felt a flush of anger. Tarring was right. Someone was going to have to straighten Von Ludwig out. He could hear Rose on the phone and knew his message had been relayed. He turned towards the entrance to the tent.

"Come on, bring them to the other tent," he said to Causey. Angrily, he entered the cold tent. Petitt followed with a blanket and spread it on the ground. As Sam lay the girl down, she opened her eyes and saw him. Her eyes widened in terror. He smoothed her hair back from her forehead.

"Don't be afraid. It's alright."

She watched him fearfully. He stood up, took off his parka and covered her with it. Causey was taking care of the other girl while Erickson still held the baby.

Rose came in.

"Sam, they say they can handle the baby, but they'll just have to set the others outside. They have our own wounded to take care of."

Sam flinched. "I don't give a damn. Tell them to do what they can," he said. He thought to himself a human is a human. He could not conceive of anyone not helping the little girls.

Within minutes, a jeep arrived from battalion aid and Sam helped load them aboard. The corpsman said that someone was trying to make a nipple for the baby out of a morphine syringe. Sam told him to do what he could for the girls. The jeep left. Sam returned to his hole. Some cooks came and tied the two bullocks each to a separate jeep and dragged them off to be butchered. They promised to bring back some hash.

Sam got down in his hole and peered out. The villagers of Koto Ri lay dead on the frozen earth. Already, the snow concealed the blood and left them like blocks of ice with the wind singing across their still forms. The wind had a life of its own, filling the voids behind the dead with snow, cutting bare on the opposite side, terrible in its intensity. Beyond, the village lay cold and bare, silent and forlorn, without any sign of life, the smoke no longer rising from its chimneys, a monument to man's inhumanity, the villagers victims of those who had been sent to help them.

The dead woman, clad only in white pantaloons, frozen to the earth, her head bowed, marked the site like a tombstone at Arlington. The bitter wind keened around her. She would not move until spring when she would fall forward upon the earth and waste away. But the image of her froze forever in Sam's mind.

The wind of Manchuria cut and howled its way across the bleak frozen landscape.

CHAPTER 22 ... Moment of Truth ...

This above all: to thine own self be true,
And it must follow, as the night the day,
Thou canst not then be false to any man.
(Hamlet, Act 1, scene 3)

From the center of the Y a small group of Marines approached. Sam watched them make their way through the snow to his position. They walked in an odd fashion, bent down as if carrying heavy loads, yet they weren't. They reached his position some forty or fifty feet away from Sam and sat down cross-legged in the snow. Erickson spoke with them and came over to Sam.

"Sam, those guys can't talk," he said.

"Can't talk?"

"No, I tried to ask them what outfit they were from and they just stared at me."

Sam climbed out of his hole and went over to the group of Marines. There were about twenty-five men in the group. They were just sitting in the snow silently looking out towards the village.

"What outfit are you guys from?" Sam asked.

No answer.

Sam studied the group. They all were young. Some had no shoes and instead had burlap sacks bound about their feet.

From the way they sat, he concluded they were exhausted. He tried to make eye contact, but the eyes he looked at were dull. They were in shock. He counted twenty-five men. Sam sat down beside one and glanced sideways at him. The Marine seemed to look right through Sam.

"What outfit?" Sam asked quietly.

"Item Company," said the Marine.

"Bad huh?" said Sam.

The Marine didn't answer. Instead he looked at Sam with incredulity on his face, as if to say, where the hell have you been?

"How bad?" Sam asked.

"This is all that's left."

There was nothing else to ask. Sam assumed that Item Company was Seventh Marines and these few had fought their way down from Yu Dam Ni. Now, they were like robots. If told to move, they would move; if told to stop, they would stop. They had gone beyond the pale of civilization and were now mechanical men. Word was passed for them to move out and they got wearily to their feet and walked back towards the center of the Y, all bent over with the heavy load of being all that were left of Item Company.

The combat they had endured had left them in severe shock from which they had not yet recovered. Such a ragged looking lot, Sam had never seen. Watching them was a sobering experience.

Word was passed along the line that further movement south was blocked. The Chinese had blown the road off the side of the mountain.

Tarring asked for one man from each squad, for a working party to report to battalion. Sam sent Vesuvius.

During the day, the skies cleared sufficiently that C141 transport aircraft dropped several steel girders for constructing a bridge across the hole the Chinese had blown in the road.

Army troops arrived from Hagaru. They had been east of the reservoir, had survived a battle for their existence which compared to Custer's Last Stand, and they too were going on reflex alone. They began assaulting the hill to Fox Company's rear against small arms fire, while Fox Company waited in their foxholes and listened to the sounds of the battle. The Chinese were resisting with burp guns and grenades. By four in the afternoon, the hill was taken and the sounds of firing died away. Then, firing broke out in the right leg of the Y. About seven hundred Chinese attacked Easy Company across the open area which bordered Easy Company's position. The first Chinese penetrated the position and wiped out a machine gun crew, but interlocking fire from other guns made up for the loss.

The roar of gunfire was tremendous. Easy Company stopped the assault. The balance of the enemy force was killed attempting to come across the open area. The few who made it, came in with raised hands to surrender.

Vesuvius returned from his working party late in the afternoon. As soon as Sam saw him he knew something was wrong. Vesuvius seemed incoherent. Sam was very brusque with him.

"Get over to your hole and get in it!" he said.

Vesuvius looked towards the hole, saw it was empty.

"I ain't stayin' in dat hole by myself!" he cried.

"For God sake, Benny, shut up and get in your hole."

"Sam, youse can't imagine what dat was like. Dey was sixteen truckloads of dead Marines. We just unloaded dem like dey was cordwood and placed dem side by side all frozen stiff. Den dey covered dem up wit a bulldozer," he said, then he began to weep.

Sam put his arm around Benny's shoulders. Petitt joined them in the hole. The three sat silently, looking out into the darkness, listening to the heavy metallic sound of the 4.2 mortars expelling rounds of ammunition and watched them fall far out beyond the Y. Vesuvius was weeping silently. After a few minutes he stopped. The wind wailed across the earth in front of them, bringing more snow.

Word came down the line. "Be alert. The Chinese are on the wire."

They did not attack, but seemed content to scout the position, occasionally striking a steel post with a gun barrel trying to draw fire, but getting a hand grenade instead.

When morning came, the cooks brought some hash, made from the two butchered bullocks and some Irish potatoes. 2nd Platoon lined up to eat. From somewhere out in front a burp gun chattered, throwing bullets into the earth beside the line. Everyone ran for cover, then came right back and lined up again, only to receive another burst of bullets. This time, they didn't run. They were out of range. The cooks served hot coffee. Ivan Jennings sent a cup of hot coffee to the command post for Captain Groff. In return, Groff ordered the cooks to pack and leave, taking their hash with them. Some of the men didn't get any hash and there was much grumbling.

They got back down into the holes. Sam attempted to get some sleep, but Rose came out and stood looking down into the hole at Sam.

"Sam, the Lieutenant wants two men to carry wood for the fire," he said.

"Is Fitwell in the tent?" Sam asked.

"Yes."

"Then you and Fitwell go get the wood."

Rose disappeared back inside the tent. Within a few moments he was back.

"The Lieutenant wants two other men," he said.

"Did you tell him that you and Fitwell were to go?"

"Yes, but he said for us not to. He said to tell you to send him two other men."

Von Ludwig was not only demanding personal service, he was interfering in the running of the squad. Sam knew the time had come to straighten Lieutenant Von Ludwig out.

"You go back and tell Lieutenant Von Ludwig that I said for him to go f--k himself."

Rose was startled. "You mean that, Sam?"

"I said it didn't I?"

"Yes, but do you really mean for me to do it?"

"You tell him what I said."

Rose had the manner of a child whose parents were having an argument which could only lead to more misery for him. He hesitated.

"Go on!" Sam said.

As Rose left, Sam climbed wearily up out of the hole. He knew his message would bring the lieutenant. It's high time someone confronted him, Sam thought. He hadn't wanted it to be him, but since the episode with the children he had known it had to be done.

Von Ludwig came out. "Rose says you sent word for me to go f--k myself. Did you send word like that to me?"

"Yes, Sir. I sure did," Sam said.

"You're gonna take it back mister, or I'm gonna kick the shit outta you," said Von Ludwig.

"Then start kicking!" Sam said, "because I'm not taking it back."

Von Ludwig stood for a moment undecided. Sam prepared to step sideways. He would knock him down in the hole when Von Ludwig swung. Von Ludwig weighed about two hundred sixty pounds. Sam weighed about a hundred seventy. He would have to get Von Ludwig in the hole and not let him wrestle.

Von Ludwig whirled about and started walking rapidly towards the Company CP.

Overhearing, the squad in the nearest holes waited in awed silence to see the drama played out. Sam waited for the inevitable, remembering the

Captain's admonition, woe be unto the first man to disobey my order. The warning now seemed a long time ago, and it wasn't exactly the captain's order that he was disobeying, but he expected the worst. Within three minutes, Saia came down to the hole. He gave Sam a grin. "Boy you are in deep trouble! Captain Groff says report to his tent right now," Saia said.

Silently, Sam followed him back up the hill. He looked back once. The squad had climbed out of their foxholes and were gathered about Petitt and Vesuvius.

Sam followed Saia into the captain's tent. Homer sat off to one side. Von Ludwig stood to one side, looking the part of a wounded dignitary. The captain sat on a blanket leaning back against a jerry can. He was watching Sam.

"I'm reporting as ordered, Sir," Sam said.

"Mr. Von Ludwig says you told him to go fuck himself." Captain Groff said.

"Yes Sir, I did," Sam said.

"You've got five years of service with a clean record. You're second on the company list to be promoted to Platoon Sergeant. If you'll apologize to Mr. Von Ludwig, here, I'll forget this ever happened. What do you say?"

Sam was surprised. Captain Groff had always seemed so threatening. Now, he was out of character. Whatever had happened to his belligerent warning? He was being reasonable.

"Apologize, Sir?" Sam asked.

"Yes, apologize," he said.

Sam looked at Von Ludwig. Von Ludwig was waiting expectantly. If he apologized he would just be prolonging the task of straightening him out. If he failed now it would only be harder later. Sam looked back at the captain. "Sir," he said quietly, "Mr. Von Ludwig can go fuck himself."

Groff didn't seem surprised. On the contrary, Sam was surprised at how calm he seemed.

"You give me no choice, do you?" Groff said quietly.

Sam did not hesitate. "No choice whatever, Sir," he said.

"Alright then, let's go down to battalion. First Sergeant, you come along," he said to Homer. He got slowly to his feet. Sam stepped out of the tent and waited. They all came out. Groff and Von Ludwig walked in front, Sam followed, and Homer brought up the rear. He supposed Homer was acting as his guard.

The wind was chilling him to the bone. He felt no fear, only a growing tension, wondering what they might do. They passed a few tents. Off beyond the tents, bulldozers were working on an air strip. They reached the farthest tent and Captain Groff went inside. It seemed like five minutes before he came out. They were lined at the entrance, Sam first, then Von Ludwig, then Homer.

"When I say march in, you'll march in. When I say halt, you'll halt. When I say face left, you'll face left. —And goddam you," he said to Sam, "you'll remain at attention!

March in!"

They marched in.

"Halt!"

Sam halted.

"Left face!"

Sam executed a left face and remained at attention.

Lieutenant Colonel Allen B. Sutter appeared to be about forty years old, was above average in height and build, but was not what you would call a big man. He addressed Sam.

"You are charged with insubordination, in that you have directly refused a lawful order."

Sam kept silent.

Colonel Sutter turned to Von Ludwig.

"Lieutenant, what do you have to say?" he asked.

"I don't know what made him do it. He's been a good combat NCO. I just don't know why he's done this."

Colonel Sutter turned to Homer. "First Sergeant, what do you have to say about this sergeant?"

Old Homer spoke very quietly. "As far as Ahm concerned, he's a damn good combat NCO and he's always done his job."

Sam could hardly believe his ears. It didn't seem possible that Homer would support him.

Captain Groff didn't like the way things were going. He hit below the belt.

"He's been a good combat NCO, but he has a tendency to whine and cry," he said.

Sam turned in astonishment. The only time he had ever cried was at the swimming pool. And he had never complained. The captain's unfairness made his blood come up. He would not take this. He looked Groff in the eye.

"Why you dirty son of a bitch," he said. "I cried once. Any one with any sense of human decency would have cried at that swimming pool!"

"That's enough!" Colonel Sutter shouted. "What have you to say for yourself?" he demanded.

Clearly, he did not like hearing an enlisted man call a captain a son of a bitch.

"Sir, Lieutenant Von Ludwig has come into the field with enough gear to support three men. He demands the men help him carry it. It's carry this and carry that. Get wood for my fire. Get me water. As long as I lead a squad I will never order another man to do a single thing for him," Sam said. "Yesterday, we were attacked . . . ."

He had intended to tell the colonel about the baby and girls, but was not allowed to finish.

Colonel Sutter leaped up out of his chair, his face livid with rage. He shook his finger in Sam's face.

"Shut up!" he shouted. "You are a derelict! Here we are fighting Chinese Communists on four sides and you choose this time to disobey orders. I order you a General Court-Martial at the earliest possible opportunity. Now get your ass out of here!"

"Face left!" Captain Groff commanded.

They faced left.

"March out!"

They marched out.

Outside the tent, Sam saw he was not to be placed under arrest. They walked back, but Sam hurried through the wind. He didn't want to associate with them. When he reached the line of foxholes, Tarring was waiting.

"Why didn't you send for me?" he asked.

"I didn't get a chance to," Sam said.

"What are they going to do to you?"

"General Court-Martial, at the earliest possible time," Sam said.

"While you were gone, I went around to the platoon. I asked each man. We're all agreed. Every man in the platoon will back you up. There's not a single man who won't testify in your behalf," he said.

Sam didn't say anything. It had been necessary for someone to confront the lieutenant. He had done it. Now, he would face the consequences, whatever they might be. Sam had that mind-set that is characteristic of those who, having once set a course, would never change it.

"He'll not be asking for anyone else to do his personal services," Sam said.

"Tell me what happened," said Tarring.

Sam related the events to him.

Later in the day, 2nd Platoon was moved further around the base of the hill. 1st Platoon took their old position. Sam wondered how much his insubordination had to do with moving the platoon. When they moved, he dug in by himself. He found a shallow hole that had been dug only about twelve inches deep. Some brush had been layered over the hole and the spaces between the limbs had filled with ice. There were only two openings to the hole, the first to fire through and the second on the rear side to crawl into. It had a straw mat in the bottom and the top had iced over like an Eskimo's igloo. He crawled into it from the rear and lay down and peered out. The whole area in front was visible and the wind didn't blow directly at the opening. He backed out of the hole and approached it from the front. Except for the narrow slit in front it was invisible. He saw to the disposition of the squad, told them where he would be, and crawled in. After a while it was not so cold. Unwittingly, he had done the same thing Eskimo dogs do in the frozen north. He lay listening to the wind whistling along the earth. The 60mm mortars were firing and their lighter sounds mingled with the 4.2s from down in battalion. All exploded at random places in the frozen hell. After a while, Sam fell asleep.

CHAPTER 23 ... Semper Fidelis ...

On the west coast of Korea, the American Eighth Army was in full retreat. The Fifth and Seventh Marines fought their way to Koto Ri. Now, only one huge mountain lay between the division and relative safety. The Chinese circled Koto Ri and at the point where they blew the only road off the mountainside they set up a roadblock. Obviously, they expected to destroy the entire force of Marines. The 1st Battalion of First Regiment was dug in at Chinhung Ni which lay south of the huge hill. In the middle of a howling blizzard, the likes of which no American had ever experienced, the 1st Battalion climbed the big hill. It took two days just to make the climb. They got in behind the Chinese, who were dug in facing the spot where they had destroyed the road. Before the Chinese knew they were being attacked, the men of the First were shooting them in the back of their heads.

Climbing the big hill in the middle of a blizzard was something so unlikely the Chinese did not even consider it could happen. Even so, they fought stubbornly to the last man. Those who weren't killed froze to death.

Simultaneously, while this battle was in progress, the engineers transported the steel girders, which the Air Force had dropped, to the site and constructed the bridge which was to carry the division across.

The air strip was completed. Those men who had been and wounded and some who suffered frostbite were flown out. Lewellyn and Causey were among the frostbite cases.

The supply problem, after the airfield was completed, became a case of oversupply. Huge stacks of supplies which could not be taken out were stacked in a central location in the center of the Y.

Word was passed.

"Destroy everything you can't carry."

Colonel Sutter's battalion would be the last battalion to leave Koto Ri.

Sam had captured a Chinese fur cap with fur-lined ear muffs that he tied together under his chin and it was very warm. He placed his steel helmet in a hole, pulled the pin from a grenade, placed it beneath the helmet and rolled away. The blast destroyed the helmet completely.

"Banzai!" he shouted.

At four o'clock in the afternoon, Fox Company followed the Confederate flag off their hill. They waited for a while beside the stacks of food while the remainder of the battalion began the march south from Koto Ri. Fox Company departed. Sam took a long last look back. The Chinese were streaming down out of the adjacent hills, not to attack, but to reach the stacks of food. Just before dark, while they were tearing at the food, several P51 Mustang planes appeared overhead and began dive bombing. Sam's last look was of a napalm bomb exploding among the Chinese who swarmed over the food.

It was dark and fiercely cold on the road. Behind them were the Chinese; in front, small bands of Chinese still found the will to fight. Inevitably, there were holdups. When these came, they sat down and tried to rest. It was hard to get back up. To sit still for too long meant freezing to death.

Lieutenant Von Ludwig was fresh. He had spent the entire time inside a warm tent but the men, after long sleepless nights, constant extreme cold and too little food, were nearing exhaustion.

The road was littered with the debris of battles fought and there were many stops. At one of these they sat leaning back against the side of the mountain. Word came to move out, but they were slow getting up. Sam and Arkie sat side by side against the mountain. A dead Chinese soldier sat between them. Von Ludwig came down the line, kicking at some, pulling at others, forcing them to stand. Sam and Arkie got up. Von Ludwig reached the dead soldier. Mistaking him for a Marine, he gave him a vicious kick.

"On your feet," he snarled.

The dead soldier didn't move.

Von Ludwig kicked him again.

"On your feet, you son of a bitch," he snarled again.

The soldier failed to respond.

Von Ludwig leaned over and grabbed him by the collar as if to jerk him to his feet. Seeing what he had, he said, "Oh."

Around him, the men snickered.

Cursing, he stalked off.

Sometime during the night, they reached the new steel bridge and were held up there for a time waiting for six tanks and some men from the Reconnaissance Company that were behind them. Four tanks crossed. The other two failed to show up. The last of the Reconnaissance Company came across.

Petitt found Sam.

"Sam those guys are opening a bottle of wine, over there," he said.

Sam's first thought was to ask for some, but he discarded the idea. Those who had the wine were engineers who were waiting nearby to blow the bridge.

Word came to move out. Sam's squad was the last of Fox Company to cross the span. The engineers blew it.

They kept marching.

Vesuvius was beginning to lag behind. His five-yard interval had become ten. Sam dropped back and walked along beside him. "Vesuvius, if you don't keep up, I'm going to kick your ass up between your shoulder blades," he said.

Vesuvius looked him right in the eye. "Sam, I'm doin' de very best dat I can do," he said quietly.

And Sam knew he was, so he lifted his BAR and handed Vesuvius his carbine.

"Now keep up," he said.

Daylight came and they were still marching. They reached some trucks which had been shot up and the dead were still lying where they had died. One Marine lay on his back in the road with his hands folded across his chest. He had a gold wedding ring on one finger.

Another, a Negro, had taken cover behind the wheel of one of the trucks. He had fired some from that position—his spent cartridges were beside him—but they had taken his rifle. There was something about him which saddened Sam; sometimes, a single death is more moving than half a dozen, and he could not get this one out of mind, but kept mourning for him as they marched along. They were left there, dead, frozen, never to see their families again, probably listed as missing in action. No one thought to take their dog tags or even to look for them. They were too numb. They marched steadily, descending lower and lower, following the mountain road as it wound around the mountain. Each passing curve raised the temperature ever so slightly, until at last they began to escape the cruel wind. Sam began to feel again. It was thrilling to be alive. The exultation of knowing he had once again escaped a horrible death was like drinking a glass of fine wine. His pulse quickened; his strength came back, and he felt good again.

Trucks met them late in the afternoon and soon they found themselves passing through Army artillery units who were firing back in the direction the Marines had come from. As they passed through someone said to smile and look happy.

They were off the trucks and into tents where they got warm for the first time in weeks. Then there was another truck ride to the docks at Hamhung and they walked aboard the U S S General Noble where they milled about the decks listening to other Marines. There were stories of both heroism and cowardice, but not much of the latter. One machine gunner told of being in a hole with two comrades who were going to break and run for it until, according to him, he threatened to turn the gun around and fire at them if they did.

Everywhere there were excited stories of battle and close calls.

Sam met Doc Stewart, whom he had known at Washington D.C. Doc was wearing a British Royal Marine parka and beret, and carrying a BAR. He had been a bulldozer operator but his dozer had been shot up and he was conscripted to the infantry where he spent his first night pinned down in an open field by a persistent Chinese machine gun. He was proud that he had fought well.

Some companies had suffered heavy casualties and were down to hardly more than squads. In some instances, the assault of the Chinese had come in such numbers and with such ferocity that one minute a company of Marines would be two hundred fifty strong and fifteen minutes later fifty would be dead. The survivors of this combat were exultant to be spared.

Sam listened, but said nothing. Somehow, saving a North Korean baby and two little girls did not seem to fit in as a great adventure or something to be proud of. But, he was. His experience was unique. He was the only survivor in the entire division who was looking forward to a General Court-Martial, but he told no one, and the men did not mention it in his presence.

A man could be shot by the order of a General Court-Martial.

He wrote to Charlotte and his mother, but did not mention it. He didn't want to have to explain getting court-martialed in a combat situation.

At the port of Pusan they left the General Noble and boarded trucks which carried them to a train station. As they marched into the station a lady in a Red Cross uniform approached and walked along beside Sam. She smiled and handed him a cookie. He took it eagerly and thanked her.

She shook her head. "No no, you have to pay for it," she said. Sam didn't have any money. Angrily, he handed the cookie back to her. This thoroughly disgusted him.

They climbed aboard the waiting train. It took some time to board the train because the entire Second Battalion was to be transported. Some Korean women came down to the train carrying baskets of apples on their heads to sell apples to the troops. As the train began to move, three Marines leaped off the train, knocked the women down, spilling apples all over the concrete floor, and began taking the apples. There was loud raucous laughter. Then, others leaped off and gathered the apples and got back aboard. No one made a move to exert any restraint. This increased Sam's disgust. He couldn't help but wonder why someone in authority did not intercede. Surely, someone was willing to stick up for right, but no one did.

Leaving the trains they again boarded trucks and made camp in a pea field north of the city of Mason. The entire division encamped there. Tents had already been erected. Immediately, they were served a hot meal and left free to rest and relax. The smell of human dung seemed not so bad in the pea field. Perhaps it was because it was winter that it was more tolerable.

Those who wanted to were free to visit Mason.

Tarring informed Sam that he was under house arrest and was not to go anywhere. "Don't leave the immediate vicinity of the tent," he said.

Next day, word was passed some unknown Marine had raped and stabbed a Korean woman in Mason. A search was begun but the woman soon gave up any attempt to identify her assailant. The guilty party was never found. This further senseless act added to Sam's disgust. Depressed, he waited patiently for his court-martial.

One morning, Lewellyn and Causey approached Sam. They had rejoined the platoon in Mason and, it turned out, had not had frostbite at all, but had been at battalion when such cases were being flown out and had climbed aboard.

Lewellyn said, "Sam, have you heard about the new platoon leader?"

"No."

Then Causey chimed in. "Yeah. Me and Lew were hitchhiking back out here last night. He stopped and gave us a ride in his jeep. When he found out we were in the 2nd Platoon of Fox Company he told us that he was being sent to take over from Von Ludwig."

Lewellyn grinned at Sam. "He asked about you, and me and Causey gave him the straight skinny."

"What did you tell him?"

"Sam, don't worry about what we told him. We said that you were Psycho Sam Lewis and we were two of your Twelve Fanatics."

"What's going to be done with Von Ludwig?"

"He's going to be executive officer to Captain Groff till they find a place for him."

"Sounds as if you guys had quite a talk with the new lieutenant. What job did he have before?"

"He was Battalion Intelligence Officer," Causey said. "He's an ex-enlisted man."

Lewellyn slapped Sam on the back, "Don't you worry Sam, we took care of everything."

Sam really didn't believe everything was taken care of, but was glad Von Ludwig would be replaced and someone had defended him even though he wasn't sure what they had told the new lieutenant or when the transfer was to take place.

Within a week, many replacements arrived from the United States and some light training was begun.

Simultaneously, a rumor swept through the camp that the division would be replaced. The story was the casualties had been so heavy at the Chosin Reservoir that the division was no longer combat effective. Sam seized upon this rumor and clung to it. Whenever someone asked he would insist that it was going to happen. He encouraged any who would listen to have faith in the rumor.

At the same time, they received a beer ration and a lot of time was spent in the tents drinking beer and singing songs.

One of the men from the 1st Platoon, a young corporal named Clifford, sang a beautiful rendition of 'Danny Boy.' Next, Joe Goggins sang 'Old Blind Barnebus' and sang it well even while Causey harassed him. Causey also sang well, which was surprising, because he seemed somewhat brutal and was inclined to become combative when drinking. He sang songs like 'Blue moon of Kentucky' and 'On the banks of the Wabash.'

One night, they were in the tent singing Irish songs and drinking beer. It got late and the beer supply ran low. Only one or two men had any left. Finally, one of Sam's squad, a reserve from Detroit, Michigan, named Westfall, broke out his last beer which was also the last beer in the tent. Someone tried to buy it from him and he refused.

"No sir, I been saving this beer all night long. I ain't selling it and I ain't givin' it away either."

"Ah come on Westfall," Petitt said, "I'll give you five dollars for it."

"No way!"

Sam said, "I'll bet Westfall will give the beer to me."

Westfall opened the can. "No way!" he repeated.

Then someone said, "I'll bet Sam gets the beer!"

This set off a chorus. Some said yes; some said no.

"Westfall is going to give me his last beer!" Sam announced.

He knelt down beside Westfall and stayed his hand to prevent him from lifting the beer. All grew quiet, watching intently. Sam whispered in Westfall's ear.

"Look, Westfall. Look at their faces. Look at the anticipation. They expect you'll give me the beer. You know you won't, but you must and I'll tell you why. Westfall, we're not going to be sent home. We're going back to the front. I know you've heard me repeat the rumor we'll be withdrawn, but I know better. You must give me the beer. Not for me, No! Not for me! but for them! And the reason why you must is in their faces. Look at them. Their confidence in Psycho Sam must not be shaken. They must follow me, immediately, without question. If they hesitate, it could cost us all our lives. It's our best chance to survive. You must do it. Not for me, but for them!"

As Sam whispered to him, Westfall looked at the faces of his comrades. That undefinable feeling Marines have for their Corps caused him to see the truth of Sam's argument. Slowly, his grip on the beer relaxed. He looked up at the smiling faces of his comrades. Westfall would die for them and they for him. Slowly, Sam took the beer from Westfall's hand. A cheer went up.

Sam took a swallow of the beer. "Banzai!" he cried. "Five thousand communists that a way! Go get em!" Then he handed it back.

Long after the tent was quiet, Sam was wide-awake. He could still see their faces smiling down at him, the faces of his comrades, the United States Marines. There's no brotherhood in the world quite like it, he thought. His depression lifted. He felt at peace with the world. As he lay in thought, feeling his depression lift, he realized that it was Christmas eve.

On Christmas day, Vesuvius got pepperoni from home. He shared it with Sam. Since the march out, Sam had let up on him and Vesuvius confided in Sam that he had written home and told his parents his squad leader was a John Wayne type.

Sam put his arm around Vesuvius.

"Benny, he said, "when we go back to combat, we're gonna get you the Congressional Medal of Honor."

Benny grinned at him.

"Chee! No kiddin'," he said.

He took Benny as a special project. He wanted to turn the boy into a real Marine. At every opportunity to do so he endeavored to build the boy's confidence. Just when Sam thought Vesuvius was going to be alright, he went to sick bay and arranged a transfer to Easy Company. He told Sam that he was unable to carry the BAR and the ammunition that went with it, so he had transferred out.

"What job are they going to assign you to?" Sam asked.

"I don't know, but nuttin could be worse dan carrying dat BAR," Benny said.

"I was only teasing about the Congressional Medal of Honor, Benny," Sam said.

Benny grinned at him. "I know dat, Sam," he said.

Then, he departed for Easy Company.

CHAPTER 24 ... The Court-Martial ...

General Matthew B. Ridgway of World War Two fame arrived to take command of all the forces in Korea. He issued a letter and insisted it be read to all, in which he quoted Thomas Paine when he was addressing George Washington's soldiers with the words, "These are the times that try men's souls." It was a letter intended to restore confidence. Ridgway wrote, "The war is being waged to contest whether or not men who enslave their citizens and shoot their prisoners will prevail. The letter was passed from man to man. Sam read it silently. The letter might have inspired Sam had he seen it before the swimming pool, but now it meant only that Sam knew something General Ridgway did not. Sam knew war lifted the restrictions of civilization and men were free to become what they were. If a man was a murderer at heart, he became one. Still, Sam felt better about the letter. At least, it indicated Ridgway did not condone the murder of prisoners of war.

The day after Christmas word was passed for Sam to report to the Battalion Command post. Sam entered the tent. He spoke to a clerk.

"I'm Sergeant Lewis. I've been instructed to report here."

Sergeant Major Ferrango looked up from behind a nearby desk. Sam had not seen him since Japan. Ferrango stood up and walked around the desk. Sam wondered if Ferrango recognized him from the incident in Japan. If he did, he gave no indication of it.

"Your court-martial is scheduled to take place tomorrow at eight o'clock. Report here at that time."

Sam nodded that he understood and turned to leave. There were several clerks in the place. Sam saw Petitt speaking with a clerk and waited for him. They left the tent together. Ferrango followed them outside. As they were walking away, he called out to Sam.

"Sergeant Lewis!"

Sam stopped. Ferrango motioned to him to come back. Sam turned and started back. Petitt followed. Ferrango waved Petitt away.

"Not you, Petitt. I just want to have a private word with Sergeant Lewis."

When Sam got close and stopped, Ferrango said, "We, down here at Battalion, know all about Lieutenant Von Ludwig. We know he's no good. We also know the whole platoon is prepared to support you at your court-martial. It would be a shame if this thing got out of hand."

Sam was surprised. He had never really considered what the platoon would testify to. With the stoicism born of military service he had been waiting for events to unfold. He hadn't spoken with anyone about the court-martial since Tarring had told him the platoon would support him. He wondered how Ferrango knew.

"What do you mean?" Sam asked. He was vaguely suspicious of the Sergeant Major.

"Think how it would look. You get court-martialed and all these men come forward and take your side against a lieutenant. A rotten lieutenant would be a blight on the record of the Corps," Ferrango said.

"Yes, that's true," Sam said.

"If this thing got out of hand, it could make the Marine Corps look very bad. Morale would be damaged. There's no telling where it might lead. Now, since we know all about this lieutenant and have taken steps to have him transferred, there's no need for a big trial. Do you agree?"

"I suppose so," Sam said. He had no idea where Ferrango was leading.

Ferrango reached out and placed his hand on Sam's shoulder. He leaned his head back and looked Sam square in the eye. "I have been authorized to make you a deal," Ferrango said, emphasizing the word 'authorized.' His whole manner indicated that he was a messenger sent with a message of huge importance.

Sam had not anticipated such a development. He hesitated, wondering. Ferrango saw him hesitate. Then, he continued, "If this thing got out of hand, it might cost lives. At best, the Marine Corps would be damaged by public knowledge that we had a rotten lieutenant."

"What's the deal?" Sam asked.

"You plead guilty to insubordination and we will reduce your Court-Martial from a General to a Deck. You would go before just one officer. It would be over in fifteen minutes."

"What would my punishment be?"

"Only a small fine." Ferrango said.

"How much fine?"

"Only forty dollars."

"I'd like to think about it," Sam said. "Can I sleep on it?"

"You must let me know tomorrow," Ferrango said.

Sam was vaguely suspicious. There had been something about Ferrango's manner that was too smooth. Something about the way he used the words, "We, down here at Battalion." Yet, Sam knew such an offer had to have the approval of Colonel Sutter, because Sutter had ordered the court-martial. He promised to let Ferrango know the next morning and caught up to where Petitt was waiting for him.

"What was that all about?" Petitt asked.

"They want to knock the court-martial down to a deck if I agree to plead guilty. They heard the men are going to back me."

"What are you going to do?"

"I don't know yet," Sam said.

They reached the company area and Sam sought Harvey Owen and told him what had transpired. As usual Harvey was stoic.

"What are you going to do?" he asked quietly.

"I don't know yet," Sam said. He highly respected Owen and had hoped Harvey would advise him.

"What would you do?" Sam asked.

Harvey said, "I don't know Sam, Boy." He shook his head. "Being court-martialed in a combat area. I'd not like that. I'd probably already have shot the son of a bitch."

Sam saw he would have to decide. If Causey and Lewellyn were correct, Von Ludwig would no longer be with the platoon. The men would be free of him. The forty-dollar fine was a cheap price to pay for freedom from Von Ludwig. Ferrango's appeal that it would be bad for the Marine Corps had swayed him. Just as Westfall had yielded his last beer to him, Sam decided to accept the deal. Like the can of beer, the forty-dollar fine was a cheap price to pay. He would not be hurt and the Marine Corps wouldn't have the embarrassment of a lieutenant shown to be less than a leader.

Next morning, he returned to the Battalion Sergeant Major. Ferrango greeted him with a smile.

"Sergeant Lewis, what have you decided?"

"I've decided to accept the deal," Sam said.

"Good," Ferrango said, then looking about, "Wait here."

He went out of the tent. A few minutes later he was back.

"Captain Cronk will conduct the court. He's in the next tent. Just go on over and go in. He's waiting for you."

Sam did as he instructed. Captain Cronk was seated at a desk. There was a single folding chair in front of the desk. He indicated it to Sam with a nod. Sam recognized him as one of the poker players at Inchon when he had stolen the rations.

"Sit down," Cronk said.

Sam sat down.

Cronk opened a manila folder and took out a single paper.

"Sergeant Lewis, you are charged with direct disobedience of a lawful order of Lieutenant Von Ludwig. It is my understanding you wish to plead guilty. Is that correct?"

"Yes Sir."

"Very well, The plea is so entered. Would you like to make a statement . . . off the record of course," he said, as he smiled at Sam.

"Yes Sir, I would like to say Lieutenant Von Ludwig was a burden upon the men whom he treated as personal servants. He ordered me to send men to cut wood for his fire. I picked two who shared the fire, but he wanted two others. I told him to go fuck himself. As far as I am concerned, he still can," Sam said.

Cronk gave him an odd look, signed the paper he had in front of him, and closed the manila folder. His friendly manner had disappeared.

"You can go now," he said curtly.

Sam got up and left. As he walked back to the platoon area he felt as if a heavy weight had been removed from between his shoulders. Tarring was waiting for him. He greeted Sam with his little girl smile, his eyes twinkling with an inner joy.

"Sam, word just came. You're free to go on liberty."

Sam saw some of 2nd Platoon preparing to leave and joined Causey, Lewellyn, Kenneth Hall, and Taylor. The five went to Mason and wandered about. They chanced upon a photography shop and had some pictures made. The owner of the shop had a little boy about four years old who roamed about the studio making friends with the customers, as children are prone to do. Sam had his picture taken and the boy climbed up on his lap and looked very somber for the occasion.

The town was full of Marines with little to do. Sam left the group and wandered about alone. The streets had been turned into street markets where stacks and stacks of C rations were on sale. How did all these military rations wind up in civilian hands? he wondered. Someone was making a lot of money. Some officers had to be getting rich because there was so much food on sale it could not have escaped anyone's attention and obviously someone high up had to be in on it. He soon tired of his visit and hitched a ride back to the pea field. He did not go in again. A few days passed uneventfully.

As a precautionary measure, in the event the enemy should show up unexpectedly, the 2nd Platoon was sent to the top of a hill which overlooked the north road which led to the pea field. A tent had been erected to sleep in, but there were no candles. At night, inside the tent it was very dark.

Back in the United States, Sam had been an avid reader of the comic strip, 'Terry and the Pirates,' which portrayed a Chinese bandit leader who liked to play the accordion. The bandit leader's name was Serge Blue.

In the early evening, inside the dark tent, Sam recalled Serge Blue. He remembered the bandit leader had always played his accordion prior to performing some evil act such as shooting prisoners. There had been one scene where Serge Blue sat under a tree playing in which he said, "When music stops, shooting starts," indicating that his ceasing to play would be the signal for his men to kill the prisoners.

In the darkness of that tent, Sam decided he would assume the name of Serge Blue.

"My name is not Psycho Sam," Sam shouted. "My name is Serge Blue!"

It was very quiet in the tent.

"Serge Blue!" he shouted.

Petitt was lying beside him.

Petitt cried out, "And I am the Centurion!"

Both Sam and Petitt were endeavoring to make someone laugh but, no matter how they tried, it seemed near impossible. All lay there in the darkness in silence. In a whisper Sam inquired of Petitt what a Centurion was. Petitt replied that it was a British tank.

"Serge Blue!" Sam cried.

"And the Centurion!" Petitt echoed.

The two wearied of trying to draw a laugh. Then, into the darkness of the tent, Lieutenant Von Ludwig muttered, "That son of a bitch is crazy."

All were silent.

In the darkness, the phone rang. Von Ludwig picked it up. Apparently the calling party was a friend, because Von Ludwig talked with him for some time, although he had lowered his voice, Sam heard bits and snatches of his conversation. "Oh no, not anymore, no. We don't have to worry about him anymore. He's a corporal . . . ."

Could he be talking about me? Sam wondered. He decided not, because he was a sergeant. But, who else would Von Ludwig have to worry about, if it wasn't him?

Since the incident at the Chosin Reservoir, Von Ludwig had never asked for anyone to help with his gear. He no longer carried the excess. But the platoon didn't like him and his presence in the tent dampened their spirits. Had he not been there, the men would have been singing.

At daylight, the men filed out of the tent and went off the hill. They reached the pea field, had breakfast, and discovered that training was beginning again. Each day they went for a short march along the road to get the replacements familiar with hand signals, tactics, and field communications.

A week after Sam's court-martial, they were ordered to fall in for a rifle inspection. The entire company stood at attention in the pea field. Captain Groff inspected the 1st Platoon and made his way over to the 2nd Platoon. Tarring saluted and reported, "2nd Platoon ready for inspection, Sir."

Groff returned his salute and followed him past the first squad.

At the head of the second squad, he reached Sam and stopped. Sam, standing at attention, brought his carbine to port arms and opened the bolt. Captain Groff stared at him silently. Tarring preceded him to the next man and Captain Groff followed. By the time they reached the third man Captain Groff seemed to be having a fit. At first, his voice was low and Sam could not discern what he was saying. Then he heard Tarring say, "But he's a natural squad leader. It's instinct with him."

"I don't give a damn." Groff's voice was rising, taking on his sarcastic nasal twang, "I'll not have that crazy bastard leading a squad!"

"But . . ." Tarring said.

"But, Hell!" Groff shouted, "Now! you beggar, or I'll have your stripes."

He was now so angry that he stalked away from the platoon without inspecting the third squad.

A few minutes later, they began the morning march. As they went along, Tarring came up and put his hand on Sam's shoulder.

"Sam, I have to take the squad away from you. They've busted you to corporal."

"They've what?"

"Your court-martial. They busted you to corporal."

Sam felt his heart skip a beat. A hot flush of anger seared him. The dirty bastards, he thought. They had double-crossed him.

"The Captain says he'll not let you lead the Twelve Fanatics. I've done all I can do. Fitwell will take over the squad."

Sam's mind was racing. Now, he knew that a week prior Von Ludwig had been talking about him. And Von Ludwig had been in on the plot to betray him, along with Colonel Sutter. The dirty rotten deed stretched from the Battalion Commander down to the Sergeant Major in support of an officer who wasn't fit to lead.

Then, because Groff had insisted Tarring do the deed immediately, Tarring called out for the platoon to halt. Fitwell came forward and took Sam's place at the head of the squad.

"I'm sorry, Sam," he said, "but you'll have to give me your carbine and take this rifle."

Sam did so silently, aware that everyone was watching. He knew Groff was trying to humiliate him and he was furious, but there was nothing he could do about it. The most painful thing was they had used Sam's loyalty to the Corps to effect their betrayal of it. The contempt Sam felt for them was boundless.

After a three-mile hike, they returned to the tents. Even though it was January, everyone had been issued field shoes except Sam. He had been told they didn't have his size, which was 12F. He was still wearing the arctic boots with big thick socks and thick pads. The hike ended, Sam went to Tarring.

"Tarring, I've made my last training march without field shoes. When the platoon falls out again, I will remain in my tent. I refuse to do anything until I get a pair of shoes that fit."

"You mean that? That you refuse to fall out?"

"I mean it," Sam said.

"They'll court-martial you again," he said.

"That's alright. Let them. Next time my statement won't be off the record, I can assure them of that," Sam said.

The very thought of Captain Cronk's words angered him. Sam knew that all courts-martial were reviewed by the Regimental Commander, who was the famous Chesty Puller. If he had seen the statement Sam had made, he would have wanted to know more. This was why Cronk had added his comment of, off the record of course. By this seeming idle remark, Sam's statement had been omitted from the record. The plot to betray him had included all of these and he didn't know who else.

Next day, the company fell out for training. Sam stayed on his cot. He was waiting for repercussion but none came. They made no attempt to coerce him.

Two days passed. Tarring entered the tent.

"Sam, go see the Supply Sergeant; your shoes have been delivered from Japan," he said with a grin.

"From Japan, huh," Sam said.

Tarring grinned broadly. "Yeah, they flew them in."

The training hikes stopped. Word came they would move north to the city of Andong up on the east coast of Korea. Late in the afternoon, the day before they were to move, Baxter returned from the hospital in Japan. Everybody gathered around him like old home week. Everyone tried to talk at the same time to tell him how cold it had been at the Chosin Reservoir, and he, in turn, was surprised at their light casualties. He had been hit in the buttock, had lost some muscle and a lot of blood, but guessed he was ready to go. Sam was surprised to learn that after he had left Baxter, the wall of the building, beside which they had placed him, collapsed and he was almost buried in rubble. When the conversation died down, Sam went outside the tent. A few minutes later, Baxter followed him out.

"What's this I hear about you, Sam."

"It's a long story," Sam said.

"Tell me what happened," Baxter said.

Sam related to him all that had happened after Baxter was wounded. He spoke bitterly about the atrocity at the swimming pool, and a lot of things, including the baby and two little girls. He related his appearance before Colonel Sutter and how he had been duped by the Sergeant Major, Colonel Sutter, Cronk, Groff, Von Ludwig, and whoever. It was impossible to conceal his bitterness.

Baxter listened all the way.

"Sam, the Colonel may not have known what the Sergeant Major told you. He may have told him that you would be reduced in rank. The Sergeant Major may have found a way to get revenge for the night in Japan when you crossed him."

"Uh huh," Sam said, "that's possible."

"One thing for sure," Baxter said. "They're afraid of you!"

"Me?" Sam was incredulous. "Why would they be afraid of me?"

"They're afraid because of what you know and what you are. It's that swimming pool. They knew that if you received a General Court-Martial you would be assigned a Counsel, and if you were, you might tell him about the pool. And that's what they're afraid of. And since you complained to Groff about it, and he failed to act, he's afraid of you too. That's the real reason they didn't give you a General Court-Martial."

Sam hadn't really thought about it till then. He had been too angry. But Baxter's logic was sound. Sobered by the revelation, he spoke softly.

"Someday, I'm going to tell the world about that pool," he said. "Everyone should know what a horrible sight it was. I wish I could scream loud enough for the whole world to hear me. Maybe then, it wouldn't bother me so much."

Baxter's face reflected concern. "Sam, don't let this bunch sour you against the Corps. These people, who have done this to you, are not representative of what the Corps is. These are shoddy people. Don't let them get you down. Look at it this way. You're still here. Von Ludwig has to move, not you. It's you the men respect, not them," he said.

Sam was very bitter and Baxter saw it.

"Come on, let's go into town," he said.

Sam hesitated.

"Come on, it'll be good for you."

So, at Baxter's insistence the two of them visited Mason again. They got off the truck and started down the street. Walking along, they chanced upon an aged Korean papa-san who had an A-frame strapped to his back which was loaded down with fish. One of the platoon, a Mexican-American named Villa, ran up and shoved the old man violently, sending him sprawling into the street. Baxter intervened. He grabbed Villa. "Man what are you doing?" he demanded.

Villa seemed to have been drinking. He gave Baxter a big sheepish grin. Baxter released him. Villa walked away.

Baxter stood looking after him.

"You would think a minority would have more feeling for another human being," Baxter mused, as if to himself. "You would think Villa, of all people, would know how it feels to be mistreated."

"Yes, you would think so," Sam said. He was puzzled. He had always liked Villa. Villa was a large youth with a big toothy grin that lit his whole face when he smiled. It made no sense for him to be cruel.

The whole affair seemed to be just one incident after another that kept making a lie of values Sam had always considered American values. More than anything else, Sam needed something tangible to cling to. The old dream they would whip the North Koreans and go home to the victory parade had died. No one ever spoke of it. When they talked of home it was about fresh milk and peaches and going out to dinner in nice restaurants. The Chinese intervention had changed everything. Where the Marines had once considered they would fight a rabble, they were going to fight the most powerful land army in Asia, which had shown itself to be utterly ruthless, cruel, and brave.

Sam felt that all vestiges of civilization had been stripped from both sides. He could no longer cling to the notion he was fighting for his country. What did the clash between communism and capitalism have to do with the ordinary Korean peasant who never got more than ten miles from the village he was born in? Sam was not sophisticated enough to answer. He was isolated. Things which caused him great pain, seemed not to bother his comrades. Sam felt alone in a crowd. He roamed from tent to tent, greeting his comrades with, "Banzai!" living out the drama of Psycho Sam, covering his bitter disappointment and disillusion with play acting. The men accepted him as Serge Blue, bandit leader—or Psycho Sam.

CHAPTER 25 ... Groff's Whorehouse ...

The inevitable came about as Sam had known it would. It was cold on the fender of the truck which carried Sam north but no cold he would ever endure would match what he had seen in the past. He had the flaps of his Korean cap tied below his chin and still wore the great hooded parka. He drew some warmth from the engine of the truck. After a long ride they pulled into the city of Andong. In the western outskirts of the town they dug foxholes on a street which had an open area in front that could have been a park but was more likely just vacant. It had a single house on the vacant side of the street in front of the line of foxholes.

Fitwell assigned a fire team to the house as a sort of outpost. The Second Platoon dug holes in front of the row of houses on the east side of the street facing the vacant lot. They maintained a watch in the holes, but were allowed to sleep in the houses. No sooner had they dug in, than some U. S. Army tankers wheeled into the park and began erecting tents right in front of Marine machine guns.

Captain Groff came stalking out, wearing Marine wool trousers, a leather jacket, and the red fox cap.

"Who's in charge of this goddam lashup?" he demanded.

An Army lieutenant stuck his head up out of a tank. "Who in hell want's to know?" he demanded.

"By God, I do. You're blocking my field of fire," said Groff.

"So what?" said the lieutenant. Apparently Groff had met his Army counterpart.

"Look goddam it. I don't want to have to shoot your men. Pull your tanks back between those houses. We'll protect em. You and me can go get a drink."

And immediately, the two left together. The soldiers stopped erecting the tents and backed their tanks up between Marine foxholes. They had extra machine guns which they loaned to 2nd Platoon, and these were set up. The soldiers were armed with crude sub machine guns, called grease guns, which had a steel bar handle that could be extended to fire from your shoulder, or you could close the handle and use the weapon as a long automatic pistol. Sam missed his carbine. The M1 rifle did not appeal to him as being a close-quarters defensive weapon. He wanted something to spray with. The grease gun seemed ideal. It was light and cheap and you could cock it on the run. When you pulled the trigger, it fired a 45-caliber bullet with more force than a standard pistol, so Sam paid one of the soldiers ten dollars for it. The same soldier had a Chinese shovel better than Sam's entrenching tool. It was half the size of a normal shovel and had a steel wire to sling it across your chest. It would be easy to carry. The soldier really didn't need it, so he gave it to Sam.

The soldier said his commanding officer was a colonel named Mchalis, who was trying to make a name for himself by volunteering his unit for hot spots. Sam sized the soldiers up. None seemed to have any particular bearing which exuded confidence. They appeared like Marines, except they had no esprit de corps; they were just a bunch of American kids thrown into a war they didn't understand. Sam questioned them.

"Who among you knows anything about communism?" he asked a tanker.

"What do you mean?" the soldier replied.

"You're supposed to be fighting communism. You should know something about it," Sam said.

"I don't know nothin' about it and I don't want to!"

"But you might die in this miserable country. And what is there here, but a bunch of mud huts. Look at these damn walls man! Mud! Just mud and bamboo. Look at these people. What do they have? Nothing! At least in North Korea, the communists built houses out of concrete. Do you think for a moment these people care anything about what kind of government they have? Hell no! They pull carts with bullocks or carry A-frames on their backs, and what do they have to eat? A few peas, some cabbage, lots of rice, and some fish. Maybe, if they're lucky, they might get an egg once in a while—if we don't kill all their chickens. They've never seen an orange or a banana. Hell, let the communists have the place," Sam said.

He was full of anger and became so enraged that he was about to lose control. He took his new weapon and started to go for a walk. He stood for a while in the doorway, looking around before he went outside. The soldier was talking to Lewellyn.

"What's wrong with him? He sounds like a damn communist!"

"He'll be alright. He gets that way in the rear. But when we go back up, he'll be hell on wheels," Lewellyn said.

"Sounds like a damn communist," the soldier muttered.

Sam left. He knew he wasn't communist. Let the damn soldier think whatever he wanted to.

When he returned it was dark. He stood his watch in the hole and then moved to the house. At daybreak, the floor of the house got warm and Sam found himself turning first on one side and then another. Awakened by the heat, he smelled smoke and went out into the kitchen area which was at a lower level. A young Korean boy about eleven years old was stuffing wood into the old fashioned cook stove. He gave Sam a huge smile.

"I am Korean schoolboy," he said, "you American soldier."

"No. No soldier. Marine!" Sam said. He loved children.

"I am Korean schoolboy. I fix fire for you."

"Fine," Sam said. "Is this your home?"

"No. I live away from here."

The men began to come into the kitchen and get acquainted with the schoolboy, who soon acquired the name of Billy Goat. As soon as he saw he was accepted, he disappeared and returned with two little girls, about six, whom the men named Mabel and Jean. They were two little darlings who were, no doubt, sent by their parents in order to survive. Sam managed to raid another stack of rations and sent them home by Billy Goat.

The kitchen stove used the space below the floor as a chimney. The smoke was drawn below floor and out the chimney on the far side. The heat was thus transferred from the smoke to the floor. The floor became to hot to lie on, so Sam shifted to a fruit shelf on the wall about three feet off the floor. It was warm and eliminated the hot side when the floor got hot. Sam was on the fruit shelf when Tarring brought two replacements in.

"This is Sam Lewis," he said, pointing toward the shelf. "Sam, these two guys will be in Ivan's squad."

Sam looked them over. One was a blond youth who had a nervous tic in the side of his face. The other was stocky, round-faced and appeared calm. Each carried a civilized look, that undefinable something which said they had never seen any horrible event.

"Blood!" Sam cried. Then at the top of his lungs, "Blood for Syngman Rhee!"

The one with the nervous tic was startled. He turned to Tarring.

"What's he mean? Blood for Syngman Rhee?"

Sam swung his feet off the shelf and sat up.

"Syngman Rhee's the president of this damn country," Sam said, "and he's shed a lot of blood. He'll shed yours too, Boy! In the tick of a second you can be dead."

He hopped down off the fruit shelf and pointed at the distant unseen imaginary hills. "Banzai!" he screamed. "Five thousand communists! That a way, go get em, Banzai!"

Nervous Tic looked at Tarring. "What's wrong with him?" he asked.

Tarring said, "Oh, I forgot to tell you. We call him Psycho Sam."

"Is he crazy?"

"Only a little bit."

Tarring shot Sam a raised-eyebrow look as he took them out to introduce them to the rest of the platoon. Sam rolled over on the fruit shelf and closed his eyes. "Poor devils," he thought.

On the third morning at Andong, they lined at the galley for food. The whole company was standing in line when out of nowhere a young attractive Korean woman came walking along the line. The men fell silent. It was as if someone had said hush. They watched her hungrily, as she went straight to the head of the line and had the cooks load her tray. Just as silently, without even looking at all at the eyes that were following her every movement, she walked back down the line and headed back to the house which served as the Company CP.

As the men followed her with their eyes, those same eyes came to rest on Captain Groff. He was standing in the doorway watching.

When Groff saw what happened he decided it wasn't right he should have a woman and the men should have none, so he sent Jackson into Andong for some prostitutes. Later in the day, Jackson returned with six. Groff had Jackson escort them to a house down the street and passed the word that Groff's whorehouse was open for business.

Some of the men went. Most didn't.

Two days passed. Sam was in his hole out in the street. Sergeant Parker from the machine gun platoon stopped by the hole and the two talked for a long time. Parker was married, had two children, and was from Toledo, Ohio. He had been with the company since Seoul.

Another Marine, a blond-haired youth from Massachusetts, stopped by. The moon was out full and it was a clear cold night. If they had been stateside, sex and girls might have been a topic, but not in Korea. Also, very rarely would religion ever be a topic, but somehow the subject of God came up. Parker ventured the thought that, wherever God was, he certainly wasn't with them. The other Marine disagreed.

"You want to know where God is? I'll tell you where God is. He's in every foxhole. That's where he is," he said.

"Do you suppose he was looking over us at Chosin?" Sam asked.

"I'm sure of it," the blond Marine said.

Sam didn't say anything. He had gotten a letter from his mother that day saying she prayed for him constantly.

"I lost six men to sick bay today," Parker said. "They caught gonorrhea in Groff's whorehouse. I wonder what God would say about that."

"Do you believe there's a God?" Sam asked.

"Oh sure," Parker said, and then, he stretched his arms skyward and yawned.

"Well, God damnit, I've got to go." He walked on towards the house.

The blond Marine looked after him. "He's Catholic, like I am," he said. "He shouldn't use God's name in vain like that."

"No, I guess he shouldn't," Sam said.

The blond Marine moved on. Sam watched him depart. He felt a great weariness, felt older than his years, and felt fear of what was coming; he had a premonition something bad was going to happen. He got down on his knees in the hole. He asked God to look after him, but that sounded selfish, so he asked him to look after all of them, but he knew God wasn't going to, so he thanked him for doing so in the past, but he still felt anxious. He began reciting the Lord's Prayer, but could not remember it. Finally, he said "Thank you God for allowing us to live in houses, even if there are no toilets and running water."

God, I would love to hear the sound of music, Sam thought, but he knew he wasn't going to. A storm was gathering and he could sense it, feel it with every fiber of his being, and he was bitter and alone and very much afraid.

CHAPTER 26 ... Hunting Guerrillas ...

Word was passed the battalion was going on a guerrilla hunt. At 5:00 o'clock in the morning they lined at the galley for a meal of mush, prunes, powdered eggs and flapjacks. As soon as they had eaten, crates of hand grenades and ammo were opened up and they began to load up. Fitwell found Sam and offered the carbine back.

"Here take this thing, Sam," he said.

Sam was surprised. "You don't have to do that Fitwell."

"No, but I want my M1. I don't feel comfortable with this thing."

They exchanged weapons. Sam felt real good about it. Now he had two automatic weapons, a grease gun and a carbine. Both were light and easy to carry by day and a real defensive arsenal at night. It lifted his spirits and he began roaming the street where the men were gathered around warming fires, warming their hands.

Sam came to the fire where Harvey Owen and Ray Joyner were standing.

"Banzai!" Sam shouted.

Harvey grinned at him. If Owen ever felt any fear or apprehension it never showed. Sam considered him to be the bravest man he had ever known.

"Hi Sam, there's supposed to be a division of North Koreans who didn't get back north when we hit Inchon," said Harvey.

"I'm gonna shoot everything that gets in front of me," Joyner said, reassuring himself, repeating what he had said back in Washington.

"Ah it's just a bunch of guerrillas," Sam said. "They probably have single shot rifles and no ammunition."

The men chuckled. There were about a dozen at the fire.

"We'll tear those bastards limb from limb," Sam said.

Someone threw another empty grenade box on the fire. As the flames leaped up, Sam warmed his hands. The trucks were always late. Several at the fire were from the barracks in Washington. Joyner grinned at them.

"How nice it would be to be back at Eighth and I getting a good breakfast every morning and going out to Arlington once a week," he said.

Joyner still clung to the dream. Sam's disillusionment did not allow him to. He listened to Joyner for a moment then grew restless and turned to go to the next fire. He took about three steps.

WHOOM!

The explosion slammed him in the back and knocked him forward, headlong into the street. Stunned, Sam struggled to get up. He got to his knees and looked back. The fire was completely gone. Even the street showed no trace of it—not even a burnt spot. The men were scattered about, blown away from where the fire had been. Some were lying still and the clothes of some were smoking. Harvey Owen had been blown across the street. He was trying to get up. He had his hand to his head and blood was running out between his fingers. He looked about wildly, as if searching for his enemy. The expression on his face said, "Where did that come from?" It was the first time Sam had seen him show fear, but there was no doubt he was afraid. Sam stood up.

The others were still down and calls of "Corpsman! Corpsman!" were ringing out.

Every man at the fire was injured except Sam. The three or four steps he had taken had made the difference.

The trucks arrived before the wounded were picked up and the others were ordered to climb aboard. As they pulled away, Sam perched on a fender, waved good-bye to Harvey and Joyner. He wondered if he would ever see them again. He guessed that someone had accidentally placed a box on the fire which still contained a grenade. He would never know.

The trucks left the city streets, got out on to a gravel road and picked up speed. It began to grow cold. They were, as near as Sam could guess, headed southwest away from Andong. The road followed a valley, twisting and turning, so that Sam lost all sense of direction. It was desolate country with mountains on both sides, and he began watching the skyline, where occasionally a lone figure was standing, watching the trucks, making no attempt to hide. After a two-hour ride, they entered a small village and the trucks came to a stop.

The truck ahead of Sam was open, its bed filled with Marines. A young Marine lit a cigarette. He took a couple of puffs on it and flipped it on to the roof of the adjacent hut, smiling at his deed. Sam slipped off the fender and took the barrel of his carbine and brushed the cigarette off. The Marine gave him a hostile look, his lips twisted in a snarl, as if to say, "Who are you?" Sam didn't say anything. If he wanted to fight about it he could get off the truck. Then the hut beyond the one Sam had knocked the butt off of began to burn. There was an outcry and the people in the village began trying to put it out.

Sam saw the futility of trying to stop wrong and yet he could do nothing else. A hut was burning for no other reason than just plain vandalism. Grimly, he watched.

Groff came stalking by, followed by Saia and the Confederate flag. He ignored the burning hut and the people trying to put the fire out. The company followed him without any command, like automatons. Sam fell in right behind Groff. Erickson was behind Sam. Groff struck out into a cornfield going away from the village. There was a layer of snow and ice on the earth and the corn stalks were dead and brittle. When it was frozen, the earth didn't stink and Sam was grateful.

Groff alone knew where they were going. Sam wondered what they might do if Groff was killed suddenly.

Saia was talking on the field radio, "Dog Robber, Dog Robber, this is Crazy Fox. Do you read me?"

"Loud and clear, Crazy Fox. We read you."

"We have left checkpoint Able, Dog Robber."

They traveled about a half mile out across the fields, with Saia talking on the radio. Suddenly, the captain stopped. He stood very still. He was listening and searching the area in front. In the distance Sam saw a small stream with scrub pine trees scattered along ridges leading down to the stream at right angles.

"Pass the word," Groff said, "keep a sharp lookout, right and left."

Sam turned to Erickson, "Sharp lookout, right and left."

He heard Erickson relay it back, it sounded like a recurring echo as it resounded down the column of men. They went two hundred yards and Captain Groff stopped again. He studied the terrain in front and then started forward and crossed the frozen stream and began following it. He stopped again and looked at Sam.

"Get away from me," he snarled.

"How's that Captain?" Sam asked. He hadn't understood.

"Get me something up here that'll knock somebody down!" Groff said.

"Erickson, stay close to the Skipper," Sam said.

Erickson trotted forward with the BAR and took Sam's place behind the captain, staying about four paces away from him. Saia dropped back with the flag.

As they went along, Groff drew his forty-five. He stopped again, looking intently at the ridges in front. Sam saw North Korean soldiers flitting across the second ridge in front. One would cross, disappear from sight, then another would cross and then another. They were moving parallel to the Marine column, but two hundred yards ahead.

"Heads up. Sharp lookout!" Groff said.

Erickson repeated it and Sam passed it back to Arkie who was following him as they began to move again.

The scrub pines began to thicken and limit visibility, and as they followed the captain into the underbrush he became like a wolf stalking a lamb. He would pause and stand very still and when he did the entire column would come to a halt. Three hundred yards into the underbrush they came out into an open valley with hills on either side, and right in front stood a single straw-roofed hut with a North Korean soldier strutting back and forth in front.

Captain Groff stopped. The men kept coming and the entire second squad filed forward and went to ground, aiming at the sentry. The captain motioned to Saia. Saia walked over and handed him the phone. The flag hung limp from the antenna.

The sentry walked about twenty paces and stopped. He did an about-face, walked twenty paces back towards the Marines, about-faced again and headed back. It was hard to believe he hadn't seen them. He had three BARs trained on him.

Sam still stood erect. He had forgotten he was no longer the squad leader. "Captain, say the word and he'll never know what hit him!" he said.

"No! No! Don't start a firefight." Groff took the phone from Saia's hand.

"Dog Robber, Dog Robber, I'm at their command post."

A voice came back. "How do you know?"

Groff became sarcastic. "How do I know!" His voice took on his nasal twang, "I've got a goddamn gook walking post right in front of me. That's how I know."

There was a period of silence on the other end. Dog Robber was trying to make a decision. Groff interrupted.

"It smells like a mouse trap to me."

More silence.

"Do I hold up or continue to advance?" Groff whined.

"Continue to advance," the word came back.

"Alright, we're going in, but it's a mousetrap."

The sentry reached the end of his post facing them, did an about-face, walked all the way to the far end of his post, hurled his rifle to the ground and darted behind the hut, using the hut to shield his escape.

As they went forward, the entire platoon fanned as skirmishers. Tarring ordered Parker to take a machine gun up the slope on the right and set up. Parker, six ammo carriers, and the corpsman took off at a run to get up on the hill as quickly as possible. The platoon moved forward at a trot. Sam studied the terrain as he went, making decisions in advance as to how to use the ground contours for survival.

"Spread out! Spread out!" Tarring shouted. "Let's not make it easy for them!"

There were rows of rock fences on the left side of the valley where farmers had stacked them to clear the field, and Sam headed towards a rock fence.

A single rifle shot rang out and they went to ground. A second later, the enemy fired at one time, a loud burst of fire, but that first premature shot had started them for cover. Sam went behind the rock fence and fired across it. The muzzle blast knocked his fence over and he slithered forward and fired more carefully. A roar of gunfire echoed up, then someone called out, "Steady! Steady now!" and the firing died away.

Up on the ridge, the machine gun crew were lying about with bullets still striking all around them. One man ran out from behind a mound of earth to drag an injured Marine back behind the mound. Bullets hit all around him, but he got back. Sam could see they had tried to set up their machine gun in an exposed position.

There was a pile of stone on Sam's left and he crawled over to it. Arkie was behind it, firing at the hillside to the left.

"The machine gunners are in trouble," Sam said.

Mortars began falling out in the valley and stepped closer. Petitt came crawling along the stone wall. Someone called out, "The mortars are friendly."

Petitt grinned his crooked grin. "Friendly or not they can kill us just as dead," he said.

The firing died out. Captain Groff stood up and came walking towards Sam, with Saia following, hunched over. A rifle shot rang out.

Groff ducked in contempt.

The rifle fired again.

Groff ducked in contempt again.

A third time, the enemy shot came.

This time, Groff didn't duck.

"See, those slope-headed bastards can't shoot," he said.

Lewellyn moved out in to the paddy and began having a bowel movement. Walking erect, Groff grinned down at him.

"Scared it out of you, did they boy?" he said.

Lewellyn grinned back at the captain, hitched up his trousers and got over next to the rock wall.

Further along on the hillside, above and on the right, were two thatched-roof huts. A flurry of gunfire broke out from them that wasn't aimed at Fox Company.

Groff stood out in the paddy in full view and, ignoring the smattering of fire, got on the radio to battalion. Word was passed that Fox Company would attempt to withdraw from the valley by running up the hill to the right towards the buildings. Dog Company would cover as Fox withdrew. Most of Fox Company had not come into the trap. They had circled to high ground on the right. 2nd Platoon followed in file out across the paddy towards the two buildings, came to a path that led up towards them and had to run single file across an area at the top that was still receiving hostile fire. An enemy machine gun was traversing back and forth across the path. Sam got close to the first hut and in a burst of energy ran rapidly towards it. He encountered a row of hedges and leaped to clear the hedges.

Airborne, he saw a North Korean soldier hiding behind the hedges. Sam whirled, shot by reflex, hit the ground, and ran around the building. The longer of the two buildings had been used as a hospital. Its occupants were dead, victims of a Dog Company BAR man. Sam ran back around the hut. Petitt was dragging a North Korean soldier by the leg. He stopped, released the soldier's leg, and aimed at him with a pistol.

"What are you doing?" Sam asked.

"This one's still alive. I'm going to kill him," Petitt said, grinning at Sam with a twisted grin.

"You don't want to do that," Sam said.

He looked at the soldier. Clearly he was already dead, but if Petitt believed he was still alive, and shot him, he would live with it the rest of his life. Sam didn't want that to happen.

"No! I'm gonna shoot him," Petitt grinned.

Sam shoved him aside. Thinking him already dead, he shot the soldier twice in the head. To his horror, the soldier grimaced. He had indeed been alive.

"If you didn't want me to kill him, why did you?" Petitt demanded.

"You were going kill him with malice in your heart," Sam said, trying to conceal his horror. "I shot him to put him out of his misery. There's a difference."

They waited in the area behind the huts. The company was beginning to move past with wounded and dead. Four men came past, struggling with a loaded stretcher. As they went past, the stretcher occupant's face was turned towards Sam. He recognized Parker. He was dead. One of his arms trailed off the stretcher. Blood was flowing out of his mouth and down his trailing arm and dripping off his fingertips. In horror, Sam turned away.

The stretchers kept coming past and Sam recognized Peterson, one of the machine gun ammo carriers. He had many times played cards with him. He was being carried along on his back. He was a freckle-faced seventeen year old from California, a nice quiet boy. If you noticed him at all you would say that he was clean cut. He was still alive, and as they passed, his eyes met Sam's, but he did not speak. He looked as if he had had the course. Sam fell in behind and they struck out on foot again across snow-covered ridges. Within an hour they reached a small clearing where Colonel Sutter and his staff were waiting. The column stopped and a debate took place among the staff as to whether a helicopter would be landed to take Peterson out.

"Where is he hit?" Colonel Sutter asked.

"In the leg," someone said.

"We'll carry him," Sutter said. "I don't want to risk losing a helicopter."

With this decision made, they continued across the snow-covered hills. After a while, it became the turn of the squad to carry Peterson. Sam, Arkie, Petitt, and Causey took the stretcher. Peterson weighed about a hundred sixty-five pounds, but they were going through snow and ice and the trails of those ahead. They slipped and skidded some, but didn't drop him. It grew dark, and still they struggled along, far into the night. They carried him up hill and down, until it seemed to Sam that they had been carrying him all their lives. They carried him, this seventeen-year-old child, until they were welded to his stretcher. Peterson began to moan and cry out weakly. Doyer, the corpsman, kept reassuring Peterson. They carried him until the weight of him was like lead and Sam felt he would never be free of the weight of him. It was past midnight. They had struggled about twelve miles. Peterson was very weak but, in the distance, they heard the sound of motors running and struggled the last hundred yards. Ten yards distant from the ambulance jeep, Peterson moaned weakly. "Stop, please stop," he said.

Sam knelt down beside him. "It's just a few more yards, Pete, and you'll be in the ambulance," he said.

"I'm not gonna make it," Peterson whimpered.

"Ah, come on Pete," Doyer said. "It's just a little ways."

They picked him up and struggled forward. As they placed him in the ambulance, he stopped breathing. Sam leaned forward, listening. There was nothing.

"He's dead," Doyer said.

Sam felt a numbness in his heart; an ache filled his chest with pain. He looked about helplessly.

Someone came up and said, "You guys come out here and lie down in front of the artillery."

So they left Pete and went along in front of the guns and lay down in an open cornfield in the wet snow. Half asleep, in shock and exhaustion, they endured the night. The guns fired. The muzzle blast rolled them halfway over, then they rolled back and fell half asleep until the guns fired again. This continued until dawn.

Whoom!

Roll away, then back.

Whoom!

Roll away, then back.

And on and on and on.

CHAPTER 27 ... Psycho Sam's Influence ...

At daylight the artillery was still blasting away. Sam got up on his knees. He had no feeling in his ears. He was wet from a night of being rolled in the snow. He stood slowly. The artillery loosed a blast which almost knocked him down. He walked out in the field to get more distant from the guns. The others followed. When all were up and moving about word was passed that trucks would transport them back to Andong. Within minutes it proved true. Trucks came and carried them back to Andong.

Billy Goat, Mabel and Jean returned, bringing a group of children who began playing around the outpost hut. Arkie, thinking to tease with them, dumped the powder out of a hand grenade, screwed the detonator back in, pulled the pin and tossed the grenade into the group of children. It exploded. Fortunately, none were seriously hurt. One little boy got a scratch on his finger.

Sam said, "Arkie what's happening to you? Are you going Asiatic?"

"Hell, I don't know Sam, I just didn't think," he said. "It wasn't supposed to explode, but it did."

Arkie was quiet and sensitive. In a normal time he would never have considered scaring children with a hand grenade, but the war was twisting all who were exposed to it in odd ways.

Tarring took him to the CP and Arkie waited outside.

Tarring reported the incident.

"Did anybody get hurt?" Groff asked.

"No. Just one tiny scratch. I put Mercurochrome on it."

"Well, let him go." Groff said.

Late in the afternoon of the second day, the machine gunners who had contracted gonorrhea returned and learned Parker, Peterson, and one other of their comrades had been killed. They blamed themselves. If they hadn't been infected they would have been there when needed and their comrades might have lived. And it followed, if Captain Groff hadn't procured the women they wouldn't have contracted venereal disease. The resentment, having long simmered against the captain for his brutal ways, boiled over. That night, they went to Groff's whorehouse, sent the women back to whence they came, and tore the house down with their bare hands; tore it right down to the floor and left only the floor, all the time shouting and screaming like prisoners in a riot. They stood out front of the CP and shouted, "Captain! Captain Groff! Come out you son of a bitch!"

Groff did not show.

"Come out and see what we think of your little gift. Come out, you son of a bitch, and see what we've done to your whorehouse!"

No Groff.

They were asking for the warden, but the warden knew how close to the edge they were.

It was a riot. Groff pretended not to hear them and remained in his CP.

Out in front of the CP, the men stormed and cursed and raved until their rage was gone.

The racket had hardly died down when Tarring found Sam on his fruit shelf.

"Sam, the Twelve Fanatics are getting drunk out in the outpost," he said.

"Why tell me? I'm not their leader. That's Fitwell's job," Sam said.

"Fitwell can't handle them. He's already tried. Lieutenant O'Bannion says he's asking you to use your influence. He wants you to go over and calm them down." (O'Bannion had taken over from Von Ludwig.)

Sam got up off the shelf and went to the outpost. They had taken the floor up, leaving only the joists in the entry room, and had dug a machine gun pit in the earth. The barrel of the gun jutted out from a slot below the outside wall. Arkie was down behind the gun on watch, peering out into the darkness. Sam walked a joist to the next room where the noise was coming from.

"Hey, Psycho Sam is here! Sit down Sam, and join the party!"

Sam sat down and looked the situation over. Causey, Rose, Petitt, Lewellyn, Rude, and Erickson were all sitting on the floor. Someone passed him a bottle. Sam turned it up and took a swig of the fiery stuff.

"Banzai!" he shouted.

They all laughed. He saw they only had four bottles and decided the best way to keep them sober was to help them drink it up. He began telling them about the machine gunners tearing down the whorehouse. It seemed to Sam it was quite a message they sent to the captain. Sam had not realized, till then, the depth of resentment against the captain. Sam's own feeling towards the captain were becoming mixed. Even though he was disappointed in the captain, Sam had to admit that he had guts.

The squad had heard the machine gunners shouting out in anger, but it seemed to have made no impression on them.

Sam passed the bottle back.

"Have another drink," someone said.

Causey began singing 'Blue Moon of Kentucky,' sitting back against a wall, his beautiful voice filled the room with the old American tune. Sam began to feel the alcohol effects almost immediately. These were his beloved comrades; his Twelve Fanatics!

By the time the booze was gone and they were complaining about it, he felt guilty for drinking them dry. He found Billy Goat, gave him ten dollars, and sent him for more drink. Billy Goat came back with five bottles in a matter of minutes.

Everyone cheered and all began drinking and singing. Someone relieved Arkie from watch and he joined in. Then Causey began to curse.

"That son of a bitch!" he shouted.

"Who?" Arkie asked.

"My mother-in-law."

"Why her?" Sam asked.

"When I heard my reserve unit was shipping out, I went back and joined up just to get away from her," Causey said.

He sang a chorus of 'My Old Kentucky Home,' then got into an argument with Petitt. Then with a crazy grin, Petitt touched the handle of his forty-five Colt.

"Go ahead! Pull it, you son of a bitch," Causey said.

Petitt took his hand away and grinned his crazy grin.

"Pull it! I'll shove the damn gun down your throat," Causey said.

"No. No!" Petitt said, "I wasn't angry at you Causey."

"Pull it and I'll kill you. I'll knock your fuckin' head in," Causey said.

"Boys," Sam said, "save your killing for the front."

"I thought you said we were going to be sent back to the States," Rose said.

"That's what I've heard," Sam said.

Causey had an empty bottle in his hand. He got to his feet and began pacing back and forth, crying out, "That son of a bitch!"

He knocked out the window panes one at a time. Each time he struck one, he shouted, "That son of a bitch."

"Get a blanket, and cover the window," Sam said. "It's cold in here."

Erickson left and returned with a blanket. They somehow wrapped it over the window frame to get it to stay in. Not satisfied, Causey kicked the whole frame out, blanket and all. The cold air poured in. Rose leaned out to pick up the window frame and Causey booted him in the seat of his pants. Rose went head first out the window.

He came right back in.

"Causey, you may be a big son of a bitch, but nobody does me that way and gets away with it," he said.

He lunged at Causey and carried him against the wall. They wrestled about. Sam began singing, "Cruising down the river on a Sunday afternoon."

They stopped fighting. Apparently, it was a draw.

Doyer, the corpsman, came to the door and yelled, "Sam!"

"In here," Sam cried.

Doyer came in, almost stumbled when he found the floor missing, then came in the room and surveyed all.

"I found out why Peterson died with a leg wound." he said. "The bullet hit a bone, and instead of going through his leg it deflected up into his abdomen. All the time, he was bleeding internally."

Everyone grew quiet.

"Sam, Lieutenant O'Bannion wants to know if he can have some of your booze?" Doyer said.

"Sure. I'll take it to him myself," Sam replied, staggering to his feet. He followed Doyer back to the platoon CP. Doyer went in the back door and Sam followed him in. O'Bannion looked up.

"Lieutenant, Doyer says you wanted a bottle of our booze," Sam said.

"That's right, Sam."

"Catch!" Sam said and hurled it at him.

O'Bannion caught it.

Sam was quite drunk and, as he turned to leave, he staggered and almost fell. Doyer caught him.

"Where do you want to go, Sam?"

"I want to go see the first squad. That's where I'm going."

"I'll walk along with you," Doyer said.

Sam entered the house where the first squad was staying. They had a blanket on the floor and were playing poker.

"Banzai!" Sam shouted.

They looked up at him, surprise written on their faces. They never would have expected to see him drunk. Even in his drunken condition he saw their disappointment. He sneered at them.

"So I'm drunk. So what? Ain't you guys ever seen a drunk before?"

They didn't answer. Martin looked at Manson and shook his head sadly. Sam saw again their disappointment.

"Well, I'm drunk, and . . . I think I'm going to faint," he said, his voice trailing off weakly.

The rafters of the room were exposed; he was hanging on to a rafter. Losing his grip, he fell headlong into the poker players. He had a sensation of being carried. Four of them placed him on his fruit shelf. He was slipping from consciousness to unconsciousness and back again.

Somehow Causey and Fitwell wound up in the room, and Fitwell was reading Causey off. As an ex-policeman, Fitwell had lots of experience with drunks. He and Causey were both big men, yet had not become friends. They were arguing, and Sam was unable to hear all because he was on the verge of total unconsciousness. Then he heard Causey say, "I never liked you anyway."

There were some muttered curses and they began wrestling. One got the other down across Sam's face and he couldn't breathe. He was so faint he could not cry out or move at all. He thought they were going to suffocate him. Finally, they rolled away and Sam passed out completely.

When he woke it was daylight. Tarring was standing over him.

"Thanks—Thanks a lot. Some influence. Come and see what your influence did," he said.

"My head hurts, Tarring. Tell me what it is."

"For one thing, it's Arkie. He's hanging out the front door of the outpost, half in and half out. I can't even tell if he's alive."

Sam got slowly to his feet. His head was breaking open with pain. Tarring wouldn't leave him alone.

"Come on, I want to show you what your influence did." he insisted.

Sam followed him out to the outpost. Just as Tarring said, Arkie was draped over the front steps with his face down in a pool of vomit. His legs and feet from waist down were inside the building. Sam knelt down and roused him from his condition while Tarring looked on.

"I'm sorry Arthur," Sam said to Tarring. "I just overestimated my capacity for booze. I thought I could keep them sober by helping them drink it up."

"We're moving out of here today. Trucks will be here within an hour," Tarring said, ignoring the apology.

"Where're we going?" Sam asked.

"Wonju. It's up on the coast, just below the 38th parallel," Tarring said.

Tarring went about telling the men to prepare to move out. Sam went looking for Billy Goat. He found him and sent him to get the girls, then went to steal some food for them.

With regret he left Billy Goat, Mabel, and Jean. They were the only human thing he had seen in many months. He managed to leave them with a small supply of food, and they left the whole platoon with smiles they would not soon forget.

Within two hours, hung over, his head pounding from over indulgence and filled with self-loathing for having done so, he was on the move again, back on the fender of a truck.

CHAPTER 28 ... The Vivid Dream ...

Sam became very ill. He would have given anything for just one Alka-Seltzer. The truck ride was a nightmare. He hung onto the fender of the truck and tried to convince himself that he wasn't going to vomit but, after he did, he felt better. It was rumored they would relieve some Army outfit near Wonju, which was supposed to be thirty miles from the front lines. They arrived at the Army's rear late in the day. By the time they got there, Sam had recovered, except he was weak. The Marines did not dig in, but stood fifty-percent watch.

The Army had been living in tents. They had posted sentries spread out about one hundred yards apart and were signaling each other with flashlights. Sam could hardly believe this. Each in turn sent a beam of light to the adjacent station, and in doing so, their position was outlined in detail for any observing enemy. It was a blueprint for disaster. It was dumb. Whoever issued such an order was derelict. Although he would not have obeyed such an order, Sam blamed it on whoever was in charge. He felt some of his leaders were cruel or arrogant, but they weren't stupid.

The following day, the Army moved back. The Second Battalion moved into the position and set about digging foxholes. Nightfall again brought a fifty-percent watch, one man in each hole awake at all times. Some of the soldiers laughed at them as they were leaving.

"You Marines are thirty miles behind the lines," one said, "Why dig in?"

They dug anyway.

Within four days they moved again, back towards the east coast to a place called Hoengsong. They arrived at Hoengsong, without seeing any part of a city, and again dug foxholes in a defensive perimeter. A single tent was erected inside the perimeter for each platoon, and a fifty-percent watch was ordered in the holes.

The day following the pullout, Chinese forces attacked the Army troops they had relieved at Wonju while they were watching an open-air movie. They suffered heavy casualties.

Sam and his comrades rarely knew the reasons behind the moves but took pride in staying alive. Part of staying alive was to be prepared for the unexpected. They didn't know why they were sent to Wonju, nor why they left. They never saw the city. Sam supposed whoever was calling the moves was looking for Chinese. When the Marines had left Hungnam, the country was, in effect, abandoned to the Chinese. The Chinese could be anywhere.

Sam chanced to be close to a jeep which had a radio. The Chinese put American prisoners of war on the radio to broadcast surrender messages and he overheard one of these. The soldier said he was Private Jones from Nitro, West Virginia. "I am being well treated and have become a lotus eater. The Chinese Communist Peoples Volunteers appeal to all Americans fighting in Korea to surrender and become lotus eaters." Apparently, the Chinese did not realize the mere fact the man was parroting their propaganda was an indication he was not being well treated. Sam resolved that he would not be taken prisoner.

Late in the second day at Hoengsong, Petitt came out to Sam's hole. "Sam, the whole platoon is to assemble in the platoon tent," he said.

As Sam walked along with him, Petitt told him that he had overheard a conversation between Tarring and O'Bannion, that they were being committed to combat.

"They're worried about you, Sam," he said.

"Why me?"

"Because you've believed the rumor the division was to be withdrawn," Petitt said.

"Is that what they said?"

"Something like that," Petitt said.

"Thanks, Petitt," Sam said.

He arrived at the tent. Most everyone was there. He went in and waited while two or three others filed in.

Lieutenant O'Bannion waited until everyone was there and it grew quiet in the tent.

"Men, while we've been resting and reorganizing, the Chinese Army has been making its way down through Korea. Only the Army 2nd Armored Division has stood in their way, and the 2nd Armored has taken heavy casualties. We're going to relieve them, but we're not going to take up defensive positions. We will attack. As you know, General Ridgway has taken command of all forces in Korea. He says we're going to move away from the roads and move out into the hills and fight the Chinese on new terms. We're not so much interested in real estate as we are in killing Chinese. The operation has been named Operation Killer. We'll go forward until we meet the Chinese. When we find them, we'll kill 'em. They're approximately twenty miles north of here. Tomorrow morning, we'll board trucks that'll take us ten miles north. We'll then proceed on foot until we can start killing Chinese."

O'Bannion ceased talking. It was so quiet in the tent you could have heard a leaf fall. The very thought of being pitted against the Chinese Army in this land of mountains and smelly rice paddies with no roads for supply was depressing. Sam felt a great fear touch his heart. He had not been so afraid since the night the train had stopped in the tunnel.

"Does anyone have any comment?" O'Bannion asked.

There was no answer. He looked all about the tent searching their faces with his eyes. At length, his eyes rested on Sam.

"How about you, Sam?" he asked.

Sam did not hesitate.

"We'll tear those Chinese to pieces with our bare hands," Sam said.

And everyone laughed.

O'Bannion was surprised. Sam saw it in his eyes. Suddenly, he felt grateful to Petitt for warning him. Although filled with fear, he didn't want to show it.

"That's the spirit," O'Bannion said.

They filed out of the tent.

Sam wondered why they had announced the coming action. It seemed as if they were saying, "You may die tomorrow, so you must worry about it all night." It was somewhat like being a prisoner on death row and being told your last appeal had been turned down. A few minutes later, a shot rang out.

"Corpsman! Corpsman!"

The cry was coming from the hillside above him. A few minutes later four Marines came down the hill carrying another Marine on a stretcher. He had shot himself in the foot. It was Brown, the company sniper. Sam called out to him.

"Hey Brown, did you do a good job?"

"Yes Sir, Sam, that was a sniper's rifle."

Obviously Brown had been so depressed by the news he had shot himself in the foot. An hour later, he was back. Sam went to talk to him.

"Shit, Brown, I thought you would be on the hospital ship by now," Sam said.

"Sam, I got so depressed. They got me to the battalion aid station, and took my shoe off. The bullet had just passed between two of my toes and didn't do anything except take some meat off each one. By the time we got there I was okay so I said, 'Just bandage it up and I'll go back.' The corpsman asked me if I was okay and I said, 'Yeah, I'm fine.'"

Sam went back to his hole. He had never considered shooting himself, but couldn't blame Brown, or anyone, for doing so. There was no light at the end of the tunnel. All the naive dreams of quick victory and a return to the soft life in the United States were long gone. There wasn't going to be any victory parade and all knew it. The idea of fighting for their lives with the sole purpose of killing was horrible. Sam feared what tomorrow would bring. He did not sleep that night.

At daybreak, they had their last hot meal and loaded up with grenades and ammunition and spent some time waiting for the trucks. The trucks were on time and Sam soon found himself on the right front fender traveling a narrow gravel road which followed a valley between two mountains. They traveled for about two hours, then left the trucks and began a route column approach, a column of men on each side of the road. Fox Company was at the head of the column and the entire battalion was on the move. In front of Sam, Captain Groff led the way, behind Saia who had the flag of the Confederacy unfurled. Joe Perrigo, the Battalion Operations Officer, was at the head of the other column.

Quite suddenly, a jeep came forward and skidded to a stop. General Ridgway got out of the jeep and shook hands with Perrigo. Then, as they continued to move along, Ridgway put his arm around Perrigo's shoulders and walked along with him. Sam heard him tell Perrigo,

"We need you Marines out here."

Perrigo grinned at him, a big toothy grin. It looked as if Ridgway was walking beside an ape. Perrigo's long arms reached almost to his knees. Ridgway had two live hand grenades taped to the suspenders of his pack. He talked with Perrigo and Groff for about three minutes, then hopped in the jeep which his driver turned around and drove back down the road to the rear. Within a few minutes, the artillery shrilled overhead and began falling far in front. As they marched forward, the shells fell with regularity.

An old Korean man made his way towards them with an A-frame of possessions on his back. When he reached them, the shells shrilled overhead and he gestured with his arms skyward, speaking in Korean, protesting the bombardment which had forced him out of his home. They met a thin trickle of old men, women, and children, and then there was no one.

The columns marched silently forward. Every few minutes the wounded tigers shrilled overhead and fell like thunder, making balls of fire and smoke on the road ahead. They kept marching towards the smoke.

Suddenly, a burst of fifty-caliber machine gun bullets struck the center of the road between the two columns. Sam's fear became a reflex. In an instant, he was off the road and across the ditch, running fast out across a cornfield. The field was wet with snow and mud, and the mud clung to his feet like lead. He slowed and looked back. Fitwell was still on the road, waving his arms, shouting orders to a squad that had gone with Sam. Captain Groff, too, was following Sam. When he saw Sam slow down, he shouted, "Keep going, keep going!"

Sam ran across the cornfield until exhaustion forced him to slow to a walk. There was a big hill off to the right of the road and, without being told, he began to climb it, it being axiomatic in combat to get to the high ground.

Apparently the Chinese had wanted to force them off the road, because they did not fire again, and they were able to secure the hilltop without incident except that one Chinese light machine gun kept trying to hit them as they dug in. One Fox Company gun set up and fired back at them, but both sides were out of range. They were like two barking dogs at a great distance from each other, howling out threats that could not be carried out.

After they dug in, two trucks came forward with their sleeping bags and stopped down on the road about five hundred yards to the rear. Some men from the 1st Platoon went down to get their bags and the Chinese laid an artillery barrage around the trucks just close enough to discourage them from getting their bags. There was nothing like artillery to chill Sam's heart and, although it was January, he decided he would suffer the cold night without a bag rather than chance being blown to bits.

He shared a hole with Erickson who volunteered to take the first watch. Sam got down in the hole and leaned back against the cold damp earth. It was a dark cold night.

About nine o'clock a bugle sounded three long notes from somewhere out in front.

"Did you hear that?" Erickson asked.

Sam tried to answer, but was so afraid and so cold that his teeth chattered. Finally, he said, "Yeah."

He had never felt such fear and could not sleep, so he watched until twelve o'clock while Erickson slept. When he lay back, at last, he was finally able to sleep.

In his sleep he dreamed of a large battlefield, a panoramic sight of rice paddies in front of three low hills. The paddies extended back to a range of hills that were like a distant horizon. Marines in battle gear were advancing across the paddies toward the three low hills. They were spread out as skirmishers and there were two tanks moving across the paddies with the men and, as they moved, two Corsairs, one following behind the other, swooped low above their heads and the first plane dropped a napalm bomb on one of the hills and it blossomed out red with fire. Behind this scene, on the distant horizon, the head and shoulders of a man with long hair and a dark beard and two long arms spread across the entire horizon both right and left until his arms had encompassed the entire battlefield. The face of the man was similar to pictures depicting Jesus Christ and, in his dream, Sam believed it was Jesus. Then a voice spoke in the dream and said, "Do not be afraid!"

Erickson woke him at five o'clock. Immediately, when he woke, he was calm. All his fear was gone. It was uncanny. He had been feeling fear for days and now it was all gone. He was completely free of it. Most importantly, it was so wonderful to be calm and at peace and he was thrilled to be so.

It was growing light. Tarring came to the hole and knelt down beside Sam. "Sam, Lieutenant O'Bannion wants you to take over the squad again."

"What's wrong with Fitwell?" Sam asked.

"Fitwell went to sick call last night with his feet, but it really wasn't his feet. He told me he couldn't lead a squad that followed someone else. Lieutenant O'Bannion says to tell you he'll help you get your sergeant's stripes back if you'll take the squad."

"What about Captain Groff?"

"He's cleared it with Captain Groff."

"I see," Sam said bitterly. "In the rear I'm a crazy bastard, but up front I'm needed."

Tarring ignored his bitterness. "Will you do it?"

"What happens when Fitwell comes back?"

"We'll find another job for him. Are you gonna take the squad?"

"Yes," Sam said.

"We're going to attack across the paddy at the base of this hill. Do you see that little knoll on the far side at the base of the hill beyond it?" Tarring said, pointing.

"I see it," Sam said.

"We'll regroup at that knoll and then attack the hill beyond. There won't be artillery support, but our machine guns will fire over our heads as we cross the paddy."

"Alright," Sam said.

"Be ready to move out as soon as we eat."

Out in front, a Chinese scout was trying to get back across the paddy. One of the machine gunners fired at him and he leaped behind a paddy wall. They ate. Word came to move out and they moved down the hill and paused at the bottom. There was no need to tell the men Sam was leading again. They had overheard Tarring. Sam looked back at the squad and saw fear etched on their faces. He felt none at all. It was as if he had ice water for blood. He sought to reassure them.

"If any one gives us any shit we'll blow hell out of them," he said.

Erickson grinned at him, as if to say, "Who are you trying to fool?" His face was pale with fear.

Sam stepped out into the paddy and started across. The paddy had a layer of snow on it, and it looked about a hundred fifty yards to the small knoll. He was watching the spot about twenty yards out, where the Chinese scout had gone down. Down on the left, the 1st Platoon was pausing before going out into the paddy. Sam began crossing at a trot. Behind him, the hammer of the machine guns began with all six firing at will, and tracers arced out across the paddy in a deafening din of fire. Tarring was on his left and slightly behind when Sam saw the Chinese soldier crouched behind the paddy wall. The soldier was right in front of Tarring. Sam shot him in the back with a burst of fire from the grease gun and knocked him face forward into the paddy. Tarring looked at Sam as if Sam had fired at him.

"Sorry," Sam said, "I didn't mean to shoot so close."

At that instant a spattering of bullets struck the paddy, and in the corner of his vision Sam saw the men falter as if they would go to ground. To do so would be fatal. Could they not see that?

"Come on!" Sam screamed. "What the hell's the matter with you guys!"

He waved them forward and broke into a dead run across the paddy with bullets kicking the snow all around him. A cheer broke out from the 1st Platoon and someone shouted, "It's old Sam!"

Then a voice Sam recognized as Bugarella's, "Man, look at him go!"

And indeed Sam was going, with the Twelve Fanatics right behind him, running as fast as they could. All about them the fire cut and slashed, but they were moving fast at a dead run. A bullet cut the handle of Sam's Chinese shovel in half and dropped it off his back into the paddy, but there could be no stopping. When he reached the safety of the knoll he looked back. Captain Groff was coming behind the flag, waving his forty-five overhead and Sam's squad was spilling in against the knoll. A roar of fire was going both ways, with tracers from Fox Company machine guns slamming into the hill above and answering fire still sweeping the rice paddy, kicking up ice and snow as the company crossed.

"Arkie," Sam shouted. "See where the fire's coming from."

Arkie climbed to the top of the knoll and looked across.

Sam called out to him. He stepped down a step and turned to answer. As he did, a bullet passed through a small sapling right where his head had been.

Sam looked back again. The company was crossing the paddy under a hail of fire, running like hell wouldn't have it.

Captain Groff, wearing green trousers, a leather jacket, and the red fox cap, was waving his pistol, shouting orders as he came across the paddy. Beside him Saia carried the Confederate flag. Within a minute, Groff would be at the knoll. At that moment, Sam knew Groff would order a charge as soon as he got there, but Sam didn't want him to order him. This time you bastard, Sam thought, you'll follow me.

"Charge!"

He screamed and leaped up and went across the knoll, then down and up the hill beyond. The squad went with him. They might as well have been Confederate soldiers, because there were rebel yells coming out of them as they went up the slope, hurling grenades into the holes. Groff came right behind them. The charge carried them all the way to the top and Sam threw himself to ground panting for breath, literally gasping for breath, and as he lay exhausted on the ground he looked out to the left and was amazed. *There was the scene he had seen in his dream.* The head and shoulders of Jesus were not dream there, but everything else—the horizon, the tanks, the infantry, and the two planes boring in low against the three low hills and the lead plane dropping a napalm bomb—was there. It was surreal.

Captain Groff reached the top and went to ground. Saia sat down beside him. When Groff was able to breathe, he took the phone from Saia and called Perrigo, "Dog robber, this is Crazy Fox. I'm up here with a squad," he said; then he looked directly at Sam and said, "My best squad."

Captain Groff had never praised anyone. Groff's praise, compared to the message of the dream, was unimportant, but Sam had forced Groff's respect with his life and Sam knew it. What Sam gained, in the end, was respect for himself. From then forward, he felt he was special. He had lost all fear.

After they got their breath, Groff said to Sam, "Lead out."

Sam began to lead the squad in column across the face of the hill and over a second hill, and the entire company followed. He reached the crest of a hill he knew would be better for a skirmish line to cross the crest rather than a single lone individual, so instead of crossing the crest he went parallel to it, intending to wave his arm in a skirmisher's signal. Sam had been leading for about two hours. Prisoners had been taken from the holes he had passed on the charge up the first hill, and they were beginning to get sniper fire popping across the ridge that he was going parallel to when the order reached him to go across the ridge. Expecting to be shot as soon as he went over, he went anyway. Not a single shot was fired. Sam passed over two more ridges in this manner, feeling the loneliness of being the first potential target. Then, the order came up the line to let someone else lead. Now, he knew in his gut, the captain didn't want him to gain too much recognition. He stopped and let the column file past.

Within a few minutes there was gunfire at the head of the column. The company was pulled back to the crest of the ridge Sam had gone parallel to and they began to dig in. Sam sent Westfall out to lie on his belly and cover while the squad dug. He borrowed Westfall's shovel and dug a deep hole with a shelf on the side to sit on. He still felt no fear.

He marveled at the dream. What a memorable thing! He retraced the events of the day in his mind, feeling as if he had been given a precious gift. He felt chosen, yet humble. He had no explanation for the dream. It was something so powerful it had a profound effect upon him. It was not something of his doing; he was its recipient. He knew that he never again would have to fear anything—not poverty, not disgrace, not rejection, not death, not anything!

While he was well aware of the absence of fear, he wasn't troubled at all by the killing of the Chinese soldier in the rice paddy. He had made the complete journey from civilization to barbarism. Sam had become a killer. The change in him was subtle but, from that day forward, there was a new deference towards him from his comrades. His counsel and his viewpoint were often asked on anything and everything.

A day or two later, the men would refer to that day as the day they crossed the rice paddy at Hoengsong. They had crossed the paddy under continuous fire, yet not a man had been scratched. Captain Groff had had a bullet pierce his trousers. And when this had happened, Groff had shook his fist at the enemy.

One day the men were gathered about a fire on the leeward slope of the hill. As they talked, the conversation shifted to Sam's action.

Joe Goggins said, "Sam is a hard man to get in de saddle. You almost can't get him in, cause he don't want to mount up. But once he's in de saddle, man—he is *gwine* to ride."

Baxter looked at Sam and grinned a quiet grin. "It took a lot of guts," he said.

Sam never told anyone about the dream. He was humbled by it. He was not its initiator and did not pretend to understand almighty God, but it was not difficult for him to believe, because he had seen Jesus in his dream and its reality had been confirmed when he saw the exact same picture of the battlefield in his wakefulness after leading the charge across the paddy and up the hill.

A few days later, Causey came and said, "Sam, would you think less of me if I applied for a hardship discharge?"

"Of course not, Causey."

"Then that's what I'm going to do. My father is sick and can't work and my mother needs help. They've looked into it and they've been told I can be sent home if I fill out the papers. I just wanted to see what you thought," he said.

Causey left a day or so later. He didn't make a big deal out of it. Just shook Sam's hand.

"Sam, you take care, you hear?"

It seemed to Sam that his comrades thought he was invincible. He knew he wasn't. He couldn't say he would live another day, but he no longer had the fear of death. It would have been possible to let it come back, but life was so much better since he wasn't afraid, he decided to stay that way. He had a small pocket-sized testament his mother had sent and from it he memorized the Twenty-third Psalm.

Thereafter, if he began to feel fear he would whisper it to himself, ". . . Yea, though I walk through the valley of the shadow of death, I will fear no evil, For the lord my God is with me . . . ."

Sam believed the voice in the dream. Sam believed that God had spoken to him in the night and told him not to fear. He accepted the message.

CHAPTER 29 ... Tragedies, and Savagery ...

Three days later, Tarring came around to Sam's hole. Sam saw immediately something was different. Tarring's face was aglow. He stuck out his hand towards Sam and Sam grasped it. His eyes were alight with joy. Sam could not imagine what had happened to put such a twinkle in them.

"Sam, I'm saying good-bye. I'm leaving. Jennings will take my place."

"Leaving!" Sam said.

"Yes. I'm being rotated home," Tarring said.

It was a bombshell out of the blue. Sam felt awkward. He could see how happy Tarring was, and yet Sam felt sad and tried his best not to show it. He had grown close to Tarring. "Home!" Sam thought. He thought of Charlotte, of how happy she would be to see him. But it wasn't him who was going. Emotion welled up within him. The very thought of home was hard to handle. He was glad for Tarring, but envious it wasn't himself. A wave of homesickness welled over him. He was unable to bear it so he forced it from his mind. He did not dare think of home.

"That's great Arthur," he said. "When are you leaving?"

"Right now."

Tarring laughed a delighted, joyous laugh. He had been an integral part of Sam's life, had been repelled by the swimming pool and had always supported Sam. Sam tried, but words wouldn't come to express what he felt. Tarring was joyous. Sam was sad. "I wish you luck," Sam said.

And that was all. Tarring had been closer than a brother. Now, he was more distant than a stranger.

He was joining the living; Sam was remaining with the dead. He watched Tarring go from man to man saying his good-byes. Tarring was in a hurry. Within fifteen minutes he was gone.

First Sergeant Homer left at the same time. If he said good-bye to anyone Sam didn't hear of it. Ever since he had killed Carpenter the men had held him in contempt. Sam didn't know of a single friend Homer had made. He was one of those people one meets only once in a lifetime, whom one sees and observes, but never gets to know and doesn't want to. Homer's job was taken over by a tall athletic American Indian named Hemphill. Just what that job was no one ever said. One might suppose he would have been a spare Company Commander in the event all the officers were killed.

Hemphill managed to bring a little dignity to the job. He respected the men and the men respected him.

An hour after Tarring and Homer left, darkness fell and the Chinese opened on Fox Company with a combination of mortars and artillery. The shells fell exactly into the position and blew craters in between the foxholes and shook the earth, striking terror into Marine hearts. Marine artillery radioed instructions to watch for the flash of the enemy guns and count the seconds before the shell landed. By this method they were trying to get the range, but the Chinese mortars foiled the scheme, which was why the Chinese used them in the way they did. Sam could see the flash of Chinese artillery, but when a shell fell there was no way to distinguish whether it was artillery or mortar. He pulled his head down and endured the shelling.

Next day, Fox Company went on patrol. They left one platoon and some machine gunners behind to guard the camp, and went down the hill in front of the position past the bodies of three dead Chinese soldiers who appeared to have been dead for two or three weeks. It was hard to tell how long because the weather was cold, and they had just turned blue like rotten Irish potatoes, tending to dry out rather than rot. From the position and manner in which they lay Sam concluded they had probably been killed from the air. By habit, he noticed everything about them.

2nd Platoon was first. Sam was on the point of the patrol. Jennings instructed him to head south towards the road they knew was there. A valley led all the way in that direction and Sam set out through fields of rice, peas, and corn, all now gripped in the gray dead of winter.

As he went along, he saw a small thatched roof hut in the distance and approached it warily. As he neared it, he was repelled by an intense odor. He booted the door open and looked in. Three Chinese soldiers lay side by side on the floor. One raised himself to a sitting position and stretched his arms out saying something in Chinese Sam could not understand, but common sense told him the soldier was asking for help. All three were suffering from gangrene, which was causing the odor. Sam stepped back out of the hut.

"Pass the word, three wounded Chinese in hut."

He heard the word go back. Lieutenant Von Ludwig came running around the hut.

"Kill em. Kill em!" he shouted to Sam.

"Fuck you Lieutenant," Sam said deliberately. "Do your own killing, if you want them killed."

The thought of being court-martialed again did not even enter his mind. He had no regard whatever for Von Ludwig. Sam kept moving down the valley. He had gone fifty yards when he heard three shots ring out. He did not know who shot them, but didn't believe Von Ludwig did.

A half mile further, he saw something lying on the ground in the distance and wondered what it was. As he drew nearer, he saw it was the body of a man. Warily, Sam approached, keeping a watchful eye all about, lest it be some kind of trap. He was very near when he stopped and looked. The body was naked from the waist down, lying on his face, feet and buttocks towards Sam. Warily, Sam approached. Sam walked up and stood looking down at him. It was a young American soldier. He wore only an olive drab undershirt. He had been shot in the back of the head, while he was kneeling, with his head bowed, and had pitched forward into the grass. Sam saw the marks on his wrists where his hands had been bound. They had wanted his wedding band and had shot his finger off to get it. Sam's heart skipped a beat and he began to ache inside. Something about the boy was so pitiful. He had a shock of blond hair and his eyes were open, glassy, lifeless, staring at the world. He could not have been more than twenty and looked younger.

"Pass the word, young soldier has been executed," Sam said.

Captain Groff had been working his way up the column and now he came forward rapidly and stood looking down at the soldier. He too was affected by the sight.

"Don't let him lay there like that!" he shouted. "Get him up off the dirty stinking earth!"

It was the first time Sam had seen the captain let anything bother him, and it was a revelation. Beneath Groff's hard cruel exterior there yet lay some softness. Sam left the soldier lying there. The captain was calling for stretcher bearers and crying out, "Don't let him lay there like that!"

"So," Sam thought, "the great man has a heart after all," and he smiled to himself. "Now who is crying?"

And yet, he ached. War is hard on all men, but most particularly on idealists.

Petitt was carrying a stretcher. He and three others gently placed the soldier on it and turned back to camp.

Sam kept moving, but looked back to see what was being done. He saw them start back with the dead soldier and he continued to lead the patrol south.

Within a half mile, he saw the road. There were vehicles on the road, and as he drew closer he saw they were American trucks. The lead truck had been hit with a flamethrower. The driver still held to the wheel in death and beside him sat an Army officer, both fried to a crisp and shriveled up. They looked like two fried grasshoppers.

The officer had been a major and his insignia had not melted, but was still on the side of his head. A convoy of death stretched out behind the lead truck. It was apparent that, once the Chinese had knocked out the lead truck, they had finished the occupants of the others off easily. Some had died in the trucks and some had gotten out, but had been killed on the road.

In the cornfield beside the road the corn had been cut and shocked, and some soldiers had gotten out into the cornfield, hid behind the shocks, and then been hunted down and shot.

There were too many bodies for them to carry so they left them where they had died and headed back to camp. Sam led the way back. Jennings suggested he find a different route back so as not to encounter an ambush. Sam decided to follow the road west for a while and then turn back north. He had gone no more than a half mile when he began to see bunkers on both sides of the road.

Suddenly a Corsair swooped low overhead, so low Sam could feel the air from its propeller. Someone shouted, "Air panels out!"

Within seconds the plane circled and buzzed them again. Word was passed the pilot had reported there were Chinese in the bunkers on both sides of them.

The bunkers were only about fifty yards distant from the road, but they faced each other. If they chose to shoot at the Marines they would be firing at each other, so Fox Company marched right between them, pretending not to see them. It was a gauntlet about three hundred yards long, and as the Marines marched between the Chinese, the Corsairs kept buzzing overhead. When they cleared the position by two hundred yards the planes came back and began bombing and strafing.

Sam turned north and traveled north till he came parallel with the camp, then turned east towards it. When he reached the bottom of the hill where the three dead Chinese soldiers lay, he saw their heads had been cut off.

Back at the hole, Petitt told him what had happened.

"When we brought the dead soldier back, two of the machine gunners were down there cutting the heads off those chinks."

"My God, what for?" Sam asked.

"They wanted the skulls for souvenirs. They boiled them in their helmets to get the flesh off."

"How do you know?" Sam asked.

"I saw them do it. I've reported it to Lieutenant O'Bannion."

"What did he say?"

"He told me to pass the word when he finds out who cut the heads off those three Chinese there isn't going to be anything left of their asses but greasy spots."

This word came down the line of foxholes that night. It was especially gratifying to Sam. At last, someone, besides himself, had spoken out.

During the night, two machine gunners fired a burst from their gun. One shot the other in the leg. The one who was shot in the leg shot his comrade in the hand. They claimed they had been attacked, but everyone knew better. They had chosen not to face O'Bannion.

They stayed several days in that position. The Chinese were making a determined stand in front of the battalion on the left and 2nd Battalion was held up waiting for them to knock out some bunkers. Each night they were shelled by the Chinese. They had the range and they laid the shells right in on 2nd Platoon, as close as two or three feet away. Sam kept improving his hole each day. He dug straight down for five feet and then tunneled off to one side. He was sharing a hole with Rude. None of the others wanted to. They said his feet stank, and called him Kruddy Rude. Rude had been wounded once and a second Purple Heart would send him home. He showed Sam a cut on his finger which he said was from shrapnel the day they crossed the paddy at Hoengsong.

"Do you think this will get me out of here?" he asked.

"Rude, I've already told O'Bannion no one was hit that day," Sam said.

"By golly, I've got to do something, Sam. I can't stand this anymore," he said innocuously.

While Rude was on watch, Baxter came over to talk with them. Sam was down in the tunnel part of the hole. Rude told Baxter that Sam was asleep. He had almost been, so he lay for a while. Baxter talked to Rude for a while and was about to leave when he saw that Rude was barefooted.

"Why Rude, where are your shoes?" he asked.

"Well, by golly," Rude said. "I forgot to put them on."

"How could you forget something like that?" Baxter asked softly.

"I just did," Rude said.

When Baxter left, Sam said, "Rude, you can't freeze your feet if the temperature is above freezing."

The remarkable thing about Rude was that he never caused anything to happen. Sam could not remember seeing him fire his rifle. He went where they went, but he didn't do what they did. What Rude did was suffer. He never once packed to march anywhere that his poncho or something else was not hanging loose. If it was cold, snot froze in his mustache. His speech usually began with, "By golly." He was from Minnesota and had experienced cold weather, yet he failed to understand you couldn't freeze your feet at thirty-seven degrees Fahrenheit. Sam felt sorry for him. He did not attempt to change him.

A day later, news came that others were being sent home on rotation. No one seemed to know who it would be and they were left to speculate. It seemed to Sam it should be done in some way that would let a person know how he stood, but no such ever was announced.

Then, Baxter came around saying good-bye. They had been friends since Sam had first met him in San Diego, and they had had many long serious conversations.

"Sam, I'll never forget you coming down the street in Seoul with the door to carry me," he said.

Sam grinned at him. "Nor will I," he said.

"There's something else, Sam. You should never forget you've lived up to the highest tradition of the Marine Corps. You're one of the real Marines Sam, and you know it."

Sam smiled at him. No response was called for. What he said gave Sam a feeling of well being. After all that had happened, he was still an idealist. Being told he was a real Marine was a compliment.

"When you go home you don't have to tell anyone what you've done out here," Baxter said gently.

"Why is that?" Sam asked.

"Because you know." He put emphasis on the word 'you.' "—*You know*, and that's enough. I'll tell you something else. The day you led the charge across the rice paddy at Hoengsong took guts. You know it, and so does everyone else. So you don't ever have to tell anyone about it."

"Do me a favor," Sam said. "Loan me your forty-five. You won't need it and it might make the difference in my surviving or not."

Without a word Baxter unstrapped his shoulder holster and handed it to Sam. Sam strapped it on.

"Now I've got two weapons that use the same bullets," Sam said, grinning at him.

He gripped Sam's hand. "May God bless you Sam." And then he walked away, without looking back.

That same day, Captain Cronk, who had presided at Sam's court-martial, was rotated to the United States. Lieutenant Von Ludwig was promoted to captain, and transferred to Cronk's company as Company Commander.

CHAPTER 30 ... Footsteps in the Dark ...

It was late February. The battalion on their left was still fighting to take the bunkers which were holding up the advance. After being repulsed several times, they brought a tank forward which had a 90mm gun. They laid a shell right in the slot of the bunker which had been the toughest to take and blew it away.

In the early morning, during a steady rain, Fox Company moved out in column, five to ten yards apart, trying not to let the rain interfere with watching for the enemy. This took discipline. It was easy to be looking down, to escape the rain, when you should be looking right and left to avoid being ambushed. They marched all day without any slackening in the downpour. When night came, they halted in a pea field, formed a perimeter, and dug holes. It was still raining. Even as they dug, the holes filled with water and stayed full. Sam scooped out a hole two feet wide, one foot deep and six feet long. He lay down in it and displaced the water over the sides of the hole. There was no escaping it. Nothing could be kept dry. Finally, he lay beside the hole. At least, that way, he wasn't soaking in the cold water. He placed his weapons on the ground and tried to sleep.

Next morning, with the rain still coming down, they saddled up and continued marching. About ten o'clock the rain stopped and the wind picked up and gradually dried their clothes as they marched. By nightfall they were almost dry. They dug in again and struck out next morning. Finally, they reached a large low hill.

Some rocket trucks pulled in behind them and loosed several racks of rockets that were all up in the air at one time and then crashed like thunder on the hill in front of them. Three tanks pulled up abreast and they spread out as skirmishers on both sides of the tanks and began an assault on the hill. Some rifle fire was coming, but they kept moving. Here and there you would see someone fall down, hit by the fire that was coming at them.

Sam came upon Blackfoot, the runner. He was down on the ground on his knees in front of a depression in the earth which was too small to give him any protection. He looked as if he was trying to make himself smaller. His eyes were wide with fear, and Sam saw that the popping of the enemy rifles and occasional man falling had literally terrified him. He was crouched on his hands and knees. Sam stopped and stood looking down at him.

"What are you doing, Blackie?" he asked.

Blackfoot looked back and didn't answer. He was not doing anything.

"Come on boy. Get up. You can't stay here," Sam said.

He stared at Sam, his eyes wild with fear. With his eyes he spoke what he did not dare utter, "—Why don't you just leave me alone?"

"You can get killed just as easy where you are, Blackie," Sam said "Besides, they might court-martial you for cowardice. You wouldn't want that would you?"

He shook his head negatively, got up and started forward. A tank caught up to Sam and rolled past.

WHOOM!

A roar of sound pushed Sam sideways and knocked him down. A big steel wheel sailed through the air and fell in front of him. Black smoke poured out of one of the tanks. He got to his feet and approached the tank. The hatch popped open and the crew scrambled out. An anti-tank mine had torn away part of the track. Seeing they were unhurt, Sam kept going. The crew stayed with their tank. Sam envied them. The sound of fire on both right and left increased and they moved forward a little faster. They reached the crest at a fast trot and the firing died away.

They climbed the next hill, which was so huge they could not defend the entire hill, and dug a perimeter which left a ridge to the west, including one knob, unoccupied. To the south, a tremendous hill looked down on their position, from a thousand yards away.

The earth was still frozen three inches deep. Sam dug in at the crest of the hill where the spine led from the knob down the path to his position. He dug a one-man hole and had Arkie dig in Rude, his BAR man, right in front of him, but at about three feet lower elevation. A worn footpath led from the knob down the spine to his position. This appeared to Sam like the place where an attack would come from. By interrupting the path with the two foxholes, It became a defense in depth. Sam had his hole one and a half feet deep, two feet wide and six feet long when Joe Goggins stopped him.

"Sam, de lieutenant say fo you to take yo squad downhill a way. He wants my squad on this path. I sho does like that hole you been diggin fo me."

"Joe you black slave," Sam said.

Joe laughed gleefully. "I sho figured this move out. Yessuh. That hole you jus dug is mine."

Sam pretended to be angry, cursed a little, and then moved his squad downhill. "Joe, you better put a BAR man in that hole in front of you. If they hit us they'll come right down that path," he said.

Sam didn't like the looks of the new position. A small finger of earth extended out ten yards in front of the main line. It had to be occupied. He decided to dig another hole right at the tip of the finger and occupy it himself.

The night passed uneventfully. Morning came and Sam waited five minutes after the men had gotten up and began to stir around, then he got up and began trading C rations.

Rose had a can of sausage patties and gravy he would trade for a can of peaches. Sam walked over and exchanged cans with Rose. They stood about three feet apart. From somewhere far off, Sam heard the hollow sound of a mortar leaving the tube. A moment later, he heard the rustle of dry oak leaves, heard the impact of the shell, and looked down. A four inch diameter hole appeared in the earth and white smoke curled up. No need to leap away. A single mortar shell had come within eighteen inches of each of them, broke through the crust and exploded in the soft dirt below.

While they were considering the near miss, word came that Rose was to report to the Company CP and Rose left.

A few minutes later two Korean women came down the path and Jackson intercepted them, questioned them for a few minutes, and released them to pass through the position.

A working party came back from battalion and brought some mail. They had a mail call and, while they were reading letters from home, Rose returned. He could not conceal the big grin on his face.

"I'm going home boys," he said, smiling broadly at his comrades.

"Home," Erickson said. "How'd you do that?"

Rose grinned at him. "When I saw Causey do it I decided I could too. I just made out my application."

"Then you're not goin' yet," Erickson said.

"No, but I'm sure it'll be approved," Rose said.

Sam thought about the shell that had narrowly missed. It was a white phosphorus shell which, had it exploded above ground, would have killed both him and Rose. Small wonder Rose was happy. By a stroke of fate he had escaped being burned to death. It seemed to Sam that it was unnatural for all, so young as they were, to be living each moment on the verge of sudden violent death.

February yielded to March and found them still on the same hill. Almost every day a platoon-sized patrol would go out and scout for the Chinese, but they saw no sign of them.

Replacements came and two were assigned to Sam's squad. One was a tall slender youth from Philadelphia, named Joe Walsh. He was blond and blue-eyed with freckles. His father had passed away while he was on the ship coming over, and he had not learned of his father's death until two weeks afterward. On his first patrol Walsh volunteered to walk the point and Sam let him do it. He seemed to be observant and to possess a lot of courage.

The other replacement, a lanky hotel clerk from Austin, Texas, named Apelt, was twenty-eight years old and a veteran of World War Two. The day he arrived, he told Sam he wanted to talk to him privately. They walked a few feet away from the foxholes.

"Sam," he said, "all the way over, all I heard was how bad this war is. I decided I wouldn't listen to any rumors. I would wait till I got here and ask someone who knew. They tell me you've been here since Inchon."

"That's right," Sam said.

"Tell me. Just how bad is this war?"

Sam wanted to give a reasonable answer, but he wasn't sure there was one.

"It's the only war I've ever been to. So I'm in doubt about what to tell you. It's not a bad war, as wars go, but has there ever been an easy one?" Sam said.

Instantly, he saw Apelt wasn't satisfied. So he said, "We've been lucky. Just hope our luck holds out."

"Then you're saying that it isn't such a bad war," he said.

"I'm saying it could be worse," Sam said.

Apelt seemed satisfied.

A day or two after the replacements arrived came an especially dark night. It was so dark you couldn't see your hand in front of your face. Sam was thirty yards downhill from the hole Goggins had taken from him and could barely see the silhouette of the ridge that led into it. He and George

Baker, who had replaced Jennings as squad leader, had strung trip flares in front, but they failed to string one across the ridge because it would be like stringing a wire across the top of the capital letter A. This proved to be a mistake. It left the path leading into their position unprotected. Anyone who attacked straight down the path would not hit a trip flare.

Sam peered out into the darkness. Had he heard something or was it his imagination? He listened intently. All was quiet. Then he heard a sound like a flock of quail taking flight.

What was that?

Too late!

It was the sound of many running footsteps in the dark.

WA WA WA WOwww!

From a hundred yards out a Chinese machine gun split the darkness with a short burst of fire and tracers streamed through the air at the hole Goggins had taken. They had set up a machine gun on the knob and, in the darkness, they used the earth Sam had piled around the hole to sight in their machine gun. Sam had made the mistake of digging it on the skyline at the end of the path. As the Chinese came in, their machine gunners triggered short bursts of two to four rounds.

Joe Goggins had followed Sam's advice and put Villa, his BAR man, in the hole in front. Poncho Villa heard the footsteps coming and pulled the trigger on his BAR.

When Villa fired, the machine gun found him. Two bullets struck him in the face, just below his left eye and pulled him up out of his sleeping bag. As he came up, two more bullets struck him in the chest. A terrible scream broke out of him as he came right up out of his hole and into the hole beside him, which was occupied by Dunmore and Kuhn. He fell across Dunmore, threw his arms about him, splashed him with blood, and with a terrible shudder sank to the bottom of the hole.

Dunmore screamed!—A terrible scream which rent the air as if it had come from an animal. He jerked loose from Villa and cowered over against the side of the hole moaning incoherently, then went into shock and became catatonic.

Sixteen-year-old Kuhn was firing his rifle as fast as he could pull the trigger and cursing. Hand grenades fell like rain and in the flashes of the explosions Sam saw Chinese running towards the point and fanning out to hit the line broadside. They hit and threw hand grenades at the same time. A dozen more explosions lit the night. One landed in the hole with Kuhn. He didn't look for it. His right hand went down, found it immediately, hurled it back at the man who had thrown it, and kept on firing and cursing. Mortars and hand grenades were raining down.

That single mortar shell the Chinese had put between Sam and Rose was to get the range and now they had it.

Out in front, their machine gun chopped away. In the darkness, their grenades went too far, and instead of killing 2nd Platoon, went over their heads and bounced in on O'Bannion. He got up and ran a few yards.

A grenade landed in the hole with Taylor. He threw it back. A second grenade landed and blew him out of the hole. Miraculously, he got fragments only in his hand and arm. He kept on fighting.

The platoon was hurling grenades and firing as Chinese came rushing in, illuminated by the yellow flashes of exploding grenades. One of 2nd Platoon's machine guns was set to fire at the knob, but the gunner saw the Chinese about to overrun 2nd Platoon's line. He reached out, picked up the tripod of his gun, replaced it, and fired straight down the line. The fire from this machine gun kept Sam pinned in the hole out on the finger. He kept his head down as the fire came across.

Joe Goggins finally left the hole he had taken from Sam. He ran to the platoon CP and grabbed a case of hand grenades. He came back with the case of fifty hand grenades and hurled them all.

O'Bannion got the artillery on the phone and the wounded tigers began to shrill overhead and fall on the knob in front. The sounds became a din of noise. Machine guns from both sides chopped and sawed away and mingled in with the mortars falling on Marines and artillery falling on Chinese, coming low overhead, whining through the air, and in the interludes between explosions you could hear O'Bannion's calm voice directing fire, saying, "Left fifty; drop fifty."

The wounded tigers passed overhead and fell like a firestorm on the ridge in front. More mortars fell, there were sharp blasts from a whistle as Marine machine guns fired long bursts, while grenades went both ways in a crescendo of noise. They fought for two hours. Then it stopped as suddenly as it began.

In the darkness, Joe Goggins knelt down beside Sam's hole.
"Sam!"
Sam could barely see him, though he lay less than three feet away.
"Yeah," Sam said, clutching Baxter's pistol.
"Sam, that hole you dug was the point of the whole attack."
"Who got hit, Joe?"
"Villa's dead. Taylor's hurt. Dunmore gone crazy. How about you?"
"We're all okay."

Joe said, "Man those bullets was jus poppin' through that soft dirt. I tried to get my bayonet on my carbine and I couldn't. So I quit trying. I jus lay there with my bayonet in my hand and listening to those feet running. If one hop in my hole I was gwine rise up to meet him, but when their machine gun quit I got outta that hole fast."

"You wanted it, Joe."

"Poor Villa," Joe said.

It began to grow light out. After a few minutes, Sam climbed out of his hole and went over to take a last look at Villa. They had dragged him out of the hole. Now he lay beside it. In death he didn't look like himself. Sam couldn't see his big toothy grin, and Villa had turned darker. Sam remembered Villa shoving the old Korean. Now, he couldn't help but wonder whether Villa had sensed his own death.

It got a little lighter out. Sam went out in front of the line to check the bodies for living. Petitt followed. Several dead Chinese lay just eight or ten feet in front of the holes, and the earth was littered with the strings from Chinese grenades. The strings were so close to the line they had thrown most of the grenades over Marine heads. Most of the bodies had been carried away, but in the darkness they failed to get them all.

One of the dead soldiers was really arrogant looking. Even in death, he had a mean look. He was lying on his back. His right hand was extended in the air in front of his face. His left hand was down across his waist. His lips were curled back in a snarl. Petitt stuck a cigarette in the soldiers mouth. In the left hand, Petitt placed an opened book of matches, in the right hand, a single match. Petitt backed away and smiled down at the dead soldier who looked as if he were lighting a cigarette. It was really weird. Petitt was becoming twisted. The broad grin on his face showed a peculiar delight in what he had done. Sam marveled at Petitt's conduct, which he thought odd. At the same time, he was unaware of any change in himself. Sam felt nothing. He was looking for any who might be alive. The gentleness had left him. He was not the same person he once had been and he was unaware of it. Ice water flowed in his veins.

CHAPTER 31 ... In the Trenches ...

An almost imperceptible change took place in the war. Those who did the fighting cared little for policy and knew little about it. In the higher levels, there was no longer any thought of unifying Korea under one government. At the combatant level the only chance to learn what was transpiring at the United Nations were letters from home, which did not usually mention war policy. The platoon had only Joe Goggins's Kiplinger Letter. Most held a narrow view. There were two worlds. One was the world of the diplomats, where the two sides did not even dare slap each other with white gloves, the other was the platoon's world, where they killed each other on sight. The enthusiastic zeal for killing the enemies of their country gave way to a struggle for survival. The attitude of the men towards the Chinese began to change. They began to view the Chinese soldiers as somewhat like themselves, suffering the daily shocks and hardships of war, caught between two governments. If it were left to those who were doing the fighting, they could have sat down and drunk beer together and compared experiences. They didn't feel that way about the North Koreans. The North Koreans had always seemed unusually cruel, and the Marines' view of them remained that way.

The Chinese held the initiative and the Americans and United Nations were struggling to contain them. A series of daily patrols took place. Each day they went out, drew some kind of enemy fire, usually snipers, but there were no heavy exchanges. One day they went on patrol along the ridge tops, keeping to the high ground, and about two miles from their perimeter they reached the crest of a high hill enabling them to have visibility for miles. They lined along the crest and lay down. In the valley below, they saw massive columns of Chinese infantry marching four abreast and extending back for hundreds of yards. As far back as they could see, the road was full of them. They were making no attempt whatever to disperse and it was as if they had no fear at all of air attack. They were on a narrow road and their column curved with the road like a huge brown lazy snake. When Sam first saw them, he immediately expected Corsairs to come over and bomb them.

O'Bannion came running along the ridge.

"Get back! Get back!" he said. "Don't let them see you."

Sam crawled away from the ridge line from which he had been watching.

"We've got to get back to camp. If those chinks see us we're goners," O'Bannion said.

They hurried back. There had been enough Chinese that if Fox Company had opened fire it would have been overwhelmed. This single episode of getting a real clear look at the massive numbers of the enemy made the idea of fighting the Chinese style of war ludicrous. How do you beat someone at his own game when he has a hundred times more men than you? Apparently they had not seen the Marines, because they did not attack. In a strange twist of events they were holding to the road while Americans held the hills.

The morning after, Sam woke to a loud scream. He looked out to see Walsh running down the hill as fast as his legs would carry him. Arkie was right behind him. Arkie had his trench knife out and was swinging at the back of Walsh's neck, barely missing him. Walsh outran him.

Normally, Arkie was even tempered, but he was becoming more and more irritable. Sam inquired what was wrong. Walsh had just gotten on his nerves.

The war was beginning to get to Arkie. Whenever they would be told the 2nd Platoon had patrol duty, Arkie would begin to bitch vehemently.

"You would think this was the only goddam platoon in the division," he would say.

All Marines bitch, but not insubordinately, and Arkie directed his bitching directly at the officers. He was becoming as grouchy as an old man who had lived an unhappy life. Arkie was Sam's best fire team leader and Sam relied on him. Sam began to be concerned.

On one of the company-sized patrols they approached an aged Korean who was driving a cart pulled by a bullock. The old man had a leather whip in his hand and Munson, a Marine from the first squad, snatched the whip from the old man's hand and began to whip him with it. Sam intervened.

"Quit it," he said. "You've no cause to be using a whip on him."

Munson was defiant. His blue eyes glinted with meanness. He just wanted to be cruel.

"The hell I don't. I've just as much right to whip him as he has to whip the bullock."

"The bullock is an animal."

Munson pointed to the old man. "So is he," he said.

As was the usual case, he did not continue to whip the old man. Always, whenever Sam interceded, it left the offender angry at him and Sam angry at the futility of it. To Sam, the constant cruelty exhibited towards the people they had allegedly come to help made the whole endeavor futile. Baxter and he were the only two people who had ever intervened in such conduct. Captain Groff set the example in Japan when he drove the Japanese mess cook out of the line. Thereafter, no one was ever intimidated from maltreating civilians.

On that same march they entered a small South Korean village and began checking to see if it was occupied. Sam pushed open the door to a hut and found three Korean men, dressed in white pantaloons, lying on the floor, pretending to be asleep. Sam prodded one with his bayonet and he immediately sat up with his eyes wide open. The other two then sat up. Sam motioned them to go outside and Jackson interrogated them. Jackson became satisfied they were civilians and Sam was going to turn them loose, but the squad persuaded him they should load the Koreans with firewood and have them carry it to the top of the big hill they were preparing to climb. It was always hard to find firewood to heat food with, since every place they camped was soon picked bare, so Sam agreed.

Lewellyn found three A-frames, loaded the Koreans with firewood, and preceded to climb the hill behind the three. It was a steep hill which had to be climbed diagonally, and it took over two hours to ascend. No sooner had they reached the top than word came they should come back down. Sam allowed the Koreans to unload the wood and go back without loads. When they reached the bottom, Sam said, "Let's give them some C rations for their work." The men agreed, handed over some food in payment for services, and left the three beside the road.

Obviously, a big change in plans took place because they marched for about fifteen miles and well into the night. They reached the objective and began digging in. Another company passed them. They had taken the same three Koreans, taken their food away, loaded each one down with three men's gear, and marched them the entire distance.

A little later, the three came back past Sam empty-handed and headed back towards their home. One of them had a bloody nose.

The whole incident bothered Sam. The constant mistreatment of the people they had been sent to help was always on his mind. Next day, while eating breakfast, he brought the subject up.

"You guys wonder why people don't understand Americans?"

Erickson grinned at him. No one said anything.

"I'll tell you why. A company of Marines passes an old Korean. The first guy feels sorry for him and gives him food. The next guy says to himself, if it weren't for that old son of a bitch, I wouldn't be in this God-forsaken country. So he goes over and hits the old man in the face and bloodies his nose. The next guy is kind and says look at that poor old Korean, so he gives him some more food. The next guy kicks him. The man after that gives him food. After the company passes the old man is standing there. He's had the shit beat out of him for nothing, and he has an arm load of chow. How's he supposed to understand Americans?"

They just looked at Sam.

"If you want to mistreat someone, let it be the enemy," Sam said.

Before they finished eating, Jennings came around.

"I want one man from your squad to stay behind and guard supplies," he said.

"What's happening?"

"We're going so far out in the boonies that trucks can't follow, so someone will have to be left behind for a week or so to guard our gear. There'll be several, but I only want one from your squad."

"Arkie," Sam said, "that's you."

Arkie's facial expression did not change. "If you say so Sam!" he said. He did not show any enthusiasm.

Rude spoke up. "By golly, if he doesn't want to I'd like to stay behind."

"No," Sam said, "we're going to leave Arkie. He needs a rest before he cuts someone's throat, or mails a hand grenade to Mrs. Finwilly."

The men began to laugh and Arkie managed a sheepish grin.

"Oh," Jennings said, "from now on two machine gun crews will be a part of the Second Platoon. You'll have one with your squad. We're gonna move out in a few minutes."

"Where to?"

"I'm damned if I know," Jennings said. "Some unknown hill someplace." He looked out into the distance. They were in a valley and all about were an endless range of mountains. The valley led off to the west and Sam assumed that would be their direction.

As they waited to move, Joe Goggins came around saying good-bye. At first, Sam thought Goggins was kidding; then he saw he was serious. He was being sent to the rear.

"How do you rate that?" Sam asked.

Joe gave him a big grin. "They said I wasn't even supposed to be up here. I was trained as a cook, not infantry."

Sam took his hand. "Take care of yourself, Joe." To his surprise, Sam had tears in his eyes.

"Sam, you watch out for those gooks, you hear?"

He left on the same truck which took Arkie and some of the others who had been assigned to the guard detail.

Taylor was one of these. Ever since the grenade had exploded in his hole, grenade fragments had been working their way out of his arm and hand.

They were becoming like a big family. Each time one would be sent somewhere you immediately wondered whether or not you would ever see him again. In a normal situation if a friend or brother departed for the grocery store you would think nothing of it. In their situation, the truck they rode on might hit a mine or be ambushed or any one of hundreds of mishaps might occur to take their lives or yours. Every moment of their lives was on the precipice of eternity.

They moved out and headed west as Sam had presumed. For two or three days they climbed high hills so high they had to be traversed at an angle. They dug in each night in a temporary defensive perimeter. Each day they came under sniper fire. It was as if the Chinese were just keeping them under observation as they wound deeper and deeper into the mountains. Each hill they began to climb would force the question of who might be killed there. Petitt grew increasingly uptight. He expected to be killed each day when he woke. There was not an optimistic bone in his body. When the war had begun Petitt had left the Navy base at Scotia, New York, in company with Jennings and three other Marines. Now, the other three were dead. Only he and Jennings had survived. Sam tried to reassure him whenever he could.

They went down the far side of a big hill and entered into another valley. Sam's squad was leading and Joe Walsh had the point. Far behind, Sam saw the Confederate flag, and wondered about the logic of the situation. He was picking the way to go and didn't know where he was going. By instinct, he tried to find a route that would provide some cover in the event they were shot at. Sam reached a hill used as a Korean cemetery where the dead are buried sitting up and facing downhill. Instead of in a hole, they are placed in mounds of earth about three feet high and ten feet in diameter at the base. The mounds would provide cover, so Sam led the way through the cemetery and began ascending the hill beyond. As they climbed the hill he could see another hill on either side of it. As they went up, the squad spread out as skirmishers.

Petitt was on his left and Apelt on his right. They got within a hundred feet of the crest without being shot at. Sam sought to reassure Petitt.

"Looks like we've got it made on this one."

No sooner had he said this, when a sporadic burst of fire came at them. To Sam's astonishment, Rose turned and ran all the way to the bottom of the hill and leaped behind a grave mound.

"Rose!" Sam shouted, "get your ass back up here!"

He didn't come and it made Sam very angry. There was a chatter of gunfire all about. Everyone else had gone to ground and were firing at the enemy, but Sam was standing up and cursing Rose. Rose stuck his head out from behind a grave mound.

"Did you call me, Sam?"

"Get your ass back up here!"

Rose started back. Apelt called out to Sam.

"Sam, if you don't get down, you're gonna get shot for sure!"

"They're not shootin' at me," Sam said.

A bullet clipped a one-inch limb off a small pine beside him less than two feet away and he went to ground beside Apelt. Apelt was firing at the hill on the right and Sam could see several Chinese on it in trenches. Those on the hill above were throwing hand grenades downhill at the squad. These were popping like firecrackers on the Fourth of July. Sam looked at the hill on the left. The 1st Platoon had come forward and were beginning to attack it. Sam shouted orders to the squad dividing their fire, having some fire at the left hill, Apelt at the right hill, and the others firing at the hill in front.

Petitt saw that Rude wasn't firing. He reached for the BAR.

"Here give me that BAR," he said.

Rude passed it over and began feeding him ammo magazines.

Apelt didn't like the situation.

"Sam I ain't trying to tell you what to do, but those gooks can come bouncing over that hill any minute and there ain't enough of us here to stop em," he said.

A soldier popped up out of a foxhole in front with a burp gun and a stream of bullets struck the ground around Sam and Apelt. Two hit between Sam's legs. He saw instantly Apelt was right.

"Cover me. I'm going back for a machine gun," Sam said. He leaped up and ran back. When he got to the bottom of the hill, he found the rest of the platoon hiding behind the mounds.

"I'm taking a machine gun up," he told Jennings.

"What's happening?"

"We got gooks in front. We're being shot at from two sides and in front."

"Take a bazooka too," Jennings said.

Sam found the machine gun squad and a bazooka team.

"You guys follow me," he said. He turned and loped back up the hill hunched down low to avoid the fire, with the machine gun crew strung out behind him.

When Sam reached Apelt he was still firing at the soldiers on the right ridge. Sam went to ground and motioned for the machine gunners to set up beside him. He pointed at the ridge line in front and uphill. Petitt opened up with the BAR and cut down some bushes.

A brown hand came up out of the ground and replanted one of the bushes.

"Did you see that?" Petitt shouted.

He was becoming very excited. The gunners were setting up and hadn't seen it.

"Every fifth round in my carbine is a tracer." Sam told them. "Just watch my tracers and I'll mark your target." He aimed and fired at the earth where the hand had come up and watched two tracers arc into the position. McChann was on the gun and Marvin Childers, from Texas, was feeding the belt. They began to traverse the ridge with short bursts of fire. The ammo carriers had been lugging the ammo all day and seemed anxious to get rid of it. They brought can after can up to be fired.

They were in a situation where they must do more than use up ammo. The enemy was popping up and down and firing bursts of burp gun fire, but couldn't stay up long enough to aim, so they were missing. Sam sent one of the ammo carriers back to tell Jennings that he was going to assault the hill, and when Jennings heard the bazooka fire he should be prepared to follow up.

"Second squad!" Sam shouted. "When I give the word we're going up!"

He crawled over to the bazooka team. The machine gun fire was still sweeping the ridge. They had cut a lot of bushes down and exposed a mound of earth that seemed to indicate where there was a bunker. Sam showed it to the bazooka man with a tracer. "Right there," he said. "When I yell charge you put a round right there."

He looked around. The squad was ready.

"Charge!" he screamed and started up the slope. The bazooka fired. They went up shooting from the hip, screaming rebel yells, and the Chinese began to leap up and run for it.

Petitt emptied a BAR magazine at a soldier as the soldier disappeared over the ridge. In a few seconds they reached the trench. Petitt leaped into it and began running to the right. Sam hit the same trench, saw Erickson going left, and followed Petitt down the trench to the right. Petitt was in a frenzy. The trench opened into a round hole with several dead Chinese in it. One was leaning back against the back of the hole. Although he was erect, his head had been shot off so that only his neck and a portion of one jaw remained. Petitt screamed and lunged at him. At the same moment, several Chinese ran down the back side. Sam emptied his carbine into them.

Petitt was hysterical. He had the soldier by the neck, shaking him, laughing hysterically, while the soldier's blood splashed all over him as he shook the man. Sam grabbed Petitt.

"Turn him loose!" he cried, but Petitt kept shaking the soldier until Sam struck him.

"Don't do that," Sam said quietly. "It's alright. We have the hill."

Behind them, the rest of the platoon was moving up the hill and occupying the trenches they had taken.

The Chinese frequently zeroed positions which they held and after giving up the position would begin dropping mortar fire on it. On a gut hunch, Sam avoided the trenches, moved his squad seventy-five yards to the right and began digging in. Within five minutes mortars were raining down on the trenches they had taken. One Marine, a replacement in the third squad, had a mortar land between his legs, splitting him right up the middle like two sides of beef.

Word came up to pull back off the hill, and they gave it up and started back down. Sam met Lieutenant O'Bannion on the way down.

"I guess it got pretty hot up there, did it Sam?" he said.

"Yessir it did. We got shot at from three sides." He was feeling the excitement of being still alive after one more event. It was like being invincible.

"No it was four," Apelt said, correcting him. "Some sniper was shooting at us from the rear."

CHAPTER 32 ... Death, Pencils, and Green Flies ...

Sam did not spend a lot of time trying to discover the details of just who it was who had engineered the plot to double-cross him. He was too busy with leading the squad and trying to survive. Yet, certain thoughts would come to him at the least expected times. In the stillness of one long night of peering out towards the enemy, Sam came to the conclusion the Battalion Commander, Colonel Sutter, had learned from Lieutenant O'Bannion the platoon was willing to testify at his court-martial. Sam reasoned that the night O'Bannion had picked Causey and Lewellyn up and given them a ride to the pea field, he learned what the situation was. It made sense. O'Bannion had been Battalion Intelligence Officer and as such he would have had the colonel's ear.

But, Sam never learned all the truth of who had masterminded the plot to persuade him not to fight the court-martial. He held no animosity towards O'Bannion. Sam thought he was the best platoon leader they ever had—not because he was a leader, but because he was decent; he was human. Soon after Villa was killed, O'Bannion was transferred. Sam hated to see him go.

O'Bannion had promised him his stripes back and as yet not fulfilled his promise. Oddly, it didn't seem to matter any longer. Sam had found his niche as a squad leader and he concentrated on doing his job.

One dark night he was dug in with Petitt. He always tried to encourage Petitt to be positive. Sam was somewhere between wakefulness and sleep, almost asleep.

Petitt woke suddenly and called out to him.

"Sam!"

Half asleep, Sam didn't answer.

Now wide-awake, Petitt was really alarmed. He called out again, excitedly. "Sam?"

Now fully awake, Sam answered.

"What is it Petitt?"

"Who's on watch here?" Petitt demanded.

Sam realized that he had been on the verge of falling asleep on watch and could tell from the urgency of Petitt's voice that Petitt was extremely distraught. As always, he sought to calm him. Petitt did not know about Sam's dream, but Sam always did. It never left him.

"Petitt," Sam said, "there's something I've been meaning to ask you."

Petitt ignored the question. He was going to insist on an answer. "Who's on watch?" he demanded again.

Sam here saw that he was very anxious.

"Do you believe in the lord, Jesus Christ?" Sam asked quietly.

"Sure, sure. what's that got to do with it?" Petitt said.

"Well, *he's* on watch" Sam said, "now shut up and go back to sleep."

When morning came a new Platoon Leader, a young Irishman from Boston named O'Curry, arrived. He called the platoon together for a get-acquainted session. He brought three fifths of whiskey and gave one to each squad. After the whiskey was distributed, he began.

"Men, I've come up to take over leadership of this platoon. I'm well aware you've been fighting the Koreans and Chinese communists for several months and you know more about it than I do. Nevertheless, I want all of you to know all you've got to do is lay down the overhead fire and I'll take the hills. I talked with Chesty Puller when I came through Regimental Headquarters and I informed him of my desire to win the Congressional Medal of Honor. I understand one of you, a bazooka man named Monegan, has already won the Medal of Honor. Is that right?"

"Yessir," someone said.

"Where is he?"

"He's dead, Sir."

"Oh, I see," O'Curry said.

After an embarrassed silence, he turned to Jennings.

"Are all squad leaders here?"

Jennings nodded affirmatively.

"Alright, I'd like to meet them," O'Curry said.

Jennings introduced him. He got to Sam last.

"This is Psycho Sam Lewis," Jennings said.

O'Curry gave Sam an odd, sort of curious look. It was something Sam sensed, but couldn't quite put his finger on. Sam silently shook hands with him. He could see O'Curry wanted to talk with him, but Sam was keeping his distance. Combat and the treachery of the court-martial had lessened Sam's regard for officers. O'Curry sounded as if he might get them all killed.

Captain Groff had ensured, by his method of command, that without exception the tactical decisions in combat were made by squad leaders. They were the keys to defeat or victory at the platoon level, and the meaning of victory was to live. Sam didn't need a platoon leader. The platoon leader needed him.

Next morning they went on patrol and climbed a tremendous hill. O'Curry was leading as they moved out and led for some time, but as they began to ascend the hill he grew weary and fell back. Gradually, the men passed him up. Sam was bringing up the rear and caught up with O'Curry. He was down on the ground breathing like a horse that had been run to hard.

"I thought I was in shape," he said, puffing heavily.

"We're like mountain goats, Lieutenant; it takes a month of this before you'll be able to keep up," Sam said.

He went past and looked back. O'Curry was struggling to keep up. The entire platoon had passed him up.

O'Curry's saving grace, which kept him from being known as lard ass number two, was that he readily admitted he wasn't in physical condition.

The hill O'Curry cut his teeth on became Rose's last hill. His hardship discharge came through. He could not conceal the joy he felt as he came around to say good-bye.

"Home!" he cried, laughing gleefully, "Home!"

The good-byes were getting harder on those who were staying behind. The contrast between the person leaving and those staying was stark. The one leaving had a pardon from death row. The ones who stayed inched closer to the executioner. Ivan Jennings summed it up. "All you can get from war is killed or wounded," he said.

The original company became known as the Inchon men. The Inchon men grew scarce, and it remained to be seen whether or not one would survive long enough to be rotated.

Rose's departure left Sam without a fire team leader.

He had been impressed with Apelt's coolness under fire and the advice Apelt had given him, so Sam approached him about taking over Rose's fire team. Apelt seemed hesitant.

"What's the matter Apelt, don't you want the job?"

"Sam, the day I joined this outfit I asked you what kind of war this was and you said it wasn't a bad war. Well, if you think this isn't a bad war, I'd like to know what you think a bad war is!"

"You're still alive, aren't you?" Sam said.

"Yes, but I've been here thirty-nine days and there hasn't been a single day we haven't been shot at. I want you to hold up on me leading a fire team. I don't feel up to that yet."

"Okay, Apelt," Sam said. His attitude puzzled Sam.

A day or two later, when the morning sun was warming the hills, they moved out and Apelt began to lag behind. Sam fell back in the column and let Apelt catch up with him.

"What's the matter, Apelt?" he said.

"It's my feet. They're killing me."

"Corpsman!" Sam called to Doyer. "Have a look at Apelt's feet."

"What's wrong with them?" Doyer asked Apelt.

"They've give out. I can't walk."

"Take off your shoes," Doyer said.

Apelt took his shoes and socks off. Doyer knelt down and looked at his feet.

"Wiggle your toes," he said.

Apelt wiggled his toes.

"You don't have any blisters," Doyer said.

"But I can't walk," Apelt said.

Doyer looked at Sam. "They're ain't nothin' wrong with his feet. Maybe it's in his head."

"What do you say?" Sam asked Apelt.

"If he says it's in my head, then it's in my head."

Doyer took out a red tag. He wrote on the tag, "This man claims he can't walk." Apelt turned and walked back down the column. Sam never saw him again.

About two weeks later, some Marine who had been wounded came back up. He was from another company, but he came over to Fox Company and asked for Sam Lewis. It was late afternoon when he found Sam and he brought a six pack of Coor's beer. "A fellow named Apelt sent this up to you. He said to tell you he's on his way to Texas."

Sam was grateful for the beer, but began to wonder just what it was that Apelt had done to be sent home. It didn't make sense that a man could just complain his feet hurt and he would be removed from combat.

Next day, Arkie returned. It was like old home week for a few minutes. He was glad to find all of the squad alive and unhurt and they began telling him about the big fight he had missed.

The days passed by, and as they did, Sam noticed Joe Walsh was having trouble with his bowels. He was still volunteering to walk point and Sam was allowing him to, but he was stopping to move his bowels every thirty minutes or so. Then they stopped moving for a day, and it looked as if they might not be moving right away, so Sam insisted that Walsh go to the battalion aid station and find out if they could give him anything for his dysentery. Two days later, he came back.

"Sam this is good-bye," he said, sticking out his hand.

"They took x-rays of my stomach and they say I'm ruined."

"Ruined?"

"Yes. The doctor said he had never seen so many ulcers in one stomach. He says my whole stomach is a mass of ulcers. They wanted to send me right away, but I persuaded them to let me come back and get my gear. I wanted to tell you good-bye and good luck."

Sam shook hands with him. "I'll miss you boy," he said, his eyes misting over. He watched Walsh walk away. He was just a slender freckled-faced kid with clear blue eyes and a lot of courage who seemed somehow far younger than the rest of them.

A sort of clan developed. The Inchon men began to exclude the others from their daily conversations, but as time wore on, they became fewer and fewer. And they had changed. In those first few days they all had the notion they would whip the North Koreans and go back home to a big parade and celebration, and then it became home by Christmas, and then that vanished. They had come to this land in all the ignorance and enthusiasm of youth and now were old beyond their years. When someone laughed, it was a laugh without mirth, more hard and cynical than anything else. They developed a tolerant scorn of almost everything on earth.

On one of the high hills they were compelled to dig in in a pine grove that was below the crest and not a good position. As Sam was placing the automatic weapons for the night one of the machine gunners came over.

"Sam, the guys and I've been talking. We don't like the looks of this position."

"Neither do I, but this is where they said to stop."

"The guys wanted me to ask if you would dig your hole next to our gun."

"I don't know what I could do for you that your machine gun can't do better," Sam said.

"You say that, but all the same, if you'd dig beside us, it would make us all feel better."

That night, peering out in to the blackness of the night, Sam thought about his remark. He considered it a high compliment. He didn't understand what there was about him that inspired such confidence. They respected him. He could see that. What none seemed to realize was that a thirty-caliber bullet was no respecter of persons. If one hits you in the right place you are going to die.

Sam still had not told anyone about the dream and about losing his fear, but they had seen it. There were times when it would begin to come back, but when it did he recited the 23rd Psalm, whispering it to himself, and his fear would leave and he would be at peace.

After a week with the platoon, Lieutenant O'Curry approached Sam. They were climbing another high hill and the weather was warming. Lieutenant O'Curry was halted by the path, sweating and breathing hard. Sam caught up with him.

"A few more days of this and you'll be a mountain goat, Lieutenant," he said.

"I hope so," O'Curry said, wiping his brow with a handkerchief.

Sam was about to move on but O'Curry stopped him.

"Sam, I've been watching you for several days. I don't see anything wrong with you. Something doesn't add up with what I've been told."

"What have you been told, Sir?"

"When I came through Battalion, they told me I was taking over the 2nd Platoon of Fox Company and they warned me about you."

"What did they say, Sir?"

"They said there's a sergeant up there, now a corporal, known as Psycho Sam, who doesn't take any shit off anyone."

Sam grinned at him. It was refreshing to know they considered him incorrigible. He wondered just who O'Curry included in the word 'they' and sought to find out.

"Then you talked to Colonel Sutter," Sam said.

"Yeah, and the Sergeant Major," O'Curry said.

"I suppose they told you right, Lieutenant. But you don't have to worry about me. If you treat me right, I'll treat you right."

O'Curry smiled, reached out shook Sam's hand.

"I'll buy that," he said.

Sam wondered how much they had told him and who it was that did most of the telling. He had to smile to himself. He might be just a corporal, but they knew who he was and what he stood for. He thought about the machine gunner's remark. He was beginning to understand the rewards of being different. But Sam knew well his understanding imposed responsibility. One whom others look up to must live to a higher standard. It meant going first, on the point. The only way to lead is to lead. He decided leading wasn't all bad nor always the most dangerous.

Eventually, they came again to a high hill that had been the scene of fighting between Dog and Easy companies and the Chinese for several days. They had been unable to take it, so Fox Company was committed. As was the usual custom there were no plans, no one organized the attack; they had been long accustomed to the fact that when they reached the enemy they were to begin killing them. As they began to pick their way up the steep slope the ferocity of the fighting which had taken place became obvious. Every single bush and tree had been shot away and the earth was black with napalm bombing.

Visibility was not a problem, and looking back on the hill as they went up they could see the Confederate flag in the bright sunlight and ahead the positions held by the Chinese who seemed now to be pulling back. Sam's squad reached the crest at about the middle of the hill. Unlike most, this hill had a broad plateau at the top which stretched for several hundred yards before turning downward on the far side.

Word was passed to hold up at the crest and they stopped the advance. The bodies of several Chinese were scattered about the hilltop and Sam began to look about for a hole to get into. The hole nearest to him contained the bodies of two dead soldiers who appeared to have been dead for two or three days. Sam reached into the hole and got the first one by the armpits and dragged him up out of the hole. The soldier felt limp and rubbery, as if he might come apart in Sam's hands, so he dragged him only a few feet, then went back for the other. For the second one, he had to get down in the hole and lift him up right against the edge, then climb out, grasp him by the armpits, and drag him about two yards.

He got down in the hole and opened a can of beans. In front of him, green flies swarmed over the dead face of the Chinese soldier. His face was bluish in color, somewhat like an Irish potato gets when exposed on the ground, except darker. Sam wished for some water to wash his hands, but there was none. He opened the can with his little two inch long opener and dipped the spoon in and slowly ate the beans. The green flies on the soldiers face repelled him. Sam looked away, watched the Confederate flag coming up the hill, and ate the beans. All the time, he expected to hear the mortar shells come raining down.

Within minutes word came to move forward, and they moved out in a skirmish line across the broad rolling top of the hill until they began to descend to the other side. Sam noticed suddenly that his squad was alone. There should have been others behind, but there weren't. At the same time the Chinese began to counterattack. They had a base of fire set up on the far slope and were beginning to trigger a machine gun to support their advance. Even though Sam couldn't see their infantry, the tracers of their gun were coming up the slope and passing skyward above his head. They were triggering in short bursts of two to three rounds and within minutes they would be coming at him.

"I'm going back to find out where everyone is," Sam said.

Westfall turned and said, "I'm going with you!"

Sam saw immediately he was afraid and that told him he could not leave them.

"We better all go. Fall back!" Sam cried.

They pulled back two hundred yards and Jennings met them.

"Didn't you guys get the word?"

"What word?"

"We passed word to pull back. When you didn't show, I came looking for you."

When they moved back the company was digging in a hundred yards north of the crest. Jennings assigned Sam a section of the line and they began hurriedly digging in. It was almost dark.

The Chinese stopped short of attacking as they were digging in and by nine o'clock they had holes at fighting depth. Sam dug in alone and slightly behind line, to allow him to observe the positions of his squad. When he dug alone he always got between two other holes, where someone would be awake to lessen the danger of having his throat cut while he slept.

Arkie and Petitt were on his right, Erickson and Lewellyn on the left. It had been a long day. Sam slipped into his sleeping bag, placed his hand grenades and weapons on the edge of the hole, and within a few minutes was sound asleep.

During the night, he had a vivid dream that a machine gun was firing at him and the bullets were coming so close they were parting his hair. Something was telling him, "Get lower, get lower," and although he was crouched down in the dream, the bullets stayed just above his head and kept parting his hair.

There was a thump and he woke to a rattle of gunfire all about. A spent round had bounced off something and hit his sleeping bag. His face was down in the dirt in the bottom of the hole and his feet were sticking up in the air. He struggled to get upright. "What's going on?" he shouted.

Erickson answered with a burst of fire from his BAR. Sam heard the telltale sound of running feet. Wide-awake now, he grabbed a hand grenade, pulled the pin and hurled it.

The firing died down. "Man, where you been; we thought you were dead," Erickson said.

"What happened?"

"We've been fighting these buggers for thirty minutes," Arkie said. "Where the hell you been, Sam?"

"I was asleep. A spent round hit my sleeping bag."

The Chinese pulled back. Word came along the line asking about casualties. A runner came downline to confirm conditions. When the Chinese had first hit they had struck the 1st Platoon.

Bugarella was in a hole with a buddy. He had been peering out into the dark night. His buddy asked him if he could smell them.

"No," Bugarella said, "but I can see them."

Another young Marine had been sitting back in his hole. In his hands he clutched a forty-five automatic, holding on to it with both hands. He heard someone crawling and he slipped the safety catch down with his right thumb. He saw a pair of hands reach over the edge of his hole and get a grip on the earth. There was a slithering noise and a Chinese face appeared and two eyes peered down, looking directly at him. He shot the soldier right between the eyes.

These things seemed humorous, and were passed along the line from man to man, to laugh and talk about. It seemed a joke was played on the Chinese soldier to reward him with a forty-five slug between the eyes. Not so humorous were the lice they had, and the filth of living in the dirt day after day.

Invariably, when Sam dug a hole and used a rock for a pillow, as soon as he lay down a clod of dirt would fall from the side of the hole and strike him in the head, resulting in ears full of dirt that he could never get out.

He grew weary of being called Psycho Sam and attempted to become known as Serge Blue, the bandit leader. Instead of screaming "Banzai," he screamed, "Serge Blue!"

This failed to replace his handle of Psycho Sam, indeed only accentuated it. Serge Blue, the comic strip character, had the habit of killing prisoners of war. He would sit under a tree, play an accordion, and say when music stops shooting starts. Then when he stopped playing, his men would murder the prisoners.

Three Chinese walked into the lines and gave up. Sam was on the reverse slope of the hill when they came in, but Petitt came and got him. Sam went onto the forward slope where the men had surrounded the three Chinese, who were squatting Asiatic-style on the ground. The three watched him approach, as did the squad. It was clear to the Chinese the squad was waiting for Sam. Sam looked down at them and drew his finger across his throat, indicating the men should cut their throats. He knew of course they wouldn't, but the Chinese didn't know that. It was very cruel.

One of the Chinese began to mumble something that sounded like, "Benzil. Benzil." Sam figured that he was asking for a pencil, so he went to his pack and got a pencil and a piece of paper and handed it to him.

He wrote in English, "We wish to be honorable prisoners of war."

Sam's cruel joke had gone far enough. He asked Petitt for cigarettes and gave each of the Chinese a cigarette. Petitt gave them a light, and told them that Serge Blue had spared their lives. Hemphill sent someone to escort them to the rear. As they were marched away Sam cried, "Banzai!"

The Chinese appeared startled, then extremely glad to be on their way.

Life at the front was a daily grind of horror, death, and cruelty over which they had little control. The only conscious motivation was to stay alive for the future, while with each passing day, the youth and tenderness necessary to enjoy that future slipped out of their grasp without their knowing it.

Sam was never able to forget the swimming pool. He really didn't know who in Easy Company had done it and it troubled him. Once, upon a high hill, a comrade from the barracks in Washington D.C. visited Fox Company. He had carried some papers over on some kind of business and stopped in looking for any with whom he had served. He stopped to see Sam. His name was Joel McVey. He was a machine gunner in Easy Company. The two stood by Sam's hole on the reverse slope of the hill and reminisced about the old days at their post, and as McVey was preparing to leave Sam broached the eternal question. "Mac, you remember that swimming pool in Seoul?"

McVey *hung* his head. He shifted his weight from one foot to the other. When he spoke, his voice was very low, almost inaudible. "That's something we *never* talk about," he said softly.

Sam was still inquisitive. "I can understand why you wouldn't talk about it," Sam said, "but why . . . ?"

McVey looked away. "We lost eight killed and thirty-two wounded that day."

He glanced back at Sam, then hung his head and shifted his weight again from one foot to the other.

"The Company Commander . . . he ordered it."

"Who, Captain Hanson?"

McVey shook his head negatively.

Sam persisted. "Captain Nelbrook?"

McVey half nodded affirmatively. It was clear he didn't want to talk. He looked about, searching for something to say to avoid the conversation. Then, he wouldn't take any more questions. He told Sam to take care of himself and left in a hurry.

Remembering the swelling burst of automatic fire he had heard when the massacre took place, Sam wondered if McVey had had any part in it. If it had been ordered by the Company Commander that would explain the coverup. No wonder they hadn't wanted Margurite Higgins to mention it.

The thing still gnawed at Sam.

CHAPTER 33 ... Rest ...

In April, after a hundred and three consecutive days of clawing in the earth, they pulled back for a rest. Filthy, caked with dirt, ragged, and alive with lice, they made their way off the line going down the slope of this tremendous hill, looking far below, where the flag of the Confederacy led the way. It had become significant in a way far removed from the issue of slavery, more representative of the fighting spirit that had permeated their ancestors almost a hundred years before.

They were battle hardened: accustomed to living among the dead. Most of the ground had been fought over two or more times and the bodies of the dead lay on top of the ground and rotted. Except for an occasional one that had been missed, Americans had been picked up, but the bodies of North Koreans, Chinese and civilians lay in various stages of decay and withered away. It was not yet warm enough for them to stink. Instead they dried out. The skin shrank tightly to their bodies as the flesh underneath dried up. The advance of the so-called Chinese People's Volunteers Army had been stopped.

The sights of war no longer impressed them. A dead man or woman was just that, a dead body, so commonplace as to cause no reaction at all. No pity, no sorrow, nothing. They wound down the hill, past the body of a Chinese soldier. Sam estimated he had been dead for two months. As he went past Sam swung his carbine around with one hand and shot him again. He knew not why. Something about it seemed right. He was dead, would always be dead, would never walk, or breathe, or laugh, or cry again. Sam wanted to add to the finality of his death.

Then the trucks took them into a valley that had a swift stream flowing through it, surrounded on all sides by high hills, and in the valley a field kitchen had been set up. They were served hot food and there was a van-type truck equipped with a record player and loudspeaker that blared lively music while they ate, and they began to live again.

The music was the most pleasant sound Sam had heard in months and it soothed him tremendously. The music made his pulse quicken, his heart light and mind aglow with pleasant memories.

They had chosen a site where the stream widened out creating a sandy bottom. Sam didn't know how to swim, but he waded in water up to his shoulders and spent alternate minutes on the beach.

He gave his dungarees to a Korean woman who had taken several Marines' clothing to wash. She took the clothing out into the swift flowing stream, squatted on a large rock, and beat the clothing with a stick of wood, in the traditional Korean way of washing clothes without the use of any soap.

Captain Groff loosened up and enjoyed himself. He showed a mischievous streak no one suspected he had. When night fell he took a group of a dozen volunteers into the valley where Battalion had pitched tents. He knew exactly which tent Joe Perrigo occupied, and led his volunteers to it. One man pulled at each stake the lines holding the tent were secured to. Then Groff rushed inside with two others, grabbed the tent center pole, and everyone walked away with the tent while Perrigo slept. Fifty feet distant they allowed the tent to fall. Joe Perrigo was sleeping under the stars.

In the tent Sam slept in things were different. He always slept with pistol in hand, hammer cocked, and safety catch on. He and Arkie were sleeping side by side. One man was to be awake at all times outside the tent. The sentry came inside to wake Arkie, knelt beside him, and shook him gently. In a flash, Sam had his pistol out, flipped off the safety and cried, "Who's out there?"

As he became aware of the situation, Arkie was speaking to him in a soothing voice, "Easy Sam, easy now."

"Is that you, Arkie?"

"Yes, you almost shot me. Go back to sleep."

Arkie went out and stood watch. It had been known to happen that the enemy would slit the rear of a tent with a knife, get inside, and kill everyone inside by silently cutting their throats. Sam lay awake wondering what the future held for them. The rumor was they were to have a week to rest, but a week to rest also meant a week to think.

Early morning, two Marines shot themselves. One took his own life, the other shot himself in the foot. Sam didn't wonder about it at all. It was easy to understand they had grown depressed and been unable to handle it.

Lieutenant O'Curry had exchanged jobs with Lieutenant Sorenson. Now Sorenson was the platoon leader and would be in the future. 2nd Platoon was picked to go on outpost duty and moved up to a high hill which overlooked the road leading into the valley. They were to spend one night up there and be relieved by another platoon the following morning. It was nice to be wearing clean clothes and to be free of lice, and Sam was looking forward to wading in the stream again when he came back down.

They spent the night on outpost. When daybreak came they observed some heavily camouflaged vehicles coming towards them on the road below. They were covered with the limbs of green cedar trees. The odd thing was the fields beside the road were still dead in appearance and this made the vehicles all the more obvious.

Sorenson got Battalion on the phone and reported that two trucks and two jeeps were coming down the road.

"We know," Battalion said, "that's all that's left of the South Korean regiment which took the place of our regiment in the line."

"What happened?" Sorenson asked.

"The Chinese hit them and they just disintegrated," came the reply.

A few moments passed. The radio crackled.

"You'll not be relieved. We're going back up. Bring the platoon down to the road. We'll pick you up there. We've got to hold a bridge on the Imjin River."

Thus ended their rest. They shouldered their gear and marched down to the road where they caught the last three trucks in the column. Sam was unable to get a fender and wound up in a truck which was unbelievably packed with Marines, weapons, sleeping bags, gear, and water cans. One Marine summed it up, "If I evah get back to Shreveport, Louisiana, fust thing Ahm gonna do is rent myself a six-by truck an a driver an ride all over town in it by myself."

His bitter humor did not even draw a grin. The mood aboard the trucks was one of depression, fear, and disappointment.

The position they were to hold lay on the north side of the Imjin river. The bridge had been blown some months before, but the engineers had replaced it with a pontoon bridge and after a two-hour ride in silence they reached it and slowed down. As they rode Sam thought the quietest ride he would ever take was on a truck headed for the front with men who had been there before. Now the rumble of heavy mortars could be heard and this was ominous.

"Thung, Thung, Thung," they sounded as they left the tubes, then sharp and loud as they fell like thunder.

They crossed the bridge and proceeded in silence, with the sounds of fighting now coming clearly from both sides of the road. To experienced ears this meant only one thing. The Chinese did not attack in daytime unless they felt they could win. As a rule, Marines went against them by day; they came against Marines by night. To find them coming now meant they thought they could win.

The trucks came to a stop. The sounds of battle on both sides came now in a steady rumble of sound. The Confederate flag was out in the open and headed uphill, and those on trucks in front were beginning to follow.

Instinctively, the squad followed Sam. He followed Sorenson. Everything was automatic. Orders were unnecessary. Ahead of them, Groff picked the spot where he would locate his CP and pulled out of the column, allowing the 1st Platoon to proceed on past. Within minutes they were digging in, while on both sides, unseen, but heard, the battle raged.

By nightfall they were dug in. Jennings came around. He knelt down beside Sam. His face was impassive, as stoic as a wooden statue. He was capable of bearing either the best or worst news without a trace of emotion. "There are three thousand Chinese approximately a thousand yards in front of us," he said. "Tomorrow, Fox Company will go look for them."

Then, he was gone, moving down the line of foxholes to give the other squads the news.

Sam wondered at this news. No one bothered to say just how a company of two hundred Marines might be able to go about killing three thousand Chinese.

Nothing ever happens as you think it will. The three thousand Chinese spared Fox Company the problem of looking for them. Instead, they came looking for the Marines. By daybreak, the tactical situation made it clear that killing them was going to have to be done in some other manner. This was clear to everyone from the Battalion Commander down to the last private. Word was passed they would pull back under cover of 4.2 mortar fire, and at the first light of dawn they began to retreat under the umbrella of fire laid down by the four-deuces.

Keeping to the high ground, they began taking a longer route than would have been necessary had they retreated in a straight line.

When they were five hundred yards distant from the hill, the Chinese mounted an attack intended to wipe them out, had they still been there. Hearing Chinese machine gunners lay down covering fire was always impressive. They triggered in short staccato bursts of two and three rounds, while Marine gunners usually fired in bursts of three to five and sometimes more. And hearing those short bursts of fire added a little speed to the retreat.

They were seven hundred yards distant and moving as rapidly as possible when the Chinese came pouring over the crest and streaming down the slope, taking a straight line for the hill Sam's comrades were headed for. The hillside was soon covered with Chinese in mustard-colored uniforms trying to cut the Marines off. There were so many it turned the hillside brown. At the same time, Fox Company began receiving small arms fire. Ahead of Fox, Easy Company set up machine guns and took the enemy under fire as they came down the slope.

Colonel Sutter was attempting to travel the road which lay at the bottom of the hill the Chinese had just taken. His jeep was roaring along until small arms fire disabled it. He and two others left the jeep and made a run for it.

Sam reached a place where he had to cross the crest of a ridge the enemy was delivering machine gun fire onto. Marines crossed one at a time. You got to the edge of the open area and made a run for it. As you did, their machine gun wrote your name in the dirt. Sam crossed, running hard, and leaped over the crest to safety. He looked back to see how the next guy made it. He came, running hard, holding a box of machine gun ammo in each hand. He looked familiar. When he made the leap, Sam recognized Benny Vesuvius.

"Benny, you made a hell of a trade," Sam said, "—twenty pounds of BAR and twenty pounds of ammo for forty pounds of ammo and a nine-pound rifle."

Benny ignored Sam's remark. His mind was still on the run he had just made. "Chee," he said, "dose guys are trying to kill us."

Then, he got up and scurried on.

They reached the next hill and began digging in. Communication had been lost with the 4.2 mortars when the commander lost his jeep, but by some unknown means it had been restored, and now as the enemy reached the jeep a burst of shells fell among them and kept coming without letup. They turned back and began retreating back up the hill while the shells fell among them.

Fox Company waited all day for the Chinese to renew their attack, but they did not, and all this time the fighting was proceeding on both flanks. At nine o'clock in the evening, word was passed to saddle up. They left the position under cover of darkness. Within a few minutes they were marching single file down the reverse slope of the hill. As it developed, 2nd Platoon was in the lead and Sam was leading. When they drew near the river, he heard the sound of motors running. Out of the darkness, a Marine appeared.

"Machine guns and mortars go that way," he said. "The rest of you follow me."

Sam followed him down to the river's edge.

"Cross over right here," he said.

"I can't swim," Sam said.

"You don't need to. Just hold on to the cable," he said.

Sam looked out at the swiftly flowing water. The river was about four hundred feet wide. A steel cable had been stretched taut across the water. He grabbed hold of it and waded in. The river was about five feet deep and had a rocky bottom that was very slippery. Holding his carbine aloft with one hand and hanging on to the cable with the other did not prove to be practical, so he slung the carbine with his grease gun and pistol and clung to the cable with both hands. In the middle of the river, the cable, being fully loaded with men, began to sag under water. Some were slipping and falling, and when they did, the cable and those who were clinging to it went under. The strap holding Sam's grease gun broke and he lost it in the swirling water. By this time, having been ducked under a half dozen times, he realized his best chance was to get across as soon as possible. He began trying to dog paddle and pull along on the cable. When he felt it go under, he held his breath and tried to stand on the bottom. In the end, by being first, he was able to pull away from the low place in the cable and get across. Had he been restricted he thought he would have drowned. At last, he climbed out of the river, grateful for having been first.

On the bank, on the far side, they milled anxiously about in the darkness. The entire battalion was grouped tightly. Had the Chinese known it, their mortars would have had a turkey shoot. After an hour or so, they began to march away from the river and made their way up to the roadway. The engineers had blown the bridge again, so there was little danger of being followed by the Chinese. As they moved away from the bridge, Sam could hear the rattle of fire coming from their last hill. The Chinese were assaulting it.

Their shoes were full of water. Wet clothes clung to their bodies and dripped more water down into their shoes. A cool wind was blowing and only the fact they were marching at a fast pace made it bearable. Dawn found them on the road strung out behind the Confederate flag, shoulders hunched against the wind and their loads. A column of trucks appeared and slowed to a stop.

"Where the hell have you been?" Captain Groff demanded angrily.

Whoever responded spoke in low tones. It was impossible to hear what he said.

There was no mistaking Captain Groff. "Turn those goddam trucks around and take 'em back where you came from. We wouldn't ride in those goddam trucks if they were the last trucks on earth." He halted the column while the trucks turned around in the road and prepared to leave.

"Tell your transportation officer to shove his trucks up his ass," Groff shouted.

They stared wistfully after the departing trucks. A low grumble rose up from the column of marching men, then died away.

They had been on the march all night and half the day when they were met by a second column of trucks loaded with U. S. Army. They approached at about twenty miles per hour.

Captain Groff stepped out into the center of the road, drew his pistol, and aimed it at the driver of the lead truck. The driver braked to a skidding halt. An Army Colonel raised up out of the open seat of the truck.

"Who are you?" he demanded.

"I'm the man who's going to blow the hell out of the first driver who passes through my men faster than five miles an hour," said Groff.

"I asked who the hell you are," the colonel said.

"I'm Captain Groff. G-R-O-F-F, Fox Company, Second Battalion, First Marines." He spelled it out slowly, deliberately.

"I'm going to report you to your commanding officer," the colonel said.

"I don't give a damn what you do. If any truck passes faster than five miles an hour I'm going to kill the driver.

He stepped to one side, waved his hand for the march to continue. Saia stepped past with the flag flapping in the breeze. The truck driver put his truck in low and inched slowly past.

At four o'clock, a column of trucks met them again. This time they boarded and rode for an hour before they circled into a pea field and began to dig in. They drew rations and Sam got the deadly three. He would have to do some trading.

"What am I offered for one can of peaches and a can of beef stew?" He chanted. Some one offered a can of chicken and vegetables.

"Ah, you can do better than that," Sam said.

"A can of pears, and a can of spaghetti?" someone cried.

"What am I offered for a half-assed squad leader?" Lieutenant Sorenson cried.

"I'll trade you jobs, Lieutenant. You take the Twelve Fanatics, I'll take the platoon," Sam said.

Sorenson shook his head negatively.

"It's been one hell of a day," he said.

Word was passed to dig in. They dug in overlooking the roadway. While they were digging, a convoy loaded with South Korean soldiers passed through on the way to the front, singing patriotic songs, acting as if they were going on a school outing.

Lewellyn stopped digging, watched them pass, and muttered with a grin, "There goes the old ladies clambake and singing society."

CHAPTER 34 ... The End of the Rope ...

The character of the war slowly changed. General Ridgway endeavored to stabilize a line across Korea which would maintain the integrity of South Korea. The Chinese struggled to protect North Korea. Slowly the war began to reach a stalemate. In the day after day combat all the United nations units became better soldiers. The South Korean Army improved, but were still referred to as the old ladies clambake and singing society. No one who knows what war is, sings on the way to the front. Going up to face death is not a happy occasion.

Sam saw Lewellyn leave the Twelve Fanatics without knowing how Lewellyn did it. Lew became overseer of a Korean labor gang whose job it was to carry water and ammunition. He had always been lazy, but was extremely good at shepherding the heavily laden Koreans up and down the hills. He began to speak their language.

With Walsh gone, Sam began to walk point for the squad again. Some said this wasn't the job of a squad leader, but Sam wouldn't send any man where he wouldn't go himself. He had the promise given to him in the dream. Moreover, he possessed the natural instinct for the job, understood how to use terrain in such a way that when shooting began the squad would not be caught in the open. He knew fire team tactics well and simply had to shout his commands and the Fanatics knew exactly what to do. They were a keen team, trying to stay alive.

Captain Groff seemed to rely upon his 2nd Platoon and Sorenson relied upon Sam. If a village was to be reconnoitered or a hill investigated they sent Sam. Each time the squad went out, Sam was out in front, nerves drawn tight as banjo strings, ready to kill in a fraction of a second, and behind came the Twelve Fanatics, watching out for their leader, nerves stretched taut, expecting any moment to be met by a burst of fire, and when the fire came to go to ground in an instant pouring out a hail of fire.

There was one difference between Sam and the Fanatics. He believed his dream. He believed that God had spoken to him in the dream and told him not to fear. The Twelve Fanatics believed it was only a matter of time until their luck ran out. Thus, they began to see they were being put at risk more than they should be. They decided they would try to change things. Erickson was the spokesman.

One day he approached Sam.

"Look Sam, you may not care whether or not you get killed, but we care if we do."

"What's the problem?" Sam asked, with a grin.

"Every time something comes up they send us to take care of it," Erickson said.

Sam looked at him soberly. "We'll be going home someday," he said.

Erickson was not to be dissuaded. "Every time the Lieutenant wants a squad he sends us."

"And we always do the job," Sam said.

"Yeah, but we shouldn't have to," Erickson said.

The whole squad was listening to the exchange. Sam had only to look at them to see he was being ganged up on.

"I have to do my job," he said defensively.

"Yes, but don't do it so well," Petitt said.

"What would you have me do?" Sam asked.

Arkie said, "Just don't be so handy. When we start up one of these hills, don't always be first. Lag behind once in a while. Let one of the other squads go first."

Under this kind of request, Sam sought to comply. The following day on patrol they began to climb a high hill. He lagged behind, as requested, taking note of the fact the squad was watching closely. George Baker, leader of the third squad, passed him on the trail, so Sam rested and allowed the other squad to pass through. When they reached the crest, they began to receive long-distance machine gun fire. Sorenson sent Baker's squad and a machine gun crew over the ridge to dig in. As night fell they learned Baker had taken casualties and one of the newer men had been killed. Sam felt really guilty. He knew that if he had crossed the ridge he would have set up a machine gun and gotten fire superiority before he attempted to dig the squad in.

The days wore into weeks. The terrain was much more rugged. They occupied a hill that was of such tremendous height that planes flew below them and there were clouds below the planes. They had climbed the hill without being shot at and had run into land mines. The result was that a path had been cleared and word was passed to stay on the path. When they reached the crest, they dug in, and next day the squad was sent to string wire in front of the holes. Arkie was depressed and began to bitch. "It ain't for dick, I tell you."

Erickson snickered.

This made Arkie more angry. He began to curse bitterly and threw his rifle down. The hill was so steep that the rifle began to slide as if it would go all the way. Arkie didn't seem to care.

"Not for nothin'!" he shouted. "The whole thing is for nothin'."

"Better get your rifle, Arkie," Sam said, "you might need it." Erickson and Petitt were struggling with the ninety-pound roll of wire.

"Did you see that?" Petitt said. "That rifle almost went down the hill."

A transport plane sailed slowly along the valley below. They stopped and looked.

"Turn loose," Erickson said. Petitt turned loose of the stick they had in the roll of wire.

"Oops," Erickson said, and pretended to trip. He let go of the wire and watched it roll towards the valley below. It made great leaps and bounds going skyward by ten feet or more as it rolled and bounced till it was lost from sight.

The plane continued.

Next day, a company from the Seventh Marines arrived. As Sam sat beside the path, watching them work their way up the hill, he saw a Marine he had served with in Washington. They had both been sergeants when Sam had known him, but he had been sent to Quantico to Officers Candidate School and was now a Second Lieutenant. He was the nephew of the famous Elliot Ness who had helped to bring Al Capone to trial. Ness and Sam had always seen the world from different perspectives. Their petty arguments had always been a source of entertainment to the other sergeants. Nevertheless, Sam was glad to see him.

Niel Ness came picking his way up the path. When he drew near, Sam greeted him. "Well, if it ain't a brand new Marine Lieutenant," Sam said.

He grinned back at Sam. "Well, Corporal Snorkle," he said.

"I see you heard I got busted," Sam said.

"Yeah, we kept track of all you guys," Ness said.

They sat and talked for five minutes. He told Sam the fate of some of their comrades, Sam told him about some. This was only Ness's second day with his platoon. He had been to OCS and then advanced infantry training and here he was, telling Sam that he had to catch up to his platoon.

"Good luck, Niel." Sam said.

Fox Company went off the hill and began working their way down a long valley. At noon when the heat was beating down, they came to a place where a high hill rose up on the right and in front. Sam was beside Sorenson. Groff ordered him to send a squad up to reconnoiter the hill. Sorenson sent Sam.

Sam waved for the squad to follow and started off at a trot. In order to be effective he had to double-time to get about five hundred yards out in front and then climb the hill. They worked their way up carefully, using proper cover, but still moving fast. When they reached the top they entered cautiously into a pine grove and discovered the hill was clear. Far below, the company circled through the valley behind the flag which gleamed in the sunlight and made an impressive sight. They went to ground, breathing hard, and rested in the cool shade watching the company below. From the valley below, came a call, "Sam!"

Sam cupped his hands and answered, "It's clear!"

"Come on back down!"

So they turned around and began going back down, which was almost as difficult as going up had been. Again they were perspiring and slipping on the steep slope. When they got within two hundred feet of the company, it seemed the company had turned and were coming directly at them. It began to look as if they were going to climb the hill that Sam had just been called off of. The Fanatics began to curse. It became clear they were correct in the assumption they were going to have to turn around and climb the same hill again, Sam felt a hot flush of anger. "Are we going to have to climb this damn hill again?" he demanded.

Lieutenant Sorenson nodded affirmatively.

"What dumb son of a bitch called us back down?" Sam said. "That's the most stupid order I've ever gotten."

Sorenson slipped his arm about Sam's shoulders, "Calm down Sam; calm down," he said.

Captain Groff stopped and looked at Sam steadily. It had been he who had called Sam back.

"Somebody better calm the crazy son of a bitch down. I'm gettin ready to shoot him," he said, ominously.

That did it. It was the straw that broke the camel's back. The reaction to all the months of combat and the captain's hard cruel discipline welled to the surface. Every nerve in Sam's body went taut. He was like a tight bundle of banjo strings.

The captain had made a mistake. Sam shook off Sorenson's arm and stepped clear of Sorenson. He held his carbine easily in one hand, to swing it in a fraction of a second. And he was not the tender youth he once had been. Sam could kill in less time than he could blink an eye.

"Captain," he said, "if you so much as touch that pistol of yours, it will be the last move you ever make."

The captain knew Sam would kill him. Sam could see it in his eyes. And Sam was ready, so he pushed it.

"Captain, I've got normal intelligence. Don't you, ever again, refer to me as a crazy son of a bitch," he said, ominously. "If you do, I'll kill you."

"Easy Sam. Easy," said Lieutenant Sorenson, standing very still.

The captain held silence. He too stood very still. He understood Sam. He knew Sam was ready to explode on whatever he came against and what Sam had come against was him. Groff was a brave man, but he was not a fool. Groff had first crossed the line. By his threat, he made it easy for Sam to kill him. The experience before Colonel Sutter told him Sam could not be intimidated. The truth was that, if he reached for his pistol, Sam would kill him before he could draw it and Captain Groff knew it. Silently, he walked away.

Sam stood very still for a few minutes, then fell in to the column to climb the hill. Thus, the incident passed. In a moment of reflection, in the dark night following, Sam realized he had no desire to kill Captain Groff. He understood him quite well. Groff had always done what he had to and Sam had always done what he had to. It was their doing so that brought them into conflict. At long last, they understood each other.

CHAPTER 35 ... Sergeant Martens ...

They climbed the high hills and crossed the streams and paddies and became accustomed to the stench of the earth and killed the enemy where they found them. If they found them dead, sometimes they shot them again. Bodies lay on top of the earth and rotted and blood stained the earth and didn't wash away. You would find one who had been dead for months and a dark pool of blood would still be visible on the ground. Marvin Childers, one of the machine gunners, had a camera and took pictures of the most compelling scenes of death. He took some pictures of Sam and McChann, his partner, behind the machine gun, and several pictures of the Twelve Fanatics, including a picture of Petitt.

Petitt was always negative. The death of Carpenter the first night and of his other three comrades seemed to have made a profound impression on him. Never once did he express a single positive thought. He had no expectation for the future whatever. Even so, he was there when needed and was a courageous fighter. He consistently expected to be killed at any moment. He had his eccentricities, such as taking souvenirs off the enemy dead, but he was an indispensable member of the squad and, like Walsh, would volunteer to walk point.

To Sam's complete surprise and even more so to Petitt's, Petitt was selected to be sent home on rotation. Early in May, he left them on one of the high hills, and they stood looking longingly after him.

Two days later, he was back. Sam saw him ascending the hill and when Petitt drew close he began to shout, "I knew it wasn't true." They gathered about him.

"What happened?" Sam asked.

"I was in a tent, by the hospital. Some lieutenant came by in a jeep. He said, 'You come go with me,' and I did and here I am." Then he grinned at them.

"I'll be going back in two days."

It appeared they wanted him to wait on the front lines instead of in the rear. To Sam, it seemed cruel they would have Petitt wait on the front line for two days. He might yet be killed.

"Sam I've got some bad news for you. That lieutenant from the Seventh Marines, who stopped and talked with you—what did you say his name was?"

"Ness," Sam said.

"Well, after they relieved us on that hill, Lieutenant Ness led a patrol on his first night in combat. He went out that first night, got in to a mine field, and lost both arms and both legs," Petitt said.

Sam looked away. There was always something bad happening. He could never become accustomed to it. Yet, on the surface, he was stoic.

Sam was relieved when Petitt left again. He knew each of his men intimately. Petitt had told Sam about leaving the duty station in Scotia, New York, for Korea. Now three had been killed, leaving only Petitt and Ivan Jennings.

After Petitt left a second time, they made another patrol. Jennings and Sam were out in front reconnoitering and climbed a knob of earth about ten feet high. They stood erect and looked out across a yawning chasm and beyond, watching a company of Marines marching through a valley.

"Crack!"

A rifle shot rang out, making a flat snapping sound as the bullet passed between them. Sam leaped off the knoll and hit the earth below, feeling a sharp pain in his right leg. Jennings threw himself flat and slid down beside Sam.

"Boy that was close," he said.

Sam nodded and flexed his leg. It didn't seem badly injured. As they went back to the area where the platoon was waiting, he found it was sore, but decided it would work out.

Next day, they moved off the hill they were on and began ascending a much higher hill. The climb was grueling. The hill was so steep it could not be climbed in a straight line, but could be climbed only at an angle. It was about two o'clock in the afternoon and Fox Company was working its way slowly towards the crest of the high hill. A path had been worn by those who proceeded first and Sam was struggling along this path when he came upon Sergeant Martens.

Sergeant Martens was in the machine gun section. He was a veteran of World War Two and an ex-Marine Raider who had fought in the Pacific. He was a quiet man who had always a somber outlook on things. He was very observant and was an original member of the company. He was fairly heavy-set, had straight blond hair and skeptical blue eyes. He went about his job quietly, very seldom spoke to anyone. He had taken over Parker's job when Parker was killed, and then when the machine guns had been divided up and assigned, two to each rifle platoon, his job was made easier because one machine gun would sometimes function under Sam's squad.

Martens was sitting beside the path with a forlorn look on his face and Sam stopped.

"How's it going, Martens?" Sam asked.

Martens's lips curled bitterly; his face took on a desperate look, reminding Sam of a cornered animal. He had his left hand inside his dungaree jacket, was sitting with his knees drawn up towards his chin.

"I've been waiting for you," he said softly.

This surprised Sam. He didn't say anything.

"You've stopped to talk me into going on, haven't you," Martens demanded.

"I just wanted to see how you're doing," Sam said.

"Admit it, damn you! I know why you stopped, but you can't possibly know how long I've waited for this day."

Sam had to think about it. Stopping was not something he had done with a conscious motive in mind. He usually functioned on instinct, not necessarily logic. Yet, he was analytical.

"I suppose I have," he said.

"Sam, it's been a long time since we left San Diego. I've watched you stop beside a hundred guys and talk them into going on when they were at the end of their rope. Now, I've got a question for you."

"What is it?" Sam asked.

"Have you ever thought about how many you've talked into going on to their death?" he said, looking directly at him, his voice very soft and low.

Sam trembled. He felt suddenly uncomfortable.

"I haven't done that," he said.

"No? The hell you haven't. Think about it!" Martens said.

Sam's mind began to wander over his dead comrades. He felt a deep sadness drag at him. He couldn't bear the truth of Martens's words. Tears welled into his eyes and coursed silently down his cheeks. He trembled again.

"I see you're limping," Martens said, reversing the situation.

"Yeah, I jumped off a cliff yesterday when a bullet almost got me," Sam said.

"Has anyone ever stopped to talk you into going on?" Martens asked.

Sam thought about it. He didn't like the answer.

"No," he said.

"You sure as hell better believe no! They don't appreciate what you've done. Do you think Captain Groff appreciates what you've done? Hell no! You know he doesn't. What have they done? They've betrayed you and busted you, but they can't break you. Do you think any of them gives a damn if you get killed? Hell no! They'd like for you to be killed because of that damn swimming pool. The Captain has been afraid of you ever since that day in Seoul."

His vehemence was forcing Sam to think thoughts he had not dared to think before. He sat silently, tears rolling slowly down his cheeks.

Martens pulled his hand out of his dungaree jacket. His fingers were bright red with blood.

"Look at me. I had my appendix taken out. I tried to tell that damn Navy doctor I wasn't ready to climb these hills. He wouldn't listen. Now, my stitches are coming out and nobody gives a damn. There's one thing I have to do before I go," he said.

"What's that?" Sam choked.

"Sam, it's time for you to quit. If you don't, you're going to die out here—and for nothing."

"I can't quit," Sam said.

"If you don't, you'll die. That day we crossed the paddy at Hoengsong, my guns were firing over your head. I thought you'd be killed for sure. I saw them shoot the shovel off your back and saw a hail of bullets strike all around you. It was a miracle you weren't killed. I want you to go back with me."

"I can't leave my squad," Sam said. He wiped his face clear of tears with his hand.

"No? Why not? Who's going to lead them when you're dead?"

"I don't know," Sam said.

"You can quit, Sam. You're the last of the original squad leaders.—You've been the last for some time. No one will point a finger at you if you quit," he said.

"Jennings is still here," Sam said quietly.

"Yes, but not as a squad leader."

"I'll stay as long as Captain Groff stays," Sam said.

"You little fool!" Martens exclaimed. "You mean you don't know?"

"Know what?"

"Captain Groff's going home tomorrow," he said.

It was as if he had hit Sam in the chest. Sam knew by the way Martens looked at him that he knew what Sam was feeling.

"Are you sure?" he choked.

"Of course I'm sure. He'll leave and he won't even say good-bye to any of us; it's his chance to escape and he'll take it."

"But my squad, what will become of them?"

"Arkie can lead them. He's been your right hand all along. He probably would like to lead a squad."

"But, I can't just turn in."

"The hell you can't! You've hurt your leg."

"So that gets me two days in the rear. So what?"

Martens was losing patience with him.

"You little fool!" he said.

Then he looked at the ground for a long time. When he looked up he looked Sam in the eye. His voice took on a gentle tone. He spoke from his heart.

"Sam, you're much too fine a person to die out here. You've done more than your share. I've watched you stop by a path a hundred times and encourage someone to go on. And never once—did anyone ever do that for you. I've had you on my mind for a long time. I've always known that someday you'd stop beside me, and when you did I would save your life. Now, I've stopped beside you, not to urge you to go on, but to urge you to live," he said.

Sam sat silently, considering his words.

"You have led many to their deaths," he said gently. "Now the time has come to save your life. It's something I've known for a long time that I must do."

Sam's chest ached. He felt the warm tears in his eyes.

Why is he doing this to me? he thought. He could not bear the truth Martens was speaking.

"My squad is alive," Sam said defensively.

"I'm not talking about your squad. I'm talking about all the others. You've led more than a squad. Open your eyes man. I'm not in your squad am I?"

"No."

"It's time for you to quit. I won't leave here without you. I made up my mind a long time ago that I'd save your life. But, if you won't quit, you'll die out here for sure. You can't keep leading patrols and going first day after day without getting killed. I know you think you lead a charmed life, but you don't. War always kills the best men. Sooner or later, you'll die. If you won't think of yourself, think of your family. And something else. I know you intend to write the story of that swimming pool. If you die, who's to tell about it?"

Sam sat silently. Martens put his hand back inside his jacket and drew it back out. There wasn't a lot of blood, but enough that Sam could see he needed help.

"If I turn in, what can I tell them?" Sam asked.

"You'll think of something. Just tell them the truth," he said.

"Martens, you go on back to the bottom of the hill. I'll tell Doyer to have an ambulance pick you up on the road," Sam said.

"Are you coming?"

"I've got to talk to Arkie. I'll be along behind you in case you have trouble," Sam said.

Martens stood up and started downhill. While they had been talking, the platoon had passed them by. Sam got up and began to climb. Within an hour he reached the crest. The men were beginning to dig in. He found the squad; Arkie was already digging. When he saw Sam he stopped. Sam knelt down beside him.

"Arkie, I'm going to turn in with my leg. You take over the squad, while I'm gone."

"You okay Sam?" Arkie's voice expressed his concern.

"Yeah, I'm okay."

Sam sat silently for a while. "Arkie, I may not come back. If I don't, you take care," he said.

He got up and walked away. When he found Doyer, Doyer was digging in near where Captain Groff was sitting down, resting. The captain was five yards away.

"Doyer, you need to get on the radio and have a jeep pick up Martens at the bottom of the hill. His operation broke open and he's bleeding."

Doyer moved over and took the phone off Saia's radio and began talking to the Medical Battalion. Sam was watching Captain Groff. Groff was looking at Doyer.

"I never thought this day would come, but I guess I was wrong," Sam said.

Captain Groff looked directly at him, and Sam could read his eyes. With his eyes, Groff said, "—Yes, I'm going! What of it?—"

"I always thought the Captain was the last man off the ship, but I guess I was wrong," Sam said.

Groff did not respond. Sam turned away to Doyer.

"Doyer, put a red tag on me," he said.

"What should I say on it," Doyer asked, his face expressionless.

"Just say, 'Jumped off cliff. Injured knee.'"

Doyer wrote on the tag and tied the tag to Sam's dungaree jacket. Sam kept watching the captain. As he walked past the captain, the captain followed him with his eyes.

Sam stopped and turned back to Doyer. "I won't be coming back," he said, "but there's one last thing I have to show someone, and I'm doing it now."

As he spoke, he looked directly at the captain. Their eyes met. Each respected the other. It was fate they did not ever agree. Both knew it. Neither had ever given the other a choice. In some undefinable way, they had changed each other. With their eyes, they said good bye.

CHAPTER 36 ... I See a Bat in a Well ...

Sam reached the bottom of the hill. Martens was not there. It was about four o'clock in the afternoon. He sat down beside the road and looked both ways. The road was little more than a path, but it had been graveled some long years past and still had a fairly hard surface. Sam felt depressed. Perhaps he had been wrong to needle the captain. Yet, he admitted to a need to show Groff that Sam had a voice in what happened to him. He wanted to show Groff that he was going to live. Not finding Martens depressed him, but there was nothing he could do. Perhaps Martens would still be at the medical battalion when Sam got there. Sam was beginning to have regrets he had let Martens talk him into going to sick call. He felt awful.

In the distance three Koreans appeared, wearing white pantaloons, coming towards him at a slow steady pace, and he began to watch them. The two on the outside were helping a third between them. He had each of his arms around the shoulders of the outside two and he walked with a limp. They came slowly even with Sam, as he sat silently beside the road studying every move they made. The one in the center had a grimace of pain on his face, and as Sam looked them up and down, he saw his trouser leg was cut just below his knee and his leg seemed to get much larger. From his knee to his ankle his leg was a solid mass of maggots. Sam flinched.

He watched until they were lost from sight. He would never forget the sight. When he stood up, his knee didn't hurt anymore and he felt ashamed. Just before dark, a jeep arrived and he climbed aboard. The driver was not talkative and Sam sat beside him in silence and wondered if they would come upon the three Koreans, but they did not, and as darkness fell they arrived at the medical battalion. Sam walked in carrying his carbine and this set off an objection from the duty corpsman who insisted he leave it outside.

"I'll lay it down outside the tent, but it better be there when I go back out," Sam said.

"What's your problem, Mac?" he asked.

"I jumped off a cliff and hurt my knee," Sam said.

"Which knee?"

"The right one," Sam said.

"Let me see you walk."

Sam took a few steps and turned around. The corpsman watched.

"Name rank and serial number," he said.

Sam gave him the information and he wrote it in a book and handed Sam two aspirin tablets.

"First tent, outside on the right. Sick call will be at eight o'clock tomorrow."

Sam went out, picked up his carbine, and went into the tent he had been directed to. It was full of lightly wounded Marines, but there were some cots not taken. Sam found a cot and lay down. Long into the night he stared at the center pole of the tent and wondered what was happening at the front. He could not get the maggots out of his mind.

After breakfast, he wandered about looking at nothing in particular. Martens was nowhere about. There were only four or five tents plus a larger field kitchen. Off to one side, there was a supply tent and a few ambulance jeeps.

It was not yet eight o'clock and Sam was restless. As he went back from the field kitchen he walked between two of the tents and almost stepped on a dead Marine. He was young, blond, lying on his side, and you could see he was stiff from rigor mortis. Someone had placed a shelter half on the ground and they had laid him on it. Sam stood looking down at him. He was fully clothed in combat gear and was wearing paratrooper boots with the two buckles and high leather tops. One of his heels had been blown off and it had taken leather, flesh, and bone, in one chunk, out of him. Sam couldn't tell where else he had been hit. His eyes were open and sightless. Sam supposed, if he were a North Korean, he would shoot him again and didn't like the thought of it. He wished they wouldn't have placed him there. It was as if he had just been thrown away, being no longer of use to anyone. Sam didn't like to see him that way, so he hurried on and went into the tent where he had spent the night.

Some other Marine, who occupied the cot next to him, introduced himself to Sam and asked what was wrong with him. Sam told him about his knee.

"They'll give you about two days of rest and send you back up," he said.

Sam inquired about him and he said that he was in Weapons Company and he had a slipped disc in his back. He thought they were going to send him to the Hospital Ship Repose to be operated on.

It was almost time for sick call when a thin ascetic looking man, with blue eyes that seemed to shine with a piercing light, entered the tent and approached a young Marine who was sitting on a cot. He knelt down and talked with the Marine, then got up and approached a second one and did the same thing. Then, he walked out the tent door.

"Who was that?" Sam asked.

"That was Lieutenant Commander Mullins. He's the shrink for the regiment. Those two guys he stopped and talked to are being sent home," Slipped Disc said.

"What's wrong with them?" Sam asked.

"They've got combat fatigue."

"And they're going home," Sam said. The memory of Bernie Welman popped into his mind, sitting on the back of the jeep with his hands clapped to his ears and screaming. That was combat fatigue. "They look alright to me," Sam said.

They went in to sick call and Sam sat down while a corpsman probed at his knee. He had Sam bend his leg a time or two asked where it was sore and gave him some more aspirin tablets.

"Doc, could you make me an appointment to talk to Commander Mullins?" Sam said.

"What for?"

"I'd just like to talk to him."

"I see. You just don't want to say. Okay. I'll ask him."

That afternoon a corpsman came to the tent and asked for Sam. Sam followed him out.

"You can see Dr. Mullins," he said.

Sam followed along beside him until he reached a tent and stopped.

"In there," he said, pointing.

Commander Mullins was seated at a desk in a folding chair. There was an empty chair in front of the desk and he indicated to Sam that he should sit down. Sam did so silently. Mullins had a manila folder in his hand. He opened it and read silently, then looked up at Sam.

"It says here, that you injured your leg," he said.

"Yes Sir."

"Why did you ask to see me?"

"This morning, I saw you stop and talk to two Marines in the casualty tent. Someone said that you were sending them home. I think the time has come for me to go home."

"Those are cases of combat fatigue; I have to send them home," said Commander Mullins.

Sam knew instinctively, from his experience, that he was as weary of combat as it was possible to be.

"I have combat fatigue," Sam said.

"You don't appear to," Mullins said.

"Yessir. You're right. But, I have it. I've had it for a long time. What do I have to do, go completely crazy, before I can go home? Or maybe wind up like that Marine lying on the ground by this tent. Maybe I should put a bullet in my head. Would that be combat fatigue?"

He hesitated for a moment; Sam could sense that it was due to something he had said, but didn't know what it was.

"We'll do some testing on you," Mullins said. "I'll have you talk to one of my assistants. He's very good at testing. He'll want to run some tests to help us determine the severity of your problem."

He made a notation in the folder. Sam got up and left the tent. Later in the day, he was told to report to a Lieutenant McMichaels. Sam went into the tent he was directed to. McMichaels was a heavy, barrel-chested individual with brown eyes and brown curly hair. He wore glasses.

"Sit down," he said.

Sam sat down and waited.

"What seems to be the problem?" he asked.

"The problem is that I have come to the end of my rope. It's time for me to go home. I understand you're sending people home for combat fatigue. I have combat fatigue. I'm tired of killing. I'd like to go home."

"What's your job?" he asked.

"I'm a squad leader," Sam said. "I'm known as Psycho Sam. My squad are called the Twelve Fanatics."

"That's unusual; how'd you get a name like that?" he asked.

"I was on a train with our corpsman. I threw his prayer book out the window of the train and he said I was psycho; the name stuck," Sam said.

"That's not a very flattering nickname," he said.

"I have another name I tried to substitute for it. I call myself Serge Blue the bandit leader," Sam said.

"How did you get that?" he asked.

"I took it out of a comic strip," Sam said.

"What comic strip?"

"'Terry and the Pirates.'"

"How long have you had that name?" he asked.

"Since the Chinese came into the war," Sam said.

"Have you ever taken a Rorschach test?"

"What's that?" Sam asked.

"It's called an ink blot test. I'd like to have you take it." He got up and walked over to a file cabinet, took out a large envelope, and came back.

"There's nothing complicated about this test. I'm going to show you several photographs of things that really are just blots of different colored ink. On each one of them, I want you to concentrate on what you see. When I ask, you tell me what you see," he said.

He produced an ink-covered paper about eight and one half by eleven inches in size and placed it in front of Sam.

"What do you see?" he asked.

"I see a paper colored by several different colors of ink," Sam said.

"No no! I mean what do you see in the ink?" he exclaimed.

Sam studied the paper.

"I see three Chinese soldiers cooking rice over a fire," he said.

He drew the ink blot back and placed it face down. Out of his folder, he produced a second. He placed it in front of Sam. "What do you see?"

Again, Sam concentrated on the paper. "I see a Chinese soldier with his leg blown off," he said.

He laid the ink blot aside, made a note on a tablet, and produced a third.

"What do you see?"

"I see a dog hanging by his hind legs from a tree limb," Sam said.

McMichaels wrote on the tablet, placed the ink blot aside, and produced another ink blot.

"What do you see?" he asked again.

"I see a bat down in a well," Sam said.

He showed him another ink blot. Sam studied it.

"Now, what do you see?"

"I see a dead woman with a baby on her back."

He kept on and on. Slowly Sam became unaware of anything except the ink blots. He produced about twenty. Each time, when Sam told him what he saw, he made a few notations on a pad. When he finished with the stack he picked them up and shuffled them to destroy the order in which he had presented them to Sam. Then he placed them in front of Sam one at a time and repeated the question, "Now, what do you see?"

"I see three Chinese soldiers cooking rice over a fire."

"Show me how you make them out," he said.

Sam pointed to the ink. "See here is the fire. Here is the cooking pot above the flame. Here is the outline of the first soldier. See how he is squatting down. Here is the second soldier with his bowl in his hand, and here is the third, squatting down beside him."

McMichaels produced each ink blot in random sequence. Each time, Sam saw the same thing he had seen the first time.

"What do you see?"

"I see a bat, down in a well," Sam replied and then, looking intently down at the ink blot, he exclaimed, "Oh, look! he's flopping his wings!"

His exclamation was followed by silence. Sam looked up at the psychiatrist. McMichaels was shaking his head in amazement. They went through the entire stack a second time. When they finished Dr. McMichaels appeared to be exhausted. He was wiping sweat off his forehead.

"Did I pass your test?" Sam asked.

"When you saw the bat flopping its wings did that bring any past experience to mind?" McMichaels asked.

Sam thought about it for a while. Finally, he remembered. "I was raised on a farm. There was a spring in our pasture with a lot of oak trees around. This spring was lined with rock on three sides. Once, my two older brothers and I went down to the spring and found a bat trying to climb up the rock wall. One of my brothers took a stick and knocked it down into the water. It was about four feet down to the water, and every time it would try to climb out we would hit it with sticks and knock it back. That's what combat is like. Every time you try to get out of the trap you get knocked back. Eventually, it kills you," Sam said.

"You go back to your tent and relax. I'll talk with you tomorrow," he said.

The following morning, Sam was called back to see him.

When Sam had sat down, McMichaels lit a pipe and began to smoke.

"I'm an ex-Marine," he said. "I fought in the Pacific, and after the war I had to have a psychiatrist straighten me out. So I know what it's all about. That's how I became interested in psychiatry. I went to college, majored in psychiatry, and here I am. Because of my experience, as well as my training, I think I know just about where you are. I think you are still capable of making a contribution. I propose to send you to another outfit."

"Oh," Sam said, "if I have to go back, I'll go back to Fox Company."

"No. that's not what I had in mind. Fox Company would not be good for your mental health."

"Why not?"

"These nicknames, this Psycho Sam business. It's definitely not in your best interest."

"If I have to go back. I want to go to Fox Company. All my friends are there. That's the only place for me," Sam said.

"What I had in mind was a job in a less stressful area. It would only be for a month or two and then you would be sent home," he said.

"What kind of job?"

"You would be at the final medical station. It involves issuing weapons and supplies to Marines who are returning to the front. You would sleep on a clean cot at night and get three hot meals each day. You look as skinny as a rail. What did you weigh when you landed?"

"One ninety," Sam said.

"You weigh one sixty now. You need some rest. What do you say?"

"I might give it a try," Sam said.

"Fine. I'll transfer you tomorrow. Oh by the way. You've been promoted to sergeant. Did you know?"

"No, I didn't," Sam said.

"Well, let me be the first to congratulate you. It's signed by a Captain Groff."

Sam didn't say anything. He wondered how long it had been so.

McMichaels interrupted his thought.

"We're moving tomorrow and I'll drop you off at your new location," he said.

Sam left the tent with mixed feelings. He had never felt so alone in his life. He tried to convince himself he should be glad that he would no longer be in combat. One would think that when you were being shot at every day, the news that this condition would cease would bring gladness and an enthusiasm for life. Sam tried to feel glad, but couldn't. What had he let Martens talk him into? He felt dead inside.

CHAPTER 37 ... The New Location ...

When morning came, Sam's depression lifted and he could not wait. He learned McMichaels had transferred him to the 141st Medical Battalion and was anxious to go there. He caught a ride on a jeep that was going there. He was met at the forward medical station by Sergeant Le blanc. Sam recognized Le blanc instantly. He had been Le blanc's Drill Instructor at Parris Island in 1948. They shook hands. Sam followed Le blanc into a tent. Le blanc sat down and grinned at him.

"I knew my replacement was coming, but I never dreamed it would be my D.I." said Le blanc.

Sam suddenly felt awkward. The last time he had seen Le blanc he had been required to stand at attention and say, "Sir, Private Le blanc requests permission to speak to his Drill Instructor."

Now, Sam was his replacement. Sam had never thought of himself as a replacement. Replacement for what?

From the startled expression on his face Sam saw Le blanc's puzzlement. It is sometimes easy to go up in life but always hard to come down. In Sam's view, he was coming down. He had failed to find his way home. Martens had overestimated him. Martens had said, "You'll think of something."

Now, Sam found himself in a situation which implied he was wasted. He was no longer a combat leader, and did not enjoy it. Le blanc tried again.

"What a surprise," Le blanc said, "I never in a million years would have expected my D.I. would be my relief."

"Your relief?" Sam asked.

"Yeah, I've been scheduled to go home for more than a month, but they didn't have a replacement for me," he said.

"Have you been in combat?" Sam asked.

"Nah," Le blanc said, "I've been back here handing out clothes and weapons all the time."

"How is it you're to be sent home if you haven't been fighting?" Sam asked.

"Why the rotation plan," Le blanc said. "Have you not heard of it?"

"We had a couple of guys who went that way," Sam said.

"This job gets awful boring," Le blanc said. "Breakfast is at seven. You have to be back in the supply tent by eight. You must carry your carbine when you go anywhere. Lunch is at twelve and supper is at five. After five, you can do what you want. Taps is at ten. You're supposed to be back here at ten. And anytime you leave the area, you have to check out with Dr. Shiller."

"Who is Doctor Shiller?" Sam asked.

Le blanc grinned at him. "You'll get to know him soon enough. He's a Navy doctor. He's in charge of this med station. Everyone who's been wounded comes through here on his way back to the front. He's the last doctor they see before going back. He's queer."

"What do you mean queer?" Sam asked. He thought he knew, but wanted Le blanc to be specific.

"Homosexual," Le blanc said, with a grin.

"When are you leaving?" Sam asked.

"Today. They said I could leave as soon as my replacement came. There's nothing to this job. All you do is make sure you give a weapon and whatever clothing they need when they ask for it. Doctor Shiller talks to them and then you take care of them. It usually happens at eight o'clock. They're not usually more than ten or twelve on any one day."

"How will I know Shiller?" Sam asked.

Le blanc grinned broadly. "He holds his sick call over there in front of that tent. Now, I'm outta here," he said.

He grabbed a packed valise, grabbed Sam's hand, wished him luck, and left the tent.

Sam went to the field kitchen to eat. When he came back, he saw a jeep pick Le blanc up and drive away. Sam went over to the cot and lay down and looked up at the center tent pole. He was beginning to get angry. How on earth did he get into this situation? To go from combat leader to flunky in three or four days was difficult to adjust to. It seemed radically unfair that anyone who had risked his life every day should be sent to relieve someone who had not risked his life at all. To Sam, it was a crowning insult. He began to curse Doctor McMichaels. Yet, he thought, McMichaels had done what appeared right. He had promised Sam would be sent home. Getting angry would do no good. Sam decided to make the best of the situation.

During the night, he dreamed he was standing in front of the swimming pool, and it was very vivid. All the blood and excrement and expressions on their faces were in the dream and Captain Groff was laughing at him again, except in the dream, Groff was standing on a beach in California and laughing and laughing. And his laughter was coming all the way across the Pacific Ocean. Sam woke screaming, clawing for his pistol, which wasn't there. He was wet with perspiration. Slowly, he became aware of where he was, and began to feel calm.

At breakfast, at the field kitchen, he recognized one of the cooks as another Marine he had trained at Parris Island. At the same time, he recognized Sam and came out from the kitchen to talk to him. He was from Brooklyn, New York, and had the New York accent. He kept picking his nose and wiping it on his apron, informing Sam that he was up for Staff Sergeant, which he thought was pretty good for three years of service. Sam thought he would be sick at his stomach and wondered how he could ever have allowed him to graduate from boot camp.

After breakfast, a line of Marines came to the tent. Sam issued each one of them the weapon he was entitled to. For some reason, they all seemed angry. The fourth one who arrived was one Sam had served with at Washington and had not seen since.

"Sam Lewis! How ya doin' Sam?" he cried.

"Dusanowsky. It's good to see you. What outfit are you with?" Sam asked.

"I'm in Third Battalion First, Item Company," he said.

"Going back up, huh?"

"Yeah. I got shot in the side. Didn't hit anything vital, but it's still tender. That goddam doctor gave me a real hard time," he said.

"What do you mean?"

"He asked me if I was ready to go back. I told him no. He started insulting me. You know, any one who's been in combat is never ready to go back. If I would have said yes, I would have been lying."

"So that's why everyone who has been through here has been mad," Sam said.

"Yeah, he did it to everybody," Dusanowsky said.

Dusanowsky had been the last in line. Sam talked with him a few minutes, told him how he happened to be giving out supplies, and how he hated being there.

"Man, I'd trade places with you in a minute," Dusanowsky said. They talked some more about the old days in D.C. and Dusanowsky asked about some Sam knew and Sam learned that several of their old comrades had been killed that he hadn't known about.

"Woolcocks died hard," Dusanowsky said. "I was with him when he got hit. He took a rifle bullet in the chest, up at the Chosin Reservoir. If we could have gotten him out, he might have lived. He prayed out loud to God not to let him die and I prayed for him too, but he went into a coma and never came out."

Then several jeeps rolled up and they climbed aboard and drove out of the encampment on their way. Sam went back to his tent and watched them leave. After lunch, he went to his cot and lay down. He felt like a bat in a well. He missed his comrades and wondered how Arkie was doing with the squad and felt guilty because he wasn't there.

The following day, one of the men of the 2nd Platoon came through. He had taken a grenade fragment in the leg and had been back for three days. Sam issued him an M1 rifle and asked about the rest of the platoon, told him to say hello to Arkie and the squad, then remembered one of the machine gunners who had been attached to the squad.

"Say hello to McChann for me," Sam said.

"McChann is dead, Sam."

"Oh God no!" Sam said. "How did it happen?"

"They sent us out at night to dig in a position. We had a tank with us and we were to dig in around the tank. Only thing was the Chinese sent men out into the same area. McChann was digging his hole and a Chinese soldier, armed with a burp gun, came up to him in the darkness. He stood looking down at McChann. McChann thought it was his partner, Marvin Childers, so when he looked up and saw the Chinese he said, is that you Marvin? And the Chinese killed him with a burst of fire from the burp gun. Marvin Childers killed the Chinese with his pistol. They were all around us, and we shot a bunch of them, and they told us to get on the tank and pull back to the main line. We got McChann up on the tank and brought him out with us. Sam it was awful. He was still there the next morning and he had the most awful bitter look on his face that I have ever seen."

Sam followed him over to the jeep which would take him to the front, and after he left, Sam went back and sat down his cot and began to weep for McChann.

CHAPTER 38 ... Shiller ...

Dr. Shiller stood in front of his medical tent. Two corpsmen were seated on folding chairs at a long table which had two folding chairs in front of it. Six Marines were waiting in the sick call line. The doctor was wearing a white smock and blue Navy trousers. He was hatless; his full head of dark hair was neatly combed, tending to fall to one side when he spoke. He had a nervous tic and a habit of raising one eyebrow. His skin was pale and smooth with little trace of a beard, seeming inconsistent with his dark hair.

Sam stood in the opening of his tent and watched. He could not say that, if Shiller was homosexual, his homosexuality was obvious. Somewhere, Sam had heard that it took another homosexual to know one. He was unable to reach an opinion as to whether or not the good doctor was; indeed it did not really matter. Sam was curious as to why the Marines always came in angry.

The first Marine had already had his blood pressure and temperature taken and was leaving. A second sat down. "Well! What have we here, another United States Marine," Shiller exclaimed. Now, when he spoke, his femininity became obvious. The Marine, a tall, gangly, good-natured type, grinned.

Shiller studied the chart.

"Let me see that arm," he said.

The Marine slipped out of his dungaree jacket and extended his right arm. A long pink scar ran up his forearm. "Let me see you move it," Shiller said.

The Marine flexed his fingers and arm.

"You're in top shape," Shiller said.

The Marine got up and came on over to Sam's tent.

"Is this where I get my M1?" he asked.

"Yeah, take your pick off the rack, and write your name and the serial number of the rifle in my book here," Sam said.

The second Marine had taken a rifle bullet through the chest. Shiller examined his wound and put a stethoscope to his chest, listening to him breathe. "You seem sound," Shiller said. "Are you ready to go back to combat?" The tone of his voice indicated that if the Marine wasn't ready, he might be excused.

"Why—why no, no. I'm not," the Marine stammered.

"Why not?" Shiller asked.

"Next time it might be a bullet in my head," said the Marine.

"I thought all you big brave Marines liked to fight!" Shiller said.

"No, Sir," said the Marine.

"What's the matter, run out of guts? My my my," Shiller said. He wrung his hands and walked in a tight little circle.

Sam suddenly became aware the first Marine was standing beside him watching.

"They warned me about that bastard," he said.

The second Marine came over. Sam issued him a weapon and some clean dungarees. Then he went back to the door to watch. The next Marine was a heavy-set burly youth whose neck had been torn with a bullet or fragment of some kind which had left a long red scar, and the places where he had been sewn together were still painfully obvious.

"Well, what have we here, Scarface?" Shiller's cruel smile added emphasis to his words.

"What did you say?" the Marine demanded.

"I said Scarface. Do you have a girl friend Scarface? You won't have one long when she sees what you look like." Shiller smiled as he spoke.

The Marine turned red and then white. The scar flamed red. He choked.

"It must be hard to kill those Chinese," Shiller said, his voice taking on a sympathetic tone.

"No. It's easy," Scarface said. "I shoot every one of the bastards I can get my hands on. I like to kill."

"My, oh my, oh my. A real killer Marine," Shiller said.

He gave his blessing that Scarface was ready.

"Return to duty. Next."

Scarface came over to Sam's tent. Sam showed him the BAR rack and turned back to watch Shiller.

The last man had been shot through his face. The bullet had entered from the right side and taken out two upper teeth, exited on the left taking out three upper teeth, and missed his tongue. Shiller asked him to open his mouth and wiggle his tongue. The Marine did so.

"OOhh," said Dr. Shiller, "another killer on his way back to the front. Are you ready to go?"

"If you had half your face shot off, would you be ready?" the Marine said.

"Then you're not ready," Shiller said.

"Nah. I'm not ready," the Marine replied.

"I thought all you Marines were supposed to be brave. I've not seen a brave one yet," Shiller said.

"I'm as ready as I'll ever be," the Marine said and walked away.

Filled with loathing of Shiller, Sam went to lunch. No doubt, this was the same doctor that Martens had told he was not ready to come back. Sam knew this was never going to do for him. There was no way he was going to remain in the situation he was in. He decided to go back to Dr. Mullins and find some other job. After lunch, he found one of the corpsmen.

"I'd like to go see the psychiatrist, Commander Mullins," Sam said.

"You'll have to ask Doctor Shiller. He's in his office. Just go on in," the corpsman said.

Sam did. Shiller was leaning back in his chair, had his right arm on the desk, still had on his white smock. "What do you need, Lewis?" he asked.

"I'd like to talk to Commander Mullins, Sir."

"What about?" he asked.

"It's personal, Sir," Sam said.

"I'll not give permission," Shiller said, petulantly.

"Then, I'll go see him anyway," Sam said.

"That would be direct insubordination. I could court-martial you," Shiller said.

"So what?" Sam said. "It wouldn't be my first time."

"Why do you wish to see Commander Mullins? It's not about me, is it?" he asked.

"Not completely," Sam replied.

"What do you mean, not completely?" he asked.

"I'm not suited for this job, Sir," Sam said.

"Oh you big brave Marines, my you are a big one aren't you. You all always want something other than what you've got. Well, I've got you. And you're staying right here," he said.

Sam was becoming angry. He could feel the blood rising.

"Dr. Shiller. That court-martial shit works both ways. I've asked to see a psychiatrist. Are you a psychiatrist?"

"No," said Shiller.

"You cannot refuse me the right to see Commander Mullins."

"Alright, you can go, but don't take your toothbrush; you'll be right back here tonight."

"Dr. Shiller, Sir, I will never be back here," said Sam.

"We'll see about that. I'm going to call Commander Mullins right now," Shiller said.

Sam got up and left.

Barton, one of the corpsmen, drove him to the regimental medical facility. When he pulled up in front of the medical tent Sam got out of the jeep.

"Don't bother to wait," he said.

"Dr. Shiller says you'll be coming back," said Barton.

"No way, Barton. Get this jeep out of here," Sam said.

CHAPTER 39 ... Commander Mullins ...

Sam entered the tent. A corpsman sitting behind a desk glanced up at him. "I'm Sergeant Lewis. I've come to see Dr. Mullins." Sam said.

"I know," said the corpsman. "Dr. Shiller called. Dr. Mullins will see you in a few minutes. Just have a seat." Sam found a seat and waited. He was wound up tight, full of anxiety, his mind racing full tilt. He waited for an hour. Finally, Commander Mullins appeared and beckoned Sam to follow him and led the way into another tent which Sam assumed to be his office and quarters. Mullins had only a desk, a phone, two chairs and a cot. Sam saw a stack of folding chairs off to one side and assumed Commander Mullins had meetings of some kind. Commander Mullins gazed at Sam with his piercing eyes. His eyes were neither kind nor unkind. It was as if he were deeply interested, yet neutral.

Sam wondered what kind of person was behind those eyes.

"What did you wish to see me about?"

"Sir, the job Dr. McMichaels sent me to was the worst possible place he could have sent me. I can't stay there. I'll go crazy."

"What's the problem?"

"Everything. The whole thing. I just can't stand it."

"Try to start from the beginning."

"It's not fair."

"What isn't fair?"

"Up where I've been it's been kill and be killed. It's a totally different world. It's not fair to take me from that world and use me to replace another man who has done nothing, has not even heard a shot fired. It's not fair and it's humiliating."

"It was only for a few weeks. Then, you'll be rotated to the United States."

"But for me, it's worse than the front lines."

Sam saw the trace of a smile on Commander Mullins thin face. His eyes seemed to shine.

"How so?" he asked.

"People I served with keep coming through on their way to the front. Yesterday a man came through who was from the same platoon. I couldn't bear to see him going back and me staying there. It's as if I've deserted my friends. I can't stand that."

"What else?"

"Why do they have someone like Dr. Shiller in that job?" Sam asked.

Commander Mullins eyes were neutral. He displayed not the slightest hint of knowledge.

"Someone has to give a final physical. That is Dr. Shiller's job."

"Is it his job to taunt and insult every one who comes through?"

"Dr. Shiller's job is not your affair. You've not shown me any medical reason why you shouldn't stay right where Dr. McMichaels put you. I'm afraid you'll have to go back."

Sam knew he would not take orders from Shiller. Shiller was of the same class as Von Ludwig. Sam knew that if he went back he would straighten Shiller out.

"If I have to go back, send me back to Fox Company."

"I can't do that," Commander Mullins said.

"Why can't you?"

"It would be bad for your mental health. Our tests show you had reached a breaking point. As a doctor I can't send you back to combat."

"Then send me home! I'll not go back to work in that job."

"You don't really have a choice," Commander Mullins said calmly. It was not like they were having a clash of wills. He appeared to be absolutely certain of himself.

"Yes Sir, I do," Sam said. "I refuse to leave this tent."

"Then I shall have to call the Marine guard and have you placed under arrest. You'll be court-martialed."

"That's exactly right. I've been court-martialed before, Doctor. Only this time I'll demand counsel, and when I get counsel I'll tell him about the swimming pool and the deep dark secret will be out."

"What's this swimming pool?" Mullins asked.

"Have you heard of the Malmedy Massacre, where the Nazis murdered about eighty American prisoners of war?" Sam asked.

Commander Mullins nodded. "Yes, I've heard of it."

"It was a war crime wasn't it?" Sam said.

"Yes. What's that got to do with a swimming pool?"

"When we took Seoul, I was in the battalion that fought its way right down the main street. At the end of the day, a whole bunch of North Koreans came into our lines and gave up. I helped take them prisoner. We turned them over to Easy Company. Some of Easy Company stripped them naked and marched them into a swimming pool in a hotel building and murdered them."

To Sam's surprise, he began to weep silently. At relating the incident, the hot tears just welled up. It was more emotion than he could handle. He struggled to get control.

"That's a war crime isn't it?" he said. "Only it's an American war crime. It's an American Malmedy Massacre."

Commander Mullins sat for a long time. He pulled out a pipe, filled it, lit it, and took a deep pull on it.

"When it happened," Sam said, "I complained to my Company Commander, Captain Groff. He laughed at me and refused to do anything. Right then and there, I told him I'd kill anyone who murdered a prisoner of war. He made fun of me. That's what happened when I reported it. Now, I'm reporting it again."

"What do you mean?" asked Commander Mullins.

"You're an officer. I'm reporting a war crime to you. What are you going to do about it?"

Commander Mullins was in deep thought. He sat without moving, gently puffing on his pipe. Sam sat there watching him and felt as if a heavy burden had been lifted from his shoulders. He was limp and relaxed the way he had been after his dream of Jesus Christ. Nothing could hurt him. Sam had taken the ache from inside and given it to Commander Mullins. He was ready to be court-martialed. They could do with him whatever they desired. He no longer cared.

For a long moment, Mullins sat in silence. When he looked at Sam, his eyes seemed to pierce right through him. His voice was low and soft.

"You'll have to wait outside the tent for a moment. I have to make a phone call," he said.

Sam got up and walked out the door. Mullins followed him.

"That's far enough," he said.

He dropped the tent flap and left Sam standing there wondering what would happen. First, Sam heard him call someone, then he heard him say, "We've got a problem." Then he lowered his voice and Sam couldn't hear anything else. Then Sam heard him say, "The boy has told me a hell of a story and I believe he's telling the truth."

There was a long silence. After five minutes or so Commander Mullins came back and opened the tent flap. He motioned Sam to come in.

"I wish I didn't have to do this. Are you sure you won't go back and work for Dr. Shiller?" he said.

"No Sir. I'll not do that," Sam said.

"When you were court-martialed, you had some problem with your platoon leader, didn't you?"

"Yes Sir. I was court-martialed, tricked and betrayed," Sam said.

"Hmnn. What was your relationship with Captain Groff?" he asked.

"I respected him as a brave man. I hated him for what he was otherwise."

"Did you trust him?"

"Hell no!" Sam said.

"Do you trust your Battalion Commander?"

"If it's Colonel Sutter, I have to say no," Sam said.

"Do you trust anyone?"

Sam laughed bitterly. "Not even my own mother," he said.

"How about your wife?"

"Dr. Mullins, if you had seen the things I've seen you wouldn't trust anyone. Neither do I," Sam said.

"If you choose to live this way you'll always be alone, cold, hard and bitter," he said.

"Who gives a damn?" Sam said.

"Cold and hard and bitter, is that how you feel?"

"Yes Sir," Sam said. He wondered what Mullins was leading to.

Mullins leaned forward in his chair and his face grew intense. "Just the type! Just the type!" he exclaimed.

Sam waited for him to continue. He leaned back and looked at Sam with a look which seemed to say you poor bastard.

"I'm going to send you to the United States," he said, then paused, then continued, "—in the only way that I can! I'm going to diagnose you as being seriously mentally ill. I wish I didn't have to do it, because it will cast a stigma upon you that will follow you the rest of your life.

"What do you mean Sir?"

"Once you have been hospitalized for mental illness, it will become part of your record. Every time you apply for a job, it will come back. It will be a stigma which will eventually cause you great shame."

"Doctor, what do you think I've felt ever since I saw that swimming pool? Nothing could make me feel more ashamed than I've felt because of that," Sam said.

"I don't know what will happen to you. Some of my colleagues may get ambitious and try to cure you. You're just a boy. You may not be able to resist."

"What do you mean, Sir?"

"I mean don't talk to anyone until you get to the United States. Open your mouth and there's no telling what may happen to you. When you get to Japan, keep your mouth shut. Do you understand?"

Sam understood the instruction, but he wasn't sure why. But, he was being sent home and that was what he wanted. Why question it?

"Yes, Sir. I understand. Don't talk to anyone," he said.

"When you get to the United States, you can talk then. They can straighten it out," he said.

Sam was too young and too naive to realize the power of his knowledge of the swimming pool affair. It was a truth which could harm his country. It had been covered up since the day it happened and would continue to be so. By declaring Sam crazy, Commander Mullins was participating in, indeed even furthering, the cover-up. In the end, the atrocity of the swimming pool, a truth which none who knew about it could face, became the thing which sent Sam home. It did not occur to him, until later, the power which lay in his hands. Nothing is more powerful than truth. Truth takes two. One to speak and one to listen.

Commander Mullins led him out of the tent and into the main medical tent where he found a corpsman. He spoke to the corpsman in low tones. The corpsman motioned Sam to follow him. Sam did. They left the tent and climbed aboard a jeep.

"Where're we going?" Sam asked.

"I'm taking you to the Hospital Ship Repose. You'll stay there until they fly you to Japan."

He fired the engine and pulled away. Three hours later, after a ride in silence, the jeep pulled up to the dock where the Repose was tied up.

Sam walked aboard, escorted by the corpsman, and was taken immediately to the sick bay. They gave him a set of hospital pajamas; Sam put them on and went to the bunk they assigned to him and lay down. A corpsman wandered over and asked him what outfit he was from. Sam looked up at the ceiling without answering. He was following Commander Mullins's instructions. They talked to him, but Sam didn't talk to them. If they told him to do something, he did it. He didn't ask questions. He lay on a tiered-type bunk with four bunks. He had the lower one, nice clean white sheets and clean pajamas. Sam put his hands behind his head and stared at the bottom of the bunk above. He heard one of the corpsmen tell another that he was catatonic. He didn't eat anything that day, but the second day he got up and walked to chow. The third day he was on an airplane bound for Yokuska.

Somewhere between Korea and Japan one of the engines began to leak fuel and the pilot announced they would make an emergency landing in Tokyo. Sam sat by the window of the plane and watched the fuel dripping off the wing behind the engine. He wondered if he was going to die out there in the Sea of Japan and remembered the voice in the dream saying, "Do not be afraid." Next thing he knew, they were setting down on the airstrip at Tokyo. Sam stayed on the plane while they corrected the leak and then flew on to Yokuska.

The plane was met by two corpsman. They took him by jeep to the Naval Hospital. He went down a flight of stairs to a bay full of patients that were in an open ward. Sam started to walk out in to the ward, but one of the corpsman stopped him. He took Sam to a large cell with steel bars on the door and two bunks inside. A man in pajamas sat on one of the bunks and looked up.

"Get in there with that other paranoid," the corpsman said. "If you get angry, you two guys can kill each other."

Sam stepped into the cell and the corpsman closed and locked the door behind him. Sam sat down on the empty bunk. Right away, the other guy came over. He was a heavy individual, not fat, but looked to weigh two hundred pounds. "What's your diagnosis?" he asked.

"I don't know," Sam said. "What's yours?"

"I'm a paranoid," he said. He seemed to be proud of it.

"You Navy or Marine?" Sam asked.

"Navy," he said.

"Why are you locked up?"

"I tried to choke one of those guys out there."

"You don't need to worry about me," Sam said. "You don't bother me and I'll not bother you."

He grinned. "That's fine," he said.

Sam lay back, put his hands behind his head and stared up at the ceiling. He wondered what a paranoid was. Apparently, he had been diagnosed as such.

CHAPTER 40 ...The Stigma

Two days passed. Sam was kept confined with the same inmate. Both were under constant observation. At breakfast on the third day a corpsman unlocked the cell and allowed Sam out.

"You can go anywhere in the hospital that you wish," he said "Just let the duty corpsman know where you're going."

Sam headed for the library. He was very curious about paranoia. He found a dictionary first and looked up the term. Then he found an encyclopedia. Within a matter of minutes he saw how Commander Mullins had arrived at the diagnosis. The questions the good doctor had asked Sam, when coupled with Sam's answers, had provided Commander Mullins with the basis he was seeking. Sam's mention of the conspiracy associated with his court-martial might seem imaginary to an ordinary person. Most Americans, raised in civilized society, would tend not to believe the swimming pool affair.

In a sense, Commander Mullins was rationalizing his knowledge of the swimming pool. He believed Sam was telling him the truth and yet he was looking for ways to keep the truth from becoming known. Combat is a form of insanity. By diagnosing Sam as paranoid, he left Sam to carry, not only the burden of the swimming pool, but the additional burden of the stigma of mental illness. Sam had left one world of insanity only to be committed to another.

The ward he was in was filled with silent people. Most were like zombies. They smoked cigarettes, ate, dressed themselves, and walked about. The things which were missing from the ward were joy and laughter.

Jack Benny, the famous comedian, was on tour of the bases in Japan. He visited the hospital Sam was in, bringing with him a pretty brown-eyed girl who wore a trick dress. The dress had a low cut to it. The trick was when the brunette shrugged her shoulders—the low square neck of the dress would drop momentarily, exposing almost all of her breasts. It was as if she had winked her eye.

Jack came out and stood in the middle of the psychiatric ward and began making his standard jokes about being tight with his money, and the girl kept letting her breasts pop out, acting as if she didn't know what she was doing, and the zombies all sat and stared at Jack and his girl as if they were two goldfish. Jack's brand of humor, which would normally have been entertaining, fell on deaf ears. He could not raise a smile. He got nervous and switched to talking about Rochester, his chauffeur, and still no one laughed.

Sam turned to the guy beside him and said, "Machine guns up."

The guy failed to see anything funny in Sam's twisted humor. Within five minutes the great Jack Benny left the ward for more favorable surroundings.

Sam went back to bed. The only question that entered his mind was how soon he would go to the United States. He did not think beyond that. Occasionally, he wondered what Martens would say if he knew what his advice had resulted in.

Each morning the resident psychiatrist, a Dr. Rogers, came past the bunks for morning sick call. Patients were up and standing at the foot of their beds. His nurse, a pretty blond, preceded him with a pad and pencil to take notes. He asked simple questions, like, "How did you sleep last night?" while looking the patients over. Sam remembered Commander Mullins's admonition to keep his mouth shut. If he slept well, when Dr. Rogers came around he said nothing.

One morning, Dr. Rogers stopped beside Sam.

"How did you sleep last night, Lewis?" he asked.

"Not very well, Sir," Sam replied.

"What was the problem?" he asked.

"I dreamed I was choking my father to death with a necktie, Sir."

"Oh, I see," he said, and started to move on.

"Sir, what does a dream like that mean?" Sam asked.

"It probably means you are angry," he said.

After the sick call was over, Sam climbed back into bed. Most of the zombies were up walking around or playing checkers. The nurse came in and sat down on Sam's bed.

"Why don't you get up?" she demanded.

Sam looked up at the ceiling, wishing to avoid conversation.

"You brat," she said, "do you think you're the only person who's been shot at?"

Sam stared at the ceiling. There was no point in even attempting to discuss the reality of life with her.

"Do you think you're the only one who has seen friends killed? Others have suffered besides you," she said.

Sam moved his head ever so slightly. "What would you know about it?" he asked.

"My husband is a lieutenant in the Marines. He's aboard an aircraft carrier," she said.

Sam shrank back from her. She grew alarmed.

"What's wrong with you?" she asked.

"An officer!" Sam shouted. "I hate officers. Get away from me. Leave me alone."

They moved him into a room where they could keep a closer watch. Sam failed to understand the reasoning behind this move. There was no way they would send him back to combat. Both Doctors McMichaels and Mullins had made that decision and Sam knew it would not be reversed. He wanted to go home. What were they waiting on? He began to see them as obstacles.

He stopped eating. Within a week, he was on a plane bound for Hawaii. The plane stopped at Pearl Harbor and he was taken to a Navy hospital for a day's rest.

General Lemuel Sheppard, the Commandant of the Marine Corps, visited the hospital. Sam was in the same ward as those with wounds. Sheppard made his way down the line of patients talking with each one. Those who were able were standing and, from long training, Sam stood at attention. Sheppard stopped and looked him over.

"What's wrong with you, Son?" he asked.

At one time, Sam would have been in awe of the Commandant of the Marine Corps. Now, he saw a balding man with a kind face who was a little too fat.

"They say I'm crazy, Sir," Sam said.

"And what do you say?" Sheppard inquired.

"I say I'm not, Sir," Sam said.

He passed on to the next man, leaving Sam to his thoughts. If Sheppard had spoken to him three weeks prior, Sam would have grinned at him, and shouted "Banzai!" and Sheppard would have been startled. Then,

Sam would have screamed, "Five thouusand commuuneests, that a way, go get em!" and Sheppard would have laughed. Sam was in the insane world and finding it difficult to adjust.

The plane ride ended at Treasure Island, California. Marine green uniforms were issued and he was allowed to go to the mainland on liberty. Sam went with a Marine who had been shot between the eyes. The bullet which struck him had passed through a sapling before it hit him and had imbedded in his skull. He had walked around with the bullet still in his head for three days before they had extracted it. Somewhere along the line, he had been diagnosed as schizophrenic. They got into a bar and began to feel the effects of the whiskey they were drinking. They began to sing crazy songs.

"Sitiamus J, pasqulai,
Sitiamus prosus jaraa,
Ching, Oh sing, a moraa,
Sitiamus Bre Ha Ga."

Each time they finished the song Sam shouted, "Banzai!"

The waitress decided the schizophrenic was sane and Sam was crazy. She made friends with the schizophrenic Marine and persuaded him to get Sam back to the hospital where he belonged.

"He—is crazy!" she said.

Next day, Sam was aboard a plane which was approaching San Antonio, Texas. Suddenly the plane hit an air void and fell for many feet before it stopped falling. Just when Sam thought he was going to die, the pilot got it under control and landed. The plane refueled and took off for Washington D.C. It landed at the airport in Washington about eight o'clock in the evening. Sam walked down the portable stairway and stood on the paved earth. Four Sailors approached him.

"You Sam Lewis?" one asked.

"Yeah," Sam said.

The four surrounded him. They grabbed him. One had a straightjacket.

"What the hell are you doing?" Sam demanded. "There's no need for that thing."

"Cooperate with us and it will be easier. Oppose us and we'll put you in it anyway," one said.

Sam meekly submitted. They took him to the van and placed him in back. One of the Sailors asked, "Say Marine, do you hear voices?"

"Yeah I do," said Sam.

"What do the voices say?" he asked.

"They say all Sailors eat shit and bark at the moon," Sam said. That ended the conversation. The van pulled into the grounds of the Naval Hospital at Bethesda, Maryland, and stopped. They led him inside to an elevator that had steel bars in front of it. One unlocked the bars and they rode up, got off and unlocked another set of barred doors, went down the hallway, unlocked another steel door, and went into a room where all the walls were covered with white padding. Even the door bars were padded. They took off the straightjacket, went out, closed the door behind them, and locked it.

"Now you can scream all night if you want to," one said. "This place is soundproof."

Sam shouted, "Banzai!"

At last, he lay down and fell asleep. He had finally come home.

He spent several days in the padded cell. Food was delivered with only a plastic spoon and a close eye was kept while he ate. As soon as the meal was finished the attendant took the tray away and locked the door behind him. Sam had asked to speak with a psychiatrist on the first day. He had been assured as soon as possible one would be assigned. On the morning of the fifth day, two Sailors came to the door and escorted him out through the series of barred doors and opened the door to an office. Sam went in and the two Sailors came in and stood behind him.

Sam recognized the doctor right away. There were two gray-haired Navy officers sitting over to one side. All of them were watching him intently. The doctor told the attendants to leave, and then turned to Sam.

"I'm Dr. Lowry," he said." This is Captain Jones and Captain Smith."

Sam nodded to the gray hairs. To Dr. Lowry, he said, "Yes Sir, I know you. When you were at Parris Island, I used to send recruits who had mental problems over to see you."

"We would like to chat with you," Dr. Lowry said.

Sam didn't say anything.

"What do you think of the treatment you've had so far?"

"What do you mean, Sir?"

"The doctors and nurses you've come in contact with, have they treated you right?" he asked.

"I don't consider anything that's happened to me to be treatment. I sure as hell don't consider a padded cell as treatment. I may be in a zoo, but I'm not a monkey," Sam said.

"I see," Dr. Lowry said.

"Sir, with all due respect, perhaps you don't see. Four or five weeks ago, I decided it was time for me to return to the United States. Now I'm here. I'd like to go home. I'd like to live again. Is there something wrong with that?"

"Did you decide, or did the Navy decide?"

Sam shrugged his shoulders. He did not intend to answer.

"How do you feel about killing?" Captain Jones asked.

"Have you ever killed a man, Sir?" Sam asked.

"No," he said.

"Then don't ask me about how it feels. I've killed too many. I still remember the first one. I see him many times in the dead of night. How should I feel about it? Should I rejoice?" Sam asked. Everyone was silent for a moment. The doctors all looked at each other. Sam was watching them.

"Dr. Lowry," Sam said, "how about letting me out of that cage?"

"We'll let you know," he said.

He got up and opened the door. The two attendants escorted Sam back to the padded cell.

A half hour passed. The attendants came back, unlocked the door, and Sam was again escorted to see Dr. Lowry.

"We have discussed your case," he said. "Our decision is to move you to our semi-open ward. You will still be locked up, but with a lot of other patients. You'll be allowed to leave the ward to go for walks or the library or post exchange, with permission of course. After we have gotten to know each other, we'll decide on treatment."

"How soon can I get out of solitary?" Sam asked.

"You are out now," he said. "Come with me. I'll introduce you to the duty nurse and the corpsmen on the ward." He took Sam out past one locked door.

Nurse Maloney had a pimpled face, short curly hair, and the disposition of a bitch. She was kind enough to show Sam where his bed was. Dr. Lowry introduced him to the two ward corpsmen and took his leave. He left Sam in the ward. As soon as he left, Nurse Maloney called Sam to the duty desk and began to lay down her rules and regulations. Sam listened to her without comment. When she finished, he said, "Okay Mam," and went over and lay down on his bed and looked about to see just what kind of situation he was in.

The ward was about a hundred fifty feet long with a broad aisle from one end to the other. On the west end, where Sam was, Joe and Tony, the corpsmen, had an office that contained some medical equipment and a flat bed, with a rubber mattress on it. Sam had seen all this when Dr. Lowry took him in. Nurse Maloney's desk was in the center of the room on the north side where the beds were interrupted to leave a broad hallway into the toilets. The place had lots of windows and, although they were barred, plenty of light entered and the place did not look too depressing.

From the east end, a high-pitched voice called, "Here pussy! Here pussy, pussy, pussy!"

Across from Sam, on the north side, a patient lay in his bed. Every three or four minutes he burped. He was an air sucker. He would breath through his mouth and swallow some of the air then belch it back up.

"Here pussy, pussy, pussy!" came the cry again.

Over on his right, a thin red-haired patient was trying to light a cigarette. His hands were shaking badly. He was a nervous wreck. Further down, on the right, another patient was walking about as if he was trying to find a place to hide, looking back over his shoulder furtively to see if he was being followed. He would run a short distance and cower down behind a bed until he thought whoever was following him had seen him. Then, he would move again.

"Pussy, pussy, pussy; here pussy!"

Sam decided to work his way down through the ward and find out where the noise was coming from.

At the very end, he found the noise maker, a sallow-faced man of about fifty. He had freckles, was clean shaven and had an effeminate manner. "Hi there, you," he said, to Sam.

"How are you, Chief?" Sam asked.

"How did you know I was a chief?" he asked.

"I didn't. I just guessed. You remind me of a chief I knew aboard ship in the Mediterranean."

"Oh boy, the Mediterranean; that's some sea," Chief said.

"Yeah it sure is. It can be as calm as a sea of glass, but can be choppy too, at times," Sam said.

"Here pussy, pussy," he said, looking about.

"What color is your cat?" Sam asked.

"She's black. Real shiny black."

"What's her name?" Sam asked.

"Pussy, you idiot, what did you think her name was, Miss Maloney?" he said.

Sam chuckled. "How long has it been since you last saw her?"

"I can't remember that," he said.

"Well, it's nice to meet you, Chief," Sam said and stuck out his hand.

He grasped Sam's hand and shook it.

"Same here," he said. "What's your name?"

Sam hesitated. What the hell! "Will Rogers," Sam said.

"Hey that's great. We have the Will Rogers of ward 5D!"

The other patients looked up with smiles and pleasant expressions. All except Nurse Maloney. She didn't look happy. As Sam left the chief he called out, "Here pussy, pussy."

Sam went back and lay down on his bed and closed his eyes. Well Martens, he thought, I've done it. I'm back in the United States. But, what a way to come back.

Events had moved too fast. What on earth had he gotten himself into. He was not crazy. That much he knew, but what he didn't know was what there had been in the Rorschach test that had convinced Dr. McMichaels that he should not go back to Fox Company. His mind wandered and he saw the faces of his squad in his mind's eye. He hated himself for leaving the Twelve Fanatics. He became consumed with guilt and felt tears roll silently down his cheeks. Accustomed to living in the shadow of death, he now found the shadow of despair, but the full significance of the stigma he had incurred was not yet clear to him. Miss Maloney snapped him out of it. She was standing over him when he heard her clear her throat.

"Will Rogers. There are some things you must understand. We do not lay in bed all during the day. You can have one hour after lunch. Otherwise you will be expected to be up and about until five."

"Miss Maloney, Mam, will you do me a favor?" Sam asked.

"What is it you want?" she replied.

"Will you get the chief to stop calling his cat?" Sam said.

"The chief has his problems. They're not your affair."

"And I have my problems," Sam said. "I've been too long without a bed."

Sam turned aside and ignored her. She stamped angrily away and returned with Joe and Tony. Tony was carrying a straightjacket. Joe was very quiet and calm.

"Look," he said, "would you rather go back to solitary, or would you like to stay here?"

"Would it be possible for me to go to the library, if I stay here?" Sam asked.

"Yes, if you cooperate with Miss Maloney."

"Alright," Sam said, "whatever Miss Maloney wants, Miss Maloney gets." He got up off the bed and smoothed the sheets.

Joe and Tony were satisfied. Miss Maloney wanted to beat the issue to death. She invited Sam over to her desk and went into a long harangue about regulations.

"Rule-followers of the world, unite," Sam thought, as she babbled on. Down on the end of the ward, the chief kept calling his cat. Then another patient came up to her desk and spoke to her in some kind of foreign tongue that was pure gibberish, neither French nor German nor incoherent English. Sam was unable to duplicate the sound.

"This is Albert," Miss Maloney said.

Sam extended his hand to Albert. "Will Rogers here," he said. Albert grinned and gave more gibberish.

Miss Maloney smiled and said, "Don't mind Albert, he talks to the animals."

Down at the end of the ward, the chief cried out, "Here pussy, pussy, pussy!"

CHAPTER 41 ... The End of the Dream ...

Three days passed. On the morning of the fourth day the corpsmen escorted Sam into Dr. Lowry's office. The doctor looked up from his desk and cocked his head down and peered at Sam over his glasses.

"Sit down," he said.

Sam sat down.

"I've considered your case and consulted with the other doctors."

"Really, Sir, I think the best thing that could happen to me is to allow me to go on leave and be with my wife and family."

"No. No!" Lowry said. "We're nowhere near ready for that."

"Why not, Sir?" Sam asked.

"Are you ready to go back to duty?"

"What kind of duty?" Sam asked.

"We could transfer you back to the Commandant's home at Eighth and I."

The surprise was complete. For months, Sam had carried in his mind the memories of the parades and pomp and ceremony, the firing squads and funerals of dignitaries, all as something to look forward to. These had been once a snap, a piece of cake, if you will; now, the thought of doing these things repelled him. The old dream he had carried in his mind during combat was now within his grasp, but he no longer wanted it. He struggled for words to express how he felt, but could find none. He took a deep breath and sighed wearily. The very thought of parade ground duty repelled him. He had made life-or-death decisions, not only for himself, but for his squad, on a daily, almost hour by hour basis, and such a life as he had once lived at the Commandant's home now seemed petty, boring, and repulsive.

Sam felt panic. Not only did he not want to return to it, he felt he could not. The dream was dead. The person who had once carried it in his mind was no longer Sam. Somewhere, out on one of those distant mountains, the old Sam had ceased to exist.

Surprised, he suddenly felt lost, incapable of coping. When at last able to speak, his own words surprised him.

"Sir, my days of standing at attention for any human being are over. I will never again be anyone's tin soldier," Sam said.

Dr. Lowry did not seem surprised. "I see," he said. "It's important you see you're not ready to return to duty. I believe you do. We have two methods of treating you. One method is to treat with electric shock, the other is with insulin shock. Neither method is something that you should be afraid of."

"The method I would like to see is to just let me go on thirty day leave. Really, that's all I want," Sam said.

"But to do that we have to return you to duty and you've indicated you're not ready for that," Lowry said.

"What is this electric shock treatment?" Sam asked.

"We fasten electrodes to your head and give you a shock that induces a coma," he said.

"You're not going to do that to me," Sam said quietly.

Lowry ignored Sam's statement and went on, "The other method is to give you an injection of insulin which will put you to sleep for about an hour. Then we wake you up with a glass of orange juice."

"What's the orange juice for?" Sam asked.

"It's capable of being rapidly absorbed by your blood and contains glucose which counteracts the insulin and wakes you up," he said.

"What's the purpose of this treatment?" Sam asked.

"It should help to free you of bad memories."

Sam sat silently for a long time. His thoughts ran backwards, his mind awash in impressions of horror, remembering all the things which had made deep impressions on him. He knew he would never forget these things. It had been more than a year since the night he had killed the first man beside the path in Korea. In a flash, he saw Carpenter on the ground fighting for his breath; the whole panorama of past existence, more rapidly than a modern-day computer, raced through his mind, not in any sequence, but randomly associated. He was lost in another world. When he returned from it, Dr. Lowry was saying, "You must choose one of these methods, which will it be?"

"I'll take the insulin and orange juice," Sam said.

It was against his will. He could have fought them, but in the end he would have wound up back in the padded cell, and he knew this with certainty.

He took the first treatment that same day. He lay on a hardboard mattress which was covered with a blanket and over the blanket a rubber sheet. They strapped him onto it and injected insulin into his veins in a sufficient quantity to put him into a coma. When he woke, sometime later, Joe was gently slapping his face and Sam was unstrapped from the board and they were holding him upright from his waist. He felt the slaps, heard Joe saying, "You've got to drink this."

Joe held the juice to Sam's lips. Sam began to swallow. Perhaps a minute later, he was able to take the juice on his own and gradually drank the contents of the glass. The rubber sheet was wet with his perspiration. Sam was shaky inside and his hand trembled violently as he clutched the glass.

He was allowed to rest for a few days.

Curiosity had always been Sam's habit and he became curious about psychiatry. He began to visit the library at every opportunity, to read about the manifestations of psychoses such as schizophrenia, paranoia, delusions, etc. And as he wandered about, outside the ward, he stumbled upon the ward for female personnel. There were only three patients—a blond, a brunette, and a Chinese girl. He would go in to see them each day. Sam found them eager to communicate with anyone outside their ward, and they soon caught on to his twisted sense of humor. Sam wanted to see if he could arrive at a diagnosis of each one without being told directly. The brunette told him about some of her interviews with the psychiatrist, "You know what he asked me? He asked me if I ever reached a climax."

"And what did you tell him?" Sam asked.

"I asked him whether or not his wife did," she said.

"And what did he say?" Sam asked.

"Ah, ha ha, he didn't answer. I don't think he knows," she replied.

He discerned that the brunette was being treated for nymphomania. The Chinese girl had been raped and she consistently referred to men as beasts. He was unable to discover what was ailing the blond and did not pry. Oddly enough, he was able to tell the three of them about the swimming pool. He did so one day in halting hesitant terms, feeling the emotion come welling up inside, and struggling to keep control. The Chinese girl responded with, "Beasts. They're all beasts!"

The blond, who had many times remained silent whenever Sam visited the three, suddenly spoke to him. She said, "Say, Sam, Mr. Will Rogers of ward 5D, if you really want to see something of interest, go over to the officers ward. You won't believe what you find there."

"What is it?"

"Can't tell you. You've got to see it for yourself."

Sam took her suggestion and found the officers ward, which was on the same floor of the hospital. It was guarded by a Miss Maloney type and Sam knew he would not get past her without help so he returned to the female ward and asked the blond if she would call the nurse on the phone and tell her that Commander Lowry wanted to converse with her in his office. Apparently, Blondie did this, because as Sam padded quietly back down the hall to the officers ward, the nurse passed him on her way. Sam proceeded on past her desk and found a position where he could look into the ward, which was only one large room with a bed and several chairs. Propped up in the bed was the largest baby that Sam had ever seen. He appeared to be about twenty-one chronologically, but about six mentally. His mother, Sam took her to be, two sisters, all from family resemblance, and his fiancée were with him. His summer uniform with Second Lieutenant's bars on the shoulders was hung on the hanger beside the bed and his fiancée was comforting him.

"Does my poor snookums need anything?" Then, before he could answer, "My poor, poor, precious little bun bun, what have they done to my baby?"

"They were so mean to me," he whimpered.

Then his mother came to his side with the same nonsense that his fiancée had used and she alternated with the two sisters. All, without exception, wanted to get snookums something. What snookums finally decided upon was a dish of ice cream, which his mother came back with and relieved the fiancée again, continuing with the excessive pampering.

Sam had seen enough. He no longer was curious. He left the scene and went back past the female ward, talked with his three friends and left.

Days passed. Sam hung in limbo, a virtual prisoner at the hospital. He longed to go home but couldn't, and so he waited. As he roamed about, he began to observe the manner in which Dr. Lowry made his inspections. He would stop at each patient and ask some question that seemed pertinent to him alone, but probably dealt with the patient's diagnosis. It seemed to Sam most patients restricted their answers. Occasionally, one would be told that the good doctor would see them in his office later in the day. After a month in the place, Sam was ready to try out his newfound knowledge, so he began his rounds by stopping to chat with the air sucker. Sam asked him how long he had had his belching condition, and learned that it had been several months. And, as Sam began to loosen him up a little, he confided that he had been hiccuping ever since he had been selected to be transferred to Korea.

"You have an Anxiety Reaction," Sam informed him.

"That's what they say!" he exclaimed.

The next patient he visited was a red-haired Sailor from Utah who had been ten years in the United States Navy.

"How did you happen to get in here?" Sam asked.

"One morning, we had to stand the Admiral's inspection. We were in ranks and waiting for the Captain to precede the Admiral down our ranks. I was a First Class Machinists Mate and I had stood dozens of inspections. The Captain came down the rank preceding the Admiral and all of a sudden I began to cry. I was very embarrassed and tried to stop, but the more I tried, the harder I cried, and I just couldn't stop. They had to lead me to sick bay and I still couldn't quit."

"Where were you raised," Sam asked.

"On a ranch in Utah. We have ten thousand acres," he said.

"Do you plan to return there?" Sam asked.

He began to weep. Sam did not try to stop him. Sam concluded that he had acute anxiety. When he got control, Sam asked him questions designed to find out what was troubling him. He claimed not to know.

"Hang in there," Sam said, and moved on.

He was able to engage the chief in intelligent conversation. He was friendly enough and Sam was able to persuade him to stop calling his cat. Though he would not discuss his condition, and Sam did not presume to, Sam concluded the fellow was homosexual and was having identity problems.

The most Sam could do with Albert, who spoke with the animals, was to get him to play checkers, a game that he consistently beat Sam at. During one of these games the chief came by and stood watching them. The chief lit a cigarette. Albert saw this and babbled incoherently. The chief pushed the cigarette pack at Albert with a cigarette extended. Albert withdrew the cigarette, stuck it in his mouth and nodded that he wanted a light. The chief lit the cigarette. Albert babbled some indiscernible nonsense, took a deep pull, and jumped two of Sam's men without any expression of glee whatever.

Sam had at least six of the insulin shock treatments. They made him forget some things, but left him with all the bad images of death and cruelty still intact. Midway through the treatment, Dr. Lowry asked him into his office and mentioned to Sam that he had been practicing psychology on the other patients to gain his own ends. Sam admitted that this was true.

"But Doctor," Sam said, "none of my ends are selfish or dishonorable. You don't hear the chief calling his cat anymore and Albert is playing a superb game of checkers. The only person in the ward who doesn't like me is Miss Maloney, and I couldn't begin to diagnose what's wrong with her."

"She is not a patient," Doctor Lowry said.

"No Sir, but in my opinion, she should be."

"How do you arrive at that conclusion?" he replied.

"She expects all the patients to act logically. They cannot. They act emotionally and, in many cases, illogically. In my view, she has not the kindness or consideration to be a psychiatric nurse and should be transferred to another field," Sam said.

"I think it's time for you to go on liberty," Dr. Lowry said. "What do you think?"

"Yes Sir. I'd like to visit the Marine Barracks at Eighth and I."

"Very well, you may do so. If you don't mind, I'd like you to take Sergeant Cullins along with you," he said.

Sergeant Cullins was a patient who was suffering from depression. Sam thought Dr. Lowry suggested he take him along to see if he could get Cullins to express interest in anything at all. Sam had talked to him briefly on two occasions, but found him exceptionally uncommunicative. His home was in Chambersburg, Pennsylvania, which was only thirty miles distant from Charlotte's home. When Sam approached him and inquired if he would like to go visit the barracks with him he readily agreed, and the following day they suited up in Marine green and entered the gate of the barracks that Sam had left some eighteen months before.

Cullins was a veteran of World War Two and, to Sam's surprise, he wore four rows of ribbons and many battle stars. It developed that he had been aboard a carrier that had served in both the Pacific and Atlantic and had also fought as a grunt at Okinawa in the Pacific.

Immediately as Sam entered, he did not recognize the guard at the gate, and after being duly examined as to identification, and telling him that they wished to visit the post tavern, they made their way down the broad walkway beneath the arches and entered into the post tavern where Sam had whiled away many hours drinking beer and conversing with his friends.

None were in there. One truly never can go home again. The only two persons Sam recognized in the place were Bill Williams, the mailman, and Pearshape Derwinski, the Post Supply Sergeant.

Williams was alcoholic and Pearshape was so named because his waist and rump were broader and thicker than his chest and shoulders. One did not call him Pearshape to his face unless prepared to fight, but behind his back, he was Pearshape. Sam went over to shake hands with the two of them and found both of them quite surly. He wondered If he had leprosy or something. Being greeted in an almost hostile way, Sam returned to the table where Cullins sat. Suddenly he was glad that Cullins was with him.

Bill Williams and Derwinski did not stay long. Then a Marine came in who Sam recognized immediately. He was Robert Pendarvis, one of the surviving members of the first squad Sam had led in the first three days of combat. He had later served in the same platoon, but not in Sam's squad. He right away informed Sam that Bill Williams and Derwinski were in the barracks mouthing off about him, the general gist of which was that Sam was in the nut ward at the hospital because he had gone around in the night hours looking for files that didn't exist and pretending to be crazy.

"I straightened them out," Pendarvis said. "I told them I had been in your squad in Korea and in the same platoon and you had never failed to do your job under any and all circumstances."

"And what did they do?" Sam asked.

"They shut up," he said.

The next person who came in was a sergeant Sam had known, who had been the Detachment Clerk. Only now, instead of being a buck sergeant, he was a Sergeant Major, having advanced his rank by three stripes and a diamond in the middle. He had been married to the daughter of an admiral and Sam wondered if that had had something to do with his four promotions in eighteen months. He had always been fond of talking about his wife and when Sam inquired about her his response was, "Oh—that dumb son of a bitch," which he uttered with a nonchalant grin.

Sam inquired about John Bundy and he said that he had been transferred; he didn't know where. Sam really felt quite alone now. It was easy for him to see how shallow the admiral's ex-son-in-law was and that Sam had nothing in common with any who were left there; it was as if they had split into two worlds. Of those worlds, one had gone to war, only half had survived, and many of these had lost eyes and limbs. Some, like Sam, had been scarred for life and yet didn't know it.

The other world had stayed behind and remained in the tin soldier mode, had gotten all the promotions, and had enjoyed the same soft life

Sam had previously had. But, they had not grown, and now they all seemed shallow.

Sam finished his beer with the admiral's ex-son-in-law and no longer knew or cared to know him. He asked Cullins if he was ready to go.

"Any time you are," Cullins said.

Sam was ready then. Now, he understood what Commander Mullins had tried to tell him about the stigma. He saw, for the first time, that if he should tell anyone about the pool, they would simply say that Sam was crazy and Sam saw that he would not be able to effectively deny it. If he wanted to tell the world, he would have to wait until he had lived the stigma down. They got up and walked out. Sam did not look back.

Dr. Lowry never mentioned the liberty. He did not see Sam again until after he had been given three more insulin shock treatments. These took place over a period of about four weeks. At length, the day arrived when Sam was called upon to make a decision. The good doctor asked him into his office, Miss Maloney brought his folder in, and Dr. Lowry glanced at it briefly as Sam waited patiently. When he looked up from his reading, he came straight to the point.

"How do you feel about returning to duty?" he asked.

"Do I have a choice?" Sam replied.

"Your viewpoint will be considered," he said. "I have to make a recommendation as to whether you should go back to duty or go before the physical evaluation board. If I recommend that you be discharged they will decide the degree of your disability. They may approve my recommendation and they may not. My recommendation will be, to some extent, based on how you feel about it. In some large measure, it depends on your reaction," he said.

"What does this board consist of?" Sam asked.

"Three Naval officers, one of whom will be a psychiatrist. You will be appointed counsel. A Marine or Naval officer will represent the Navy," he said.

"Sir, going back to duty is the last thing I would ever want to do. It would be the most boring thing that could ever happen to me. The very thought of standing at attention and saluting someone causes me to feel degraded. I have no desire to play tin soldier. I want to see what it feels like to do a hard day's work. I want to be tired at the end of each day. I have no education, can not even add or subtract fractions, but that can be corrected. I have seen the very worst human beings can do and also the very best. I am barely twenty-two, but I am old. Mentally, I feel no different than the day I arrived here. These shock treatments have made me forget the little things, but the cruelties, the utter brutality, of the life I've lived are still with me. At nights, I dream of death and blood and murder. Many times, I am on patrol in the Land of the Morning Calm. I dream of my friends who were killed and the men I've killed. Sometimes, I hear their cries ring out in the hills and mountains of Korea. I believe they still haunt the land and haunt me in my dreams. Me go back to duty? Never! I could not be a martinet, not ever again. If I met an officer on the street, I'd walk three blocks to avoid saluting him. I am equal to all men and subservient to none. My days of standing at rigid attention are over."

CHAPTER 42 ... The Meeting of the Board ...

Sam sat on a bench outside the board meeting room and waited for his counsel. He had no idea about who the man was. Thirty minutes passed. Sam waited stoically. At last his counsel arrived. He was a gray dapper little man, a Full Colonel in the Marine Corps who wore two rows of ribbons and no battle stars. He wore wings on his blouse which said he was an aviator. He did not introduce himself, just came and sat down beside Sam with a folder in his hand. He closed the folder.

"Look," he said, "I'm going to do the best I can for you. But, you've got to cooperate. If you go in there and start giving that board the same hostile shit you give everyone else, they not only will not discharge you, but they'll have you locked up."

Sam thought, here we go again. Always some son of a bitch threatening to put you in the brig. He concentrated on being impassive. It was clear his counsel believed Sam was a malingerer. There was no sign of friendship in his face. He looked down his nose at Sam as if he disdained the sight of him. He could not conceal his contempt for Sam and Sam met his haughty stare with concealed disgust. Sam had learned never to show a response to an enemy, and recognized him as such. He recalled a Marine Corps saying, "when under fire, keep an old cool tool," and Sam was not about to precipitate anything with the obnoxious colonel that would damage him. He sat silently, waiting.

The colonel handed Sam a statement which he had written.

"When they ask you if you have anything to say, I want you to read this statement," he said.

There was no more time. The door to the hearing room opened and a yeoman motioned them in. They went in and sat down. A Marine Corps Major, who represented the Navy, walked swiftly into the room and sat down. He had a thin narcissistic face and sported a neat mustache. He was less than average height and build, but one would not call him a small man.

It all happened fast. Sam felt as if he was in a trance. He heard the words being intoned that it was November 27, 1951, and that the physical evaluation board was convened to consider the case of Sergeant Lewis.

The major got up and opened his case against Sam. Sam was a malingerer. Sam was shocked. Absolutely no basis for such a statement, Sam thought, wondering how the major would react in the middle of a rice paddy with bullets kicking up all around him. The major continued. He said that Sam should be court-martialed and placed in the brig. His last statement was that Sam was entitled to no compensation whatever. When he had finished with his attack on Sam's character he sat down.

Sam's counsel got up and began to speak. "This board has been asked to consider the case of Sergeant Lewis. Sergeant Lewis is hostile to authority, incorrigible, and not inclined towards remorse. If his present attitude and conduct continue and he is retained in the Marine Corps, he will indeed soon be incarcerated. On the outside, he will be fired from one job after another. It is my recommendation that Sergeant Lewis be discharged from the Naval Service."

He sat down.

The board members sat impassively and stared at Sam. The board president, one of the same old Navy Captains who had scrutinized Sam the day he was escorted from solitary, asked, "Sergeant, would you like to make a statement?"

Sam stood up. "Sir, I'm here because I reached the breaking point in combat. I remind the board I had five years of service without any disciplinary problems."

Having complied with the instructions of his counsel, Sam sat down.

The president muttered something about consideration and giving a verdict in due course and dismissed the board.

Outside the hearing room, Sam's counsel said, "I'm supposed to meet my wife for lunch and I'm running late."

Sam found himself alone in the hallway. He thought about the major with his nice little thin mustache coming out to attack him. He should not be angry at the major. He was earning his living. He no doubt acted the same way for every case that came his way. The board members too had their duties to perform, and the colonel, who took dinner with his wife to be the most pressing part of his day, was no doubt just marking time before the day he would retire. There was no point in being angry.

In his time at the hospital Sam had not spoken to anyone, other than the three women patients, about his experiences in combat. He didn't mind. He felt there was no one who could be qualified. No psychiatrist could sit in a chair with his fingertips together and treat a sane man who had been in an insane world, because it was the world who needed treatment and not the man. Sam felt as unique as the Apostle Paul, whom according to the bible, God had blinded on the road to Tarsus, because he believed God had spoken to him in the dream and it was his voice saying not to be afraid. He walked slowly down the hallway to ward 5D.

A week later, Sam rode in the back of a Marine Corps truck through the gates of the Naval Gun Factory a few blocks down the street from the barracks where this story began. He lined in an office with some others who were being discharged. A pretty girl, a civilian, was typing away on a typewriter and the chatter of the typewriter reminded him of a sunlit day in Korea when they had attacked a hill. It sounded like the far-off chatter of a machine gun.

Sam drew the leave papers which would send him home. The discharge would be mailed to him at the end of his leave. Someday, when he was ready, he would tell the story. There was no way he would tell it soon. Being diagnosed as seriously mentally ill had taken care of that. They would just say he was crazy. Not only that, the story would be exploited by North Korea. Sam would just have to live with it. The memory of the swimming pool would impose upon all of the memories of the valiant acts of heroism of his comrades in such a way he would never have the pride one should have after having fought honorably. While he had not participated in the deed, it was a burden Sam would always have to carry.

Outside, it was a bright clear day, even though it was winter in Washington. Sam had no fear of the future. He was glad to be going home. With his seabag over his shoulder he began walking down Eighth Street. As he went along the familiar tree-lined street with the bright sunlight coming down, he reached the old barracks. A full-dress parade was in progress. The United States Marine Corps band was leading the Detachment Marines around the parade ground. They were playing Semper Fidelis. Sam set the seabag down and stood for a while, once again hearing the beat and roll of the drums, seeing the sunlight glitter on the flags of the color guard. He felt a sense of having lost something intangible; undefinable. His pulse did not quicken, nor did he feel the hair rise on his neck. It was as if he were standing outside himself looking on. He felt like a stranger, not the same person he once had been . He sensed something was wrong. The war; the great adventure, had taken him too far afield. He was so far distant from what had once been home that he could not find the road back. He would never again be thrilled by the sight and sound of a parade. He had a sense of what he had lost and wished it wasn't so, because he was glad to be alive. He turned his back on the parade, shouldered his seabag and walked slowly down Eighth Street towards Constitution Avenue. Moments later, a taxicab approached. Sam flagged it down and got in.

EPILOGUE

SAM LEWIS

After I was discharged, having served over six years in the Corps, and being then at the age of twenty-two, I began the process of adjustment to society. It was difficult. I drove a laundry truck in Pittsburgh, Pennsylvania, for a few weeks, before I was fired. Next, I found a job as a brakeman trainee, at the Pennsylvania Railroad. Being far back in the caboose of the train when the engine would start forward and begin to take up the slack between the cars, finally terminating at the caboose, was more than I could cope with. It was too similar to the sound of incoming artillery. No matter how hard I tried, I still had the tendency to dive for the ditch. They soon let me know that I wasn't suited.

I tried to sell life insurance, but had not the ability to misrepresent and distort, and gave it up.

Charlotte and I then moved all the way to San Francisco, California, where I found a job in the American Can factory. It was a noisy place. Cans ran in all directions, conveyed by belts, and whenever they stopped lots of noise was generated. I went looking for another job.

Marvin Childers, one of the machine gunners I had served with, sent me some photographs he had taken in Korea. Among these was the picture of a dead woman. She was lying on her back, with her face turned upward. Her flesh had wasted away in such a way that her skin had drawn taut, her eyes had rotted out, she had turned black, and her teeth looked like fangs. No Halloween mask could look so horrible. Marvin wrote that he was sending that photograph as a reminder.

"So that you don't forget what it was like," he wrote.

I put the picture in my wallet, not because I liked to see it, but so I would not forget.

I applied for a job at a steel manufacturing company in San Francisco. The personnel manager was a young personable college graduate who was twenty-three years of age. At the interview, we hit it off quite well. There was, however, a broad diversity between his background and mine. His background was in the civilized world. At the conclusion of the interview, he indicated that I had the job. He asked if I had my Social Security card. I reached into my billfold and pulled the card from its pocket. As I did, the picture of the dead woman came out and fluttered down on his desk. He reached out and picked it up.

"My God!" he exclaimed. "—What's this?"

"Oh, it's nothing," I said. "It's only a dead woman."

Seeing the shock on his face, I attempted to explain how I happened to have the picture, but I soon gave up. The gulf between our worlds was just too broad. If I could make him understand why I carried it, I would then have to explain it had been so commonplace that it was accepted as a daily experience, and he had not the preparatory background to allow him to understand. When he recovered his composure, he told me the company would call me to come to work, but they never did.

So, I left San Francisco and journeyed to Evansville, Indiana. From there, I went to Bristol, Tennessee, and then to Dayton, Ohio. And so it goes; on and on. I wandered about the United States for many years.

Henry David Thoreau, the writer, once said, "If a man seems out of step with his fellows, perhaps it's because he listens to the sound of a different drummer."

The famous English novelist, Somerset Maugham, once said that a writer could take any traumatic experience and turn it into a novel, and when the book was published he would be free of the experience forever. I believe that. To those who read this story I say, "I am free at last! Free at last!"

JAMES FLETCHER BAXTER

Sam and I had a lot in common. We both resisted evil. After I got out of the hospital, Big Jim Causey told of driving along in his police cruiser and hitting a black man in the head with his pistol. He thought it was funny how the guy sprawled into the street. When he made this comment we were in a card game. I didn't say anything, but then he said he was going to kick the shit out of Joe Goggins and I had heard enough. I said, "If you're going to try that, you'll have to go through me to get to him. I'm willing to give my life for a country that values each individual. If that isn't true, I don't want to fight for that country—but, it is true, so I'm not going to let you rob me of the very good reason I may lose my life tomorrow or next week. If you attack him, you attack me. I may lose, but I guarantee I will make it very expensive for you to get to him. Let me know what you decide."

He got up from our game and said, "I'll have to think about it."

I said, "Let me know. I'll be here.

He came back a little later and said, "You're right. I was wrong." I thanked him for his manliness.

Joe Goggins came to me later and thanked me. He had tears in his eyes.

Sam's problem was that the swimming pool robbed him of his reason to fight. So, in the end he fought for himself. What else could he do?

CHARLES GOODWIN GROFF

I'm apeshit and I had an apeshit company. When I was a 2nd Lieutenant Platoon Leader chasin' Japs across Saipan, I learned not to try to plan a battle. Too many things go wrong. When I left Bremerton, Washington, to take over Fox Company there wasn't time for training. I decided right then to make them mad and keep them mad. A good Marine is always pissed off. I wanted them to be so pissed off they'd kill the first gook they saw. To hell with the plans. When we went someplace we went in a long route column. Whoever made the first contact would start killing gooks. Then the whole damn company would just keep movin' up and blowing hell out of whoever they met. I didn't have to plan nothing. *That was my plan.*

I named that gook interpreter Jackson after Stonewall Jackson. I acted like I was Robert E. Lee. I tied that Confederate flag to my runner's radio antenna and we went out to do some fighting. Fox Company was as good as any Virginia Infantry who ever lived. By God, I did my job.

THE END

Top…Sam and Cpl. McChann- Bottom, McChann andSgt. Childers

Fox Company. Moving up an unknown Korean road.

Korea, spring 1951….The bloodstained earth

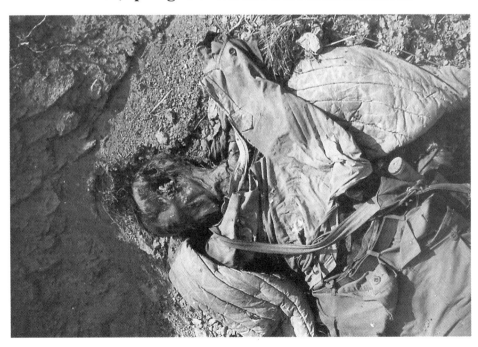

Top. Captain Groff directing air strike at bottom

Korea, spring 1951….The bloodstained earth

2nd platoon on patrol near Andong spring of 1951

Top, The Imjin River... Bottom, climbing a typical hill

The Author, Carl V. Lamb, resides in Scott Depot, West Virginia. He writes from first hand experience. He is currently working on a book of short stories. He likes to play poker and operate a bull dozer.